Scotland and Poland

Scotland and Poland

Historical Encounters, 1500–2010

Edited by T. M. Devine and David Hesse

First published in Great Britain in 2011 by
John Donald, an imprint of Birlinn Ltd

West Newington House
10 Newington Road
Edinburgh
EH9 1QS

www.birlinn.co.uk

Reprinted in 2012, 2014, 2015

ISBN: 978 1 906566 27 2

The publishers gratefully acknowledge the support of the Polish Cultural Institute, London,
in the publication of this book

British Library Cataloguing-in-Publication Data
A catalogue record for this book is available on request from the British Library

Typeset by Hewer Text UK Ltd, Edinburgh
Printed and bound in Britain by Bell and Bain Ltd, Glasgow

Contents

PART 2 POLES IN SCOTLAND, 1940–2010

Foreword

Her Excellency Barbara Tuge-Erecińska, Ambassador of the Republic of Poland to the United Kingdom

To the outside observer, the people of Scotland and those of Poland would seem to have very little in common. The early traditions of these respective nations developed in relative isolation from each other and developed their own unique, rich cultures. Yet, despite these differences, there exists an exceptional compatibility of spirit which has been discovered and explored through a series of historical exchanges. Though much work remains to be done by the archaeologists of culture, the facts that we know already about our bilateral exchanges have provided ample evidence to support this claim.

The October 2009 conference, 'Scotland and Poland: a Historical Relationship 1500–2009', was hosted in Scotland in a unique cooperation of the University of Edinburgh, the Polish Cultural Institute in London, the Consulate General of the Republic of Poland in Edinburgh, and many academics who contributed from Polish and British universities. Special gratitude must also be conveyed for the excellent work of Mr Neal Ascherson, Professor Tom Devine, and Sir Timothy O'Shea, without whose efforts this conference would not have been possible.

This groundbreaking conference and the contributions which have resulted in this publication are important first steps in giving voice to our nations' rich history of exchanges. Through these achievements a foundation has been laid upon which future work can take form. It brings me pleasure to recognise the pioneers of culture who have come before us and the many diligent scholars who have brought their stories to light.

Foreword

*Anna Tryc-Bromley, Deputy Director,
Polish Cultural Institute*

In his book, *Stone Voices: the Search for Scotland*, Neal Ascherson writes that 'the stones can be heard and should be heard'. There are more than a few stones in Poland whispering the story of Scotland and Poland's intertwined past. Graves and place names tell of the many Scottish migrants who came to Poland–Lithuania in the 15th, 16th, and 17th century.

The village of *Szkocja* (Scotland), for example, lies in the north-east corner of Poland, in the district of Gmina Raczki, within Suwałki County, Podlaskie voivodeship. Another village of the same name is found in the Kuyavian-Pomeranian region, in the Shubin municipality. *Nowe Szkoty* (New Scots) and *Stare Szkoty* (Old Scots) are well-known neighbourhoods in the city of Gdańsk. And *Szotland* (after the German word for Scotland) is the oldest area in the port of Władysławowo, near Gdańsk. These Polish place names tell of a Scottish past in Poland. And while these geographical indicators of the Scottish presence still show on the map, many other locations which were also shaped by Scottish migrants do not possess such clear labelling.

There remain tombstones of numerous Scotsmen scattered throughout Poland, for example in the town of Wegrów, 80 kilometres south-east of Warsaw, in the Mazowia region. The Radziwiłł family, aristocratic owners of Wegrow, had invited Scots to settle within the town which was a strong centre for Calvinists living in Poland. The evangelical cemetery dates back to the second half of the 16th century. There the tombs of James Hughy (Hueys), Henrietta Campbell, Archibald Campbell (1692), Hueys family, Anna Henderson-Lidell and several others are still in recognisable condition. They provide a footprint of these early travellers.

Sadly, much of the history of Scots in Poland has been forgotten or remains unexplored. This is the result of several factors, including the language barrier and the prohibition of constructive exchange due to the veiling of Poland by the Iron Curtain (1945–1989). The same obstacles prevented Polish scholars from examining the Polish presence in Scotland during World War II. Thousands of Polish soldiers came to Scotland after the Fall of France in 1940. Many of them stayed in Scotland when the War ended and Poland came under Soviet control.

These obstacles have faded since 1989. With the newly realised sovereignty of the Polish state, political barriers have fallen, and with Poland's 2004 accession to the European Union a fresh wave of migration to Scotland by young, energetic Poles has provoked renewed interest in the two nations' common past.

In the past two decades, the Polish Cultural Institute in London has been supporting Polish theatre, literature and visual arts in Scotland. The Institute cooperates with the Polish Consulate General in Edinburgh in support of many local Polish–Scottish initiatives which enrich the cooperation between our cultures. The years 2009/10 were of particular significance owing to the Polish Cultural Year celebrations in the UK under the umbrella title of 'Polska!Year', a showcase of Polish culture in the UK coordinated by the Adam Mickiewicz Institute in Poland in collaboration with the Ministry of Foreign Affairs and the Polish Cultural Institute. There have also been numerous Scotland-based initiatives which have embraced the people and culture of Poland, such as 'Polish Spring 2009' in Perth, the 'Homecoming Scotland' campaign and similar initiatives.

Traces left in Poland by early modern Scots have been largely covered under layers of history but are now slowly being unearthed. During a trip to Poland in 2008, Ms Linda Fabiani, Minister for Europe for the Scottish Government 2007–9, unveiled a plaque in Warsaw's Old Town to honour the city's first Mayor, the Scottish merchant Alexander Chalmers (d. 1703). Mayor Chalmers' original tomb had been placed in Saint John's Cathedral, the seat of the archdiocese in the heart of the city. The cathedral was destroyed by enemy action during World War II. It has since been reconstructed, but Chalmers' tomb still awaits recovery.

In October 2009, the Polish Cultural Institute and the University of Edinburgh's Scottish Centre for Diaspora Studies hosted the international conference 'Scotland and Poland: A Historical Relationship, 1500–2009'. Over a dozen distinguished scholars from Poland and Scotland came together to discuss – for the first time – the different dimensions of Scottish–Polish contact.

This book was inspired by the 2009 conference. It should be only the beginning. There is need for further research, for example for a formal, systematic query of Scottish material culture in Poland which would encourage an evidence-based consensus of Polish–Scottish historical relations in international discourse. Examples of this material culture include archaeological remains such as gravestones, written artefacts, objects of art, architecture, and even engineered landscapes. My hope is that this publication might lead the way towards the goal of unravelling the scope of historical and economic exchanges between these two cultures.

Contributors

Neal Ascherson is an Honorary Professor at the Institute of Archaeology, University College, London.

Peter P. Bajer is an Adjunct Research Associate at the School of Philosophical, Historical and International Studies, Faculty of Arts, Monash University, Melbourne, Australia.

Allan Carswell is a freelance curator and museum consultant, working mostly in the field of British military history.

Rachel Clements is a doctoral candidate at Newcastle University, School of Geography, Politics, and Sociology.

T. M. Devine is Sir William Fraser Professor of Scottish History and Palaeography at the University of Edinburgh and Director of the Scottish Centre for Diaspora Studies.

Aleksander Dietkow served as the Republic of Poland's Consul General in Edinburgh from 2000 to 2001 and from 2005 to 2009. He is currently Head of the Law Section of the Consular Department of the Ministry of Foreign Affairs of the Republic of Poland.

Grazyna Fremi is an independent art consultant based in Edinburgh.

Robert I. Frost is Professor of Early Modern History at the University of Aberdeen.

David Hesse is a doctoral candidate at the University of Edinburgh's School of History, Classics, and Archaeology.

Anna Kalinowska is a member of the Institute of History, Polish Academy of Sciences, Warsaw.

Waldemar Kowalski is Professor of History and lectures in early modern history and the auxiliary disciplines at Jan Kochanowski University in Kielce, Poland.

Peter D. Stachura is Professor Emeritus of Modern European History at the University of Stirling, and currently Director of the independent Research Centre for Modern Polish History.

David Worthington is Lecturer in History at the UHI Millennium Institute, the prospective University of the Highlands and Islands.

Introduction

T. M. Devine and David Hesse

The relationship between Scotland and Poland over five centuries and more has been long, significant and complex, though until recent times little studied. This book, based on an academic conference held at the University of Edinburgh in October 2009, seeks to provide a greater understanding of some aspects of that historic connection between the two nations. It brings together contributions from both Scotland and Poland, where academic interest in this shared history has burgeoned in the past decade.[1] In particular, the collection focuses on the two periods when migration links between the two societies became important. The first of these was the sixteenth and seventeenth centuries when Scots emigrants had a high visibility in Poland–Lithuania; the second, during World War II, when Polish soldiers arrived in large numbers in Scotland to support the allied cause against Germany. This military migration was then followed six decades later, after Poland's accession to the European Union on 1 May 2004, by the migration to Scotland of many thousands of young Poles seeking employment and new careers.

1500–1800

In medieval and early modern times it was the sea which united and the land which divided. Scotland's long North Sea coastline meant that traders had a much shorter sea voyage to Scandinavia and the Baltic than to any port in eastern England. The Baltic was Europe's inland sea with a thriving trade in grain through the ports of Gdańsk, Lübeck and Königsberg (Kaliningrad). From there the great river valleys of the Vistula and the Elbe opened up an immense network of waterways reaching more than 400 miles inland into the heart of the Commonwealth of Poland–Lithuania. This was an economic cornucopia matched by few other regions in Europe at the time, powerfully influenced by the decline in the old monopolistic structures and authorities of the Hanseatic League. The Polish aristocracy were marketing the surplus wheat and rye of their great estates to feed a rising and increasingly urbanised population in Western Europe. Scots merchants moved in first to Gdańsk in the early sixteenth century to exploit the opportunities for profit and then spread across several of the towns and cities of Poland–Lithuania. In 1569, Sir John Skene observed 'ane great multitude' of Scots traders in Cracow.[2]

Debates in the London Parliament after the Regal Union of 1603 employed 'the multiplicities of the Scots in Polonia' as a dreadful warning of the fate which might befall England if the Scots were to become naturalised subjects as a consequence of the Scots king James VI's succession to the English throne: 'we shall be over-run with them'.[3]

The question of the numbers of immigrants to Poland–Lithuania is not easily answered. One scholar has traced the names of over 7,400 male Scots in no fewer than 420 places throughout Poland but is certain that that total represented only a proportion of the total migration.[4] For the whole of the seventeenth century, T. C. Smout has estimated that something of the order of 30,000 to 40,000 Scots migrated to the Commonwealth, though this figure has been criticised as excessive by at least one recent scholar.[5] Nevertheless, even if the order of magnitude is reduced, the exodus to Poland was almost certainly the biggest single Scottish civilian emigration between 1600 and 1650, though perhaps not as significant as the huge numbers of soldiers recruited into the European armies of the Thirty Years' War.[6] The Scottish impact on Poland–Lithuania was confirmed by the rise of the twelve Scottish Brotherhoods, each organised by an elected committee of 'Elders' drawn from all the numerous Scottish 'colonies' from across the country. It was also illustrated by the ascent of a few Scots to positions of real authority in Poland. Perhaps the most famous was Alexander Chalmers (Czamer), born in Dyce near Aberdeen, who made his fortune in cloth manufacture and trading and then served four terms as Mayor of Warsaw. Some, like Robert Gordon, a wealthy Gdańsk merchant who endowed Robert Gordon's College in Aberdeen, invested some of their riches at home. Yet others, especially Scottish officers who had risen to prominence fighting under Polish command, sometimes were able to enter the ranks of the nobility and established landed dynasties.[7]

From the 1650s and 1660s, however, Scottish immigration appears to have experienced a steep decline. As the older generations died off and integration into Polish society increased, the links with the old country withered. Then the emigration to central and Eastern Europe became Scotland's forgotten diaspora, quickly disappearing from popular memory as the nation's new connections with the British Atlantic and Asian empires became dominant in the eighteenth century. The pioneering research reported in the chapters which follow begin to fill at least some of the many gaps in our knowledge of one key aspect of Scotland's ancient ties with Europe.

1940–2010

Scotland and Poland share more than one historical encounter. Almost five centuries after the first Scottish tradesmen and soldiers sought their luck in Poland–Lithuania, Scots and Poles met again on a large scale in the twentieth and twenty-first centuries. But this time, the migratory stream had reversed. Scotland became the recipient country for Polish immigration.

The first wave of Polish migration to Scotland was military. More than 20,000 Polish soldiers arrived in Scotland in the early stages of World War II to train and fight alongside the British Army. Their presence in Scottish towns and cities during and after the War created a special and lasting bond – a Scottish–Polish relationship that was not always without tension. After the War, many Poles decided to stay and adopted Scotland as their new home. When the second wave of Polish migrants arrived after Poland joined the European Union in May 2004, the newcomers met with an existing Polish community in Scotland.

The chapters in the second section of this collection take a new look at the twentieth and twenty-first century Polish presence in Scotland. They examine Polish life in Scotland and address the issue of Polish–Scottish relations. They provide insights into the interactions between the first and the second generation of Polish migrants in Scotland. And they offer analysis of the distinctive reception the Poles received in Scotland in the years after 2004. This receiving differed in several ways from the overall reception of Polish and Eastern European immigrants in the rest of the United Kingdom.

The Polish military began to arrive in Scotland following the Fall of France in June 1940. After Poland had been invaded by Nazi Germany in September 1939, the remnants of the Polish Army had joined the French and fought the Nazis as an 'Army in Exile'.[8] The unexpected defeat of France made the Polish leadership under General Władysław Sikorski (1881–1943) turn towards Britain. More than 20,000 Polish soldiers left France for England and were then relocated to Scotland. As Allan Carswell points out in his contribution to this volume, the War Office mainly chose to station the Polish soldiers in Scotland to make room for the reorganisation of the British forces after the chaotic evacuation from Dunkirk.

The Poles arrived in Glasgow and were then moved to tented camps in rural Lanarkshire, Dumfriesshire, and later to Fife and Angus.[9] Their reception in the first years was warm and supportive, as many eyewitnesses recall.[10] The Poles were greeted as 'gallant soldiers' and proud patriots who brought both continental bohème and the reality of the War to peripheral Scotland. To some, the Poles were just a bit too gallant – their well-reported success with the Scottish ladies and the disproportionate number of officers among their ranks led to tensions in both civilian and military life. Furthermore, public opinion about the Poles deteriorated when Stalin's Soviet Union entered the Grand Alliance in 1942 and the British media began to encourage pro-Soviet sentiments among the population. The Poles – with their fierce anti-Soviet stance – were increasingly rejected, as Peter D. Stachura notes in his account.

When the War ended and it became apparent that Poland would come permanently under Soviet control, many Polish veterans decided not to leave Scotland. The Polish community in Scotland grew smaller, but did not disappear. While some Scottish–Polish wartime institutions (such as the University of Edinburgh's Polish Medical School[11]) closed down fairly soon after 1945, several Polish organisations remained active in Scotland throughout the Cold War. Among them are the Ex-Combatants' Association (SPK) and the Scottish–Polish Society (founded in October 1941).[12] When Poland re-emerged from behind the Iron Curtain in 1989, the Polish community in Scotland celebrated.

The second wave of Polish influx brought economic migrants to Scotland. The phenomenon was part of a larger Polish exodus. When Poland joined the European Union in May 2004, the country struggled with the highest unemployment rate of all EU member states (19 per cent).[13] In the five years following 2004, more than 600,000 Poles seem to have left their home to find work or higher education abroad.[14] They turned almost exclusively to the United Kingdom and the Republic of Ireland – the only EU countries apart from Sweden which had opened their labour markets without restrictions to immigration from the new EU member states in May 2004.

More than 70,000 Poles seem to have settled in Scotland by the end of 2008. Precise numbers are hard to obtain, as the Scottish Registrar General's statistics do not include the self-employed and non-working spouses.[15] Furthermore, grace to newly established direct flight connections, many of the 'New Poles' are not old-fashioned emigrants but temporary expatriates who move frequently between Poland and Scotland. Mr Aleksander Dietkow, the Republic of Poland's Consul General in Edinburgh from 2005 to 2009, estimates that the number of Poles in Scotland has stabilised somewhere between 70,000 and 85,000 in the second half of 2008. According to his office, some 30,000 Poles lived in Edinburgh in the year 2009, 20,000 in Glasgow, c. 10,000 in Grampian, with many in Aberdeen, c. 8,000 in the Highlands, with most in Inverness, and c. 5,000 in Tayside, with a concentration in Dundee.

The large number of new Polish organisations in Scotland indicates the wide dissemination of Polish immigrants. Among the social and cultural clubs recently established are the Polish Associations of Inverness, Fife, and Aberdeen, the 'United Polish Falkirk' group, the Perth Polish Support Group, and the Polish Scottish Society in Ayrshire, the latter set up in 2006 by the son of a first-generation Polish immigrant.[16] The Polish presence in Scotland is evident in many other domains of public life, such as in sport, where amateur Polish football teams like the Dundee-based FC Polonia or FC Polska from Aberdeen appear in Scottish amateur league tables. The highly successful Edinburgh-based volleyball team Polonia Jets plays in the Second Scottish Division (Men).[17]

While it is not yet clear how the Polish community will react to recent financial developments and the devaluation of the British Pound compared to the Euro and the Złoty, many Poles seem to have come to stay, with their children in Scottish schools and their businesses doing well. Their networks and interactions with both host country and the Cold War Polish diaspora urgently require further research by both historians and social scientists. The essays in this collection seek to make a beginning.

The editors wish to acknowledge the kind support of the Polish Cultural Institute in London, the University of Edinburgh's Scottish Centre for Diaspora Studies, the National Archives of Scotland, and the Republic of Poland's Consulate General in Edinburgh. Special thanks go to Anna Tryc-Bromley, Neal Ascherson, Anne Brockington, and Sylwia Spooner. Most of the contributions assembled here were first presented at the international conference 'Scotland and Poland, a Historical Relationship, 1500–2009', which took place on 1–2 October 2009 at the University of Edinburgh.

Notes

1 R. I. Frost, 'Scottish Soldiers in the Service of Poland–Lithuania, 1577–1661', in *Scotland and the Thirty Years' War, 1618–1648,* ed. S. Murdoch (Leiden, 2001), pp.191–213. W. Kowalski, 'The Placement of Urbanised Scots in the Polish Crown during the Sixteenth and Seventeenth Centuries', in *Scottish Communities Abroad in the Early Modern Period. Studies in Medieval and Reformation Traditions,* eds A. Grosjean and S. Murdoch (Leiden, 2005), pp. 53–103. See also the relevant chapters in R. Unger, ed., *Britain and Poland–Lithuania. Contact and Comparison from the Middle Ages to 1795* (Leiden, 2008) and D. Worthington, ed., *British and Irish Emigrants and Exiles in Europe, 1603–1688* (Leiden, 2010).

2 Quoted in T. C. Smout, N. C. Landsman and T. M. Devine, 'Scottish Emigration in the Seventeenth and Eighteenth Centuries' in *Europeans on the Move,* ed. N. Canny (Oxford, 1994), p. 80.

3 A. F. Steuart, ed., *Papers Relating to the Scots in Poland, 1576–1793* (Edinburgh, 1915), p. ix.

4 A. Biegańska, 'A Note on the Scots in Poland, 1550–1800' in *Scotland and Europe, 1200–1850,* ed. T. C. Smout (Edinburgh, 1986), pp. 157–65.

5 Smout, Landsman and Devine, 'Scottish Emigration', p. 85. The suggestion that this estimate should be reduced was made by Professor Steve Murdoch, University of St Andrews, at the October 2009 conference.

6 T. M. Devine, *Scotland's Empire, 1661–1815* (London, 2003), pp. 13–17.

7 Ibid. pp. 9–12.

8 W. Anders, *An Army in Exile. The Story of the Second Corps* (London, 1949).

9 For general accounts of the Polish military presence in Scotland during World War II, see A. Carswell, *For Your Freedom and Ours. Poland, Scotland, and the Second World War* (Edinburgh, 1993); A. Carswell, 'Gallant Allies' in *Scots and Slavs. Cultures in Contact 1500–2000*, eds M. Cornwall and M. Frame (Newtonville, MA, 2001), pp. 241–67; P. D. Stachura, 'The Poles in Scotland, 1940–1950', in *The Poles in Britain, 1940–2000. From Betrayal to Assimilation*, ed. P. D. Stachura (London, 2004), pp. 48–58.

10 For a collection of personal memories, see D. M. Henderson, ed., *The Lion and the Eagle. Reminiscences of Polish Second World War Veterans in Scotland* (Dunfermline, 2001).

11 See W. Tomaszewski, *The University of Edinburgh and Poland* (Edinburgh, 1968), and W. Tomaszewski, ed., *In The Dark Days of 1941. Fifty Years of the Polish School of Medicine, 1941–1991, The University of Edinburgh, Jubilee Publication* (Edinburgh, 1992); H. Adcock, 'The Polish School of Medicine', *Edinburgh Review* 121 (2007), pp. 19–25.

12 L. Koczy, *The Scottish Polish Society. Activities in the Second World War. An Historical Review*, (Edinburgh, 1980).

13 *Poland Economic Survey. Poland 2004: The Challenge of Regaining Sustainable and Fast Growth*, published by OECD (http://www.oecd.org/eco/surveys/poland accessed 1 June 2010).

14 P. Ciškowicz, M. Hołda, U. Sowa, 'The New Wave of Polish Migration after EU Enlargement. Current State, Determinants, and Outlook' *MPRA Paper* No. 18596 (13 November 2009), 3, (http://mpra.ub.uni-muenchen.de/18596/, accessed 1 July 2010).

15 D. Leask, '86,000 Poles may be living in Scotland, say emigré groups', the *Herald*, Glasgow (18 May 2007).

16 See also K. Zborowicz, 'New Poles in Scotland', Seminar Paper given at the Centre for Research in Polish History, University of Stirling (7 October 2009).

17 See the Polonia Jets' website: http://www.poloniajets.co.uk/ Mr Kris Zoborowicz helpfully provided this information.

2 'Brothers and Sisters for a' that'

Rediscovering the Polish–Scottish Relationship

Neal Ascherson

Opening lecture of the international conference 'Scotland and Poland – A Historical Relationship, 1500–2009', given on 1 October 2009 at the University of Edinburgh

First of all, I would like to congratulate the organisers of this conference, which is not only about history but in itself historic. Salutes to the Ambassador, Mme Tuge-Erecińska, first of all, who has honoured us with her presence, and to the University of Edinburgh, which has maintained a rich and often generous connection with Poland for over two hundred years. Salutes to the Polish Cultural Institute, to the Polish Consulate General in Edinburgh – Consul Dietkow and his hard-working staff – to the Edinburgh publishers Birlinn under Hugh Andrew, and to everyone else who has made this meeting possible. And my thanks to you for doing me the honour of asking me to give this opening talk.

Let me add a dedication, to somebody who in his own life came to symbolise this Polish–Scottish relationship. My respects to the memory of General Stanisław Maczek, commander of the 1st Polish Armoured Division, liberator of European cities, that tough but modest soldier who chose not to return to an unfree Poland but to spend the rest of his life here in Edinburgh, where he died at the age of a hundred and two.

When Field-Marshal Montgomery first met General Maczek, soon after the first Polish troops had arrived in Britain in 1940, he asked him: 'Tell me, what language do Poles really speak among themselves at home – German or Russian?'[1] I wish I knew what Maczek replied. Perhaps he counted up to twenty before he felt himself safe to answer. But what a long way we have moved since then! There can be few people in Scotland today, or in England, who do not know that Poland is Polish, or do not have some idea of what Poland means.

But the process of making Scotland aware of the long Scottish–Polish connection has been slow. It is still only beginning. It is not that nobody has studied it or written about it. To take only a few names from those who have published in Scotland on the subject in the last half-century, there have been Leon Koczy, Anna Biegańska, Wiktor Tomaszewski, Katia Kretkowska, Stefan Zabieglik, Tomasz Ziarski-Kernberg, Peter Stachura . . . But these names are all Polish. Where were the Scottish scholars? It is only now that historians in this country have begun to realise – for example – the true scale and significance of the Scottish settlements in the Vistula basin. This neglect – a footnote or an odd sentence in accounts of Scottish military emigrations or trading connections in the Baltic – has various possible explanations, none of them very creditable: ignorance of the language, lack of written sources in Scotland, barriers to researchers imposed by politics from the Partitions to the Iron Curtain, perhaps even an element of academic sloth – that reluctance to derail accepted narratives of history. But whatever the reasons, that neglect is now over. For that change, and for the idea of this conference, we should above all thank the work in the last few years of Professor Tom Devine and of the researchers he has inspired. After this conference, Scottish historiography will never be the same again.

This meeting which begins today marks the rediscovery of a locked room, crammed with historical treasure. In some ways, I believe that it is even more important than the opening of another locked room in 1818, when Sir Walter Scott recovered Scotland's hidden regalia – the Honours of Scotland – from a chest in Edinburgh Castle.

Scotland is now beginning to repossess an extraordinary episode: those colonies in the old Polish–Lithuanian Commonwealth. This network of highly organised and tightly structured settlements, divided into at least twelve 'Scottish Brotherhoods', each with its elected council of elders, coming together at an annual general meeting at Toruń on the Vistula, represented an early and major Scottish venture into the outside world.

Much about them still remains unknown, not least the numbers involved. All historians of the period are familiar with the narrative of exuberant William Lithgow, 'Lugless Will', who trudged across Europe and the near East in the early seventeenth century. In 1616, he walked across Poland, where he found 'abundance of gallant rich Merchants my Countrey-men, who were all very kind to me, and so were they by the way in every place where I came, the conclusion being ever sealed with deepe draughts, and God be with you'. He called Poland 'for auspiciousness . . . a mother and Nurse, for the young and younglings of Scotland, who are yearly sent hither in great numbers'. And he spoke of 'thirty thousand Scots families, that live incorporate in her bowels . . .'[2]

Thirty thousand? Lithgow had no means of counting the settlers, and historians today regard this figure as a wild exaggeration. Even if an average family is counted as improbably small as three individuals, that would amount to nearly ten per cent of Scotland's population. As most of them came from eastern and north-eastern Scotland, that figure would imply almost deserted landscapes in Aberdeenshire or Angus, their fields worked by old men, old women and young children. And yet the late Rosalind Mitchison estimated that in the early seventeenth century at least 100,000 people left Scotland, counting the Scottish settlements in Ulster (50,000 at a low minimum) and the mercenaries serving in Denmark, Sweden and France. She made no guess at the figures for Poland – indeed, she does not mention the Vistula settlements at all in her 1970 *A History of Scotland* – but she admitted that her '100,000' figure 'might still be much too low'.[3]

The Polish colonies also have European significance. It is true that colonising migrations were already happening in early modern Europe. In the sixteenth century, for example, something like 150,000 people had left Castile to cross the Atlantic and settle in what was to become Latin America – but out of a total population of 6.5 million, over six times that of Scotland. The Ulster Plantations were another massive planned settlement. But in the history of this period in Europe, I can think of no comparable case of a large-scale colonial enterprise involving long-term settlement which succeeded without military conquest or political regime-change.

It may be that the unusual nature of the Commonwealth – its openness to foreign immigration and, with some lapses, its tolerance of religious and ethnic diversity – made this possible. The Scottish colonists were generally well treated by the Polish Crown, in contrast to the swarms of unlicensed Scottish pedlars with their backpacks or packhorses, who were regarded as tax-dodging nuisances. Many Scots rose to important official jobs, as bankers, officers in the forces, or urban dignitaries – Alexander Chalmers, from Dyce, was four times mayor of Warsaw in the seventeenth century.

But it is for Polish scholars to describe the impact of the Scots on Polish society. What fascinates me is that the success of this colonisation seems to have laid down so much of the future patterns and structures of Scottish overseas expansion. And some of these were repeated after the Union of 1707 as Scots fanned out across the British overseas empire, patterns which were to survive until the mid-twentieth century.

The basic model is of small, patriarchal units, usually recruited through family connections back home and from particular Scottish districts. Personal character recommendation from relatives or friends in Scotland was decisive, especially in the case of young men. These little communities were to develop into the so-called private partnerships which spread across the British Empire in the eighteenth and nineteenth centuries.[4] Their tradition of careful local recruiting by recommendation and enlightened nepotism – rather than by anything like open competition – survived into the age of giant private trading companies such as Guthries or Jardine Matheson in Asia.

Three other traditions of Scottish overseas commerce had their origins in Poland. One was the striking reluctance to repatriate profits. Fortunes were made on the Vistula and in Gdańsk. And yet little was sent home. Robert

Gordon in Gdańsk founded the college with his name in Aberdeen; and there was a collection among the Scottish community to repair Marischal College in the same city. But the general rule was to reinvest profits locally, in commerce or in charitable and educational institutions. Scotland was not seen as worth investing in – at least, not until the mid-eighteenth century, when tobacco and sugar merchants began to invest the profits of Caribbean and American plantations in early Scottish industry and in land, especially in west-central Scotland . This was a massive and decisive capital inflow, and T. M. Devine has shown that the industrial and agrarian transformation of Scotland in the second half of the eighteenth century would not have been possible without this repatriation of the profits of Empire – or perhaps it would be more accurate to call them the profits of the slave-worked sector of the imperial economy.[5] And yet in the nineteenth century Scottish private partnerships in Australia, southern Asia and many other parts of the world still preferred to plough their money back into ventures on their own territory: into Polish linen factories, Australian sheep stations, Burmese or Canadian railways. It is true that some money came home to finance the retiral of Scottish nabobs and tycoons. In the Victorian and Edwardian years, by which time Scotland had developed its own domestic capital sources, overseas fortunes were frequently used to buy Highland estates or luxurious steam yachts, or to build draughty Scottish Baronial castles in Argyll. But the serious money acquired overseas usually went into loan finance on the spot. The investments collected at home for Scottish overseas partnerships by syndicates of Edinburgh solicitors paid their subscribers well. But, with the exception of the eighteenth-century plantation profits amassed by Glasgow merchants and the younger sons of landed families sent out to make slave-driver fortunes, the capital created by these investments seldom found its way back to Scotland.

I think we have to remember that – until the 1740s at the earliest – the idea of redirecting their business towards investing in the Scottish economy would have seemed simply puzzling to most Scottish merchants overseas. Scotland, to them, was a hard, stony land without prospects of its own, and their best service to their country, they might have said, was to help the deserving young to leave it.

A second Scottish trait was the practice of high-risk banking – hazardous lending at low interest. Shrewdly selected, these risks often paid off handsomely. The Scots were already doing this in seventeenth-century Poland, advancing money to Polish landowners to improve the flow of wheat into the Vistula grain trade. Bankers like Piotr Fergusson-Tepper or William Hewson sometimes had three-quarters of their capital out on loan. It was the same in nineteenth-century Australia, a continent starving for finance, as cheap Scottish long-term loans filled the gap and laid the foundations of sheep-farming prosperity.

A third trait was lack of interest in political imperialism. In Poland and then in the British Empire, the Scots – in contrast to the English instinct – did not much care who owned a territory or whether it was coloured red on the atlas, as long as the local rulers let them trade. That connects to a fourth trait – the capacity to melt in. The Scots who made the long, difficult sea voyage to Gdańsk intended to stay, and over the generations their descendants gradually became Polonised in language, loyalties and often religion. Families of the second Scottish immigration in the 1820s went through much the same process, as Mona Kedslie McLeod has described in her wonderful book *Agents of Change*.[6] The Scottish diaspora in the British Empire acquired local loyalties much more rapidly than the English, although – with exceptions in North America – they seldom married into indigenous populations in colonised continents.

Was this 'assimilation' or 'accommodation' – two cultural alternatives anxiously debated among the Poles who stayed in Britain after World War II? The truth is, of course, that the second leads into the first. 'Accommodation' in nineteenth-century Poland was represented by Polish-speaking families who still attended a Protestant church and were proud of vaguely remembered Scottish roots. 'Accommodation' in Scotland today is represented by young Scots who know scarcely a word of Polish but treasure a grandfather's stories of Siberian captivity or of Christmas Eve feasting in a snowy countryside.

One further point before I leave the Vistula colonies. We now have the chance to correct an ancient distortion of history. This is the myth that the disastrous Darien Scheme in the 1690s showed that Scotland was incapable of colonial enterprise on its own. I suggest that we should see the Darien Scheme as a one-off, a catastrophe precisely because it ignored all the lessons and well-tried structures of the Polish colonies. Not for the last time, a Scottish attempt to copy and outdo an English commercial success – in that case, the East India Company – ended in ruin and humiliation. In our own day, we have seen what happens when respectable Scottish banks and building societies – swept away by a mania just as the old Company of Scotland was – try to copy the apparent triumph of the City of London and Wall Street in trading sub-prime mortgages and derivatives.

When Poland was partitioned and destroyed at the end of the eighteenth century, Scottish radicals were especially outraged. I will not quote what Robert Burns wanted done to Catherine II ('Auld Kate'). It's in 'Why Shouldna Poor Folk Mowe?' – the only Burns' poem Samuel Marshak didn't dare to translate into Russian.[7] But the restoration of the semi-independent Congress Kingdom in 1815 led to the second Scottish settlement in Poland. Polish nobles and intellectuals had been visiting and studying the Scottish Enlightenment since the 1790s. Now they imported Scottish engineers, managers and agricultural improvers with their families, in a heroic drive to modernise their country under the nose of Russian and Prussian occupation. Much of this was swept away by Russian repression after the failed 1830 insurrection. But enough survived – especially on the Zamoyski estates – to allow the Scots and their descendants to help build up what became the most powerful industrial economy in the Russian empire. Many of them remained until the restoration of Polish independence in 1918.

In the dark century of partition, France – the home of the 'Great Emigration' after 1830 – was the most powerful supporter of a free Poland. But Scotland, perhaps even more than England, passionately adopted the cause of the Polish exiles. Romantic Scottish patriots, while reluctant to demand their own national independence, easily identified Poland's struggles with the deeds of Bruce and Wallace and with Scotland's early proclamation of 'the freedom which no good man surrenders but with his life'. It is perhaps unfair to remember Thomas Campbell, one of the most effective friends of Poland in this period, for what has been described as the worst line in English poetry: 'And Freedom shrieked as Kościuszko fell'.

Nonetheless, direct contact between Scotland and Poland, free or unfree, was slight between about 1830 and the outbreak of World War II. The Poles did not forget the earlier Scottish presence, the merchants, the pedlars and the soldiers. Most Poles, even today, remember affectionately the figure of Ketling, the hardy, merry Scottish soldier in Sienkiewicz's historical novel *Pan Wołodyjowski*. The Scots, in contrast, lost the memory of their old relationship across the Baltic almost completely. The torrent of Polish emigration which began to flow in the later nineteenth century avoided Britain, and went instead to the industrial basins of France, Belgium and the German Ruhr, or across the Atlantic to the United States and Brazil. In the 1880s, Lanarkshire colliery owners brought in some thousands of immigrant workers from Russian Poland, the so-called 'Lithuanians'. Few of them were ethnic Poles, but their presence was resented because of the perception that they had been imported as cheap labour – and also because of their Catholic faith.

The old acquaintance was not really renewed until 1940, with the arrival of Polish Armed Forces after the Fall of France. It was Churchill's decision that they should be stationed in Scotland, to guard the east coast against invasion and to retrain for the assault on the European mainland. The soldiers, evacuated from France, together with naval and airforce personnel, numbered at first some 30,000. These numbers steadily grew. In 1942–3, some 8,000 men and women out of the mass of over 100,000 Poles who had been released from Soviet labour camps and made their epic journey to safety in Persia were transferred to the Polish 1st Army Corps in Scotland. Later still, they were reinforced by Poles who had been forcibly recruited into the Nazi armies and then taken prisoner by the Allies. At first housed in tents in the hills around

Biggar and Crawford, the Polish troops were later moved east to set their main concentration in Fife and Angus. But Polish units, army, navy and airforce, were to be found all over Scotland by the end of the war.

The impact of this Polish presence on Scottish popular imagination was enormous, and is still vividly remembered by the older generation. Scotland, used to thinking of itself as an emigrating country, now for the first time found itself receiving a massive foreign presence. The Poles were certainly exotic. They wore strange uniforms, they spoke an incomprehensible language, they had been through nightmare experiences which were hard to credit in peaceful Scotland, and they were fervent Roman Catholics. On top of all that, they possessed charm, hand-kissing manners and *joie de vivre* which seemed to come straight from the movies, and which was hard to resist. As a Glasgow woman wrote in a letter to the *Herald* last year: 'Nobody has mentioned one important reason for welcoming Poles, but perhaps only ladies in their late seventies know it. They can all dance like Fred Astaire.'[8]

The Poles liberated many places in those years, from Bologna to Breda. In a less noisy way, they liberated Scotland, too. It was not just a matter of foxtrots and promises of undying love. It was their reminder that Scotland was not just North Britain, but had been, and could be again, a small European nation. George Reid, Holyrood's ex-Presiding Officer, remembers that the village in which he grew up, Tullibody, had in the 1940s more Poles than Scots as inhabitants. As an MP, and then an MSP, Reid was to become the most experienced 'Europeanist' in Scottish politics. And the young Richard Demarco saw for the first time that there was what he calls 'a Polish–Scottish–Italian dimension to Europe' – a perception which was to change and direct his life. He has said: 'As an Italo–Celtic schoolboy, I saw this first-hand when at Sunday Mass I studied the faces of the Polish soldiers kneeling alongside those in a different uniform, that of Italian prisoners of war.'[9]

With so many men away at the war, there was a lot of love to be sought. There were many marriages (I have seen a figure of 2,500), many babies, a lot of broken hearts. In Ksawery Pruszyński's book *Polish Invasion*, he makes a Polish military chaplain rebuke his flock: 'What will be left for the women of Poland?' The soldiers reassure him: 'We will manage to have something left for them.'[10] Here's an example of how hospitality could grow into something warmer. Susan Greenhill-Gardyne, daughter of Finavon Castle near Forfar, worked in the canteen of the camp at Polmont which was training the *cichociemny*, the 'silent-shadowy ones', the parachutists to be dropped back into occupied Poland to join the non-Communist resistance. She learned Polish there, and after the war was posted to the British Embassy in Warsaw. This was a time when the new Communist regime was hunting down and arresting those parachutists, as imperialist agents. One of these fugitives, Stanisław Mazur, had known Susan at Polmont. He managed to make contact, and she arranged for him to be smuggled out of Poland through Czechoslovakia. Back in Scotland, they married and lived happily at Finavon for many years.[11]

Other women were less lucky. Some of the Scottish wives moved to Poland after the war, only to see their husbands arrested and themselves stranded – at that time, a woman who married a foreigner could lose her British citizenship. It took a change in the law to allow the British Embassy to rescue them. Returned to Scotland, many were eventually able to bring their husbands and children out of Poland, when the regime eased after Stalin's death.

But it would be wrong and sentimental to see this wartime and post-war relationship through a happy old comrades' haze. There were problems. Between people so remote from each other, how could there not be? Ksawery Pruszyński, in Scotland with the 1st Polish Corps, pointed out that the Poles often began by assuming that the Scots were a sort of English, and could not understand why they got so furious when they were told so. And the Scots in turn began by assuming that Poles were a sort of Russian, and were surprised at the outraged protests they provoked.[12] Poles, like Scots, enjoy taking offence, and the street brawls between Polish soldiers and the Black Watch were legendary.

The fact is that by 1942, that early welcoming warmth was starting to cool. International politics were mostly to blame. In the Fife coalfields where the Communist Party had a devoted following, many Scots flatly refused to believe Polish stories of their experiences in the Gulag. They were shocked at the mere suggestion that Comrade Stalin could be guilty of the Katyń massacres. Polish protests against Soviet behaviour towards their country, before and after 'liberation', were quite widely seen as selfish and disloyal in time of war, and the British Government – anxious to lubricate the Soviet alliance – did not discourage that resentment.

There were even doubts about Polish democratic credentials. Some politicians were dismayed when General Sikorski – very wisely – locked up some of his ultra-right rivals in a camp on the Isle of Snakes (otherwise Bute). A scandal over anti-Semitism in the army in Scotland was badly mishandled by the Government-in-Exile.[13] Sectarian prejudice against Catholics came into play too, especially as the war ended. And many Scottish males, not least husbands returning from the fronts, grew jealous of Polish glamour.

Many leading figures in Scotland continued to give the Poles enthusiastic support – Sir Patrick Dollan, Glasgow's Lord Provost in the early war years, and Lady Warrender of the Auxiliary Territorial Service among them. It's hard now to remember that a 'Poles Go Home' rally filled the Usher Hall in 1946, harangued by the viciously anti-Catholic John Cormack, then an Edinburgh councillor. Even Churchill had told the Poles to go home and rebuild their country, forgetting that soldiers from the regions annexed by the Soviet Union no longer had a home to go to. A few demobilised soldiers made things worse by buying up slum property in Scottish cities and rack-renting poor tenants – a variant of the much larger Rachman scandal in post-war London.

In short, the peaceful settlement of some 8,000 Polish ex-combatants in Scotland after the war, and the good reputation they won among their neighbours, is more of an achievement than it seems. When I recall such men from my boyhood in Argyll, I think of 'Tony the Pole' with his red-haired wife from Dunfermline, who worked a stony farm on the Isle of Jura – *1984* would never have been finished if Tony hadn't rescued George Orwell from the Corryvreckan whirlpool. I think of George, the Silesian miner, who could mend any engine on boat or lorry; or the wise Pole who ran the ironmongers in Ardrishaig or the Pole who founded a plumbing dynasty in Lochgilphead. Their hardiness and energy stood out in a countryside damp with gentle resignation.

Since Poland's entry to the EU in 2004, the past five years have brought a torrent of mostly young Poles to Britain. Again, some features of this immigration have had a particular effect on Scotland, not always matched in the South.

First, the demography: a large percentage of young couples, often with higher education, often in the mood to have babies.

Secondly, the spread: even in the Highlands, there are few small places without a Stas and a Zosia resurrecting dead radiators or bringing dreich public bars to life.

Third, the economic impact. The Poles have helped to fill a Scottish gap, in an ageing society which is strikingly and dangerously weak in the small business sector, above all in service enterprise formation. The Polish pattern we have seen here is roughly to accumulate money through hard manual work, and then to invest the savings in a small business. Most of them intend eventually to go back to Poland and run their business there. But many, much to Scotland's benefit, open their plumbing or decorating firms in this country.

Fourth difference: the Scottish Executive and then Government, unlike Westminster, have put some energy into encouraging and attracting young Poles to come and to settle.

So these Poles in Scotland have behaved rather like the Scots behaved in Poland four centuries ago. They have braved the collision with a strange language spoken in a way their English teachers at school had not prepared them for. They have learned the way round strict and sometimes baffling laws; they have done well for themselves 'living incorporate in Scotland's bowels', and they have made many natives wonder how they ever got by without them. Like the nineteenth-century Scots experts who went to Dowspuda or Zamość or Żyrardów, they entered a nation which feared that its creative days were over, and reminded everyone how to innovate.

To conclude, this Polish–Scottish relationship, this feeling of an unlikely brotherhood or sisterhood, is not just about sentiment. Our two histories are very different, similar only in the ways both nations read them: that the fight for freedom or independence has shaped both countries, and that bigger, less intelligent neighbours will always use their elbows on smaller, more advanced neighbours. And similar, I might add, in that both prefer to picture themselves as always the oppressed – and never the oppressors.

But this is also a solid, measurable relationship. At different times in those histories, Poland and Scotland have drawn real strength from one another in trade and in war. And shelter too: the Scottish exiles who backed the wrong side in seventeenth-century conflicts, the men and women of the Polish Armed Forces who could not or would not go home after 1945.

I will end with the ending of Ksawery Pruszyński's book. Remember, it was written in 1941, before anyone could foresee that Poland's reward for being an Ally would be to lose its freedom.

Pruszyński imagined how, when the Poles got home from Scotland, after the war was won, they would want to thank all the Scots who had shown them hospitality. So they would invite them all, from Sir Patrick Dollan ('Dollanski') to every Fife landlady, to come to visit them with their families. A fleet of liners escorted by Polish warships would approach Gdynia and Gdańsk, to be greeted by royal salutes from the guns at Hel and Westerplatte, while all Poland either lined the quayside or listened on the radio. Scottish children who had learned all about Poland during the war would be leaning over the side shouting '*Czołem! Dzień dobry!*', while Polish children shouted 'Long live Scotland!' Then, after the grand welcome ceremony, the Polish families would take the Scots off to tour their country. 'Even if you see us poor, you will know that we are happy, for we are rebuilding our own homes on our own land. May this be the last time we have to rebuild them.'[14]

Knowing what was to happen, it hurts to read that now. No happy reunion in freedom on the Baltic shore; instead, the Soviet alliance and then Yalta, and then Stalinist terror, a time when Poles felt betrayed by their British hosts and Scots lost touch with Polish feelings. All that is history now. But it shows that this relationship between two peoples has always been subject to climate change, to cooling and then warming.

Today, we are in a warm period. Scotland has done well out of the new Polish invasion, and we can hope that most – not all – of the invaders will go home with good memories of Scotland. If a day comes when Scotland asks for its own membership of the European Union, maybe those four centuries of memories will help Polish leaders to understand and support the Scottish claim. This conference will show how much these two nations have done together. May it set fire to imaginations, and show how much we can still do for each other and with each other in the future.

Notes

1 S. Maczek, *Od Podwody do Czołga* (London, 1961), p. 219

2 W. Lithgow, *A Total Discourse of the Rare Adventures and Painfull Peregrinations of Long 19 Years* (London and Edinburgh, 1906, orig. 1632), p. 368.

3 R. Mitchison, *A History of Scotland* (London, 1970), p. 183.

4 M. Fry, *The Scottish Empire* (East Linton, 2001), pp. 259–68.

5 T. M. Devine, *Scotland's Empire, 1600-1815* (London, 2003), pp. 330–2.

6 M. K. McLeod, *Agents of Change: Scots in Poland 1800–1918* (East Linton, 2000), p. 143.

7 J. Kinsley, ed., *Robert Burns, Poems and Songs* (Oxford, 1971), p. 533.

8 The *Herald*, 30 August 2006.

9 Demarco, pers. comm.

10 K. Pruszyński, *Polish Invasion* (Edinburgh, 2009, orig. 1941), p. 33.

11 Z. Siemaszko, *Lata Zanikajacej Nadzieji* (Lublin, 2006), p. 154.

12 Pruszyński, *Polish Invasion*, p. 6.

13 D. Engel, *Facing The Holocaust: The Polish Government in Exile and the Jews, 1943–5* (Chapel Hill, NC, & London, 1993), pp. 108–11.

14 Pruszyński, *Polish Invasion*, p. 112.

PART ONE

SCOTS IN POLAND, 1500–1800

Hiding from the Dogs

The Problem of Polish–Scottish Political Dialogue,
1550–1707

Robert I. Frost

This story does not begin well. In 1648, Łukasz Opaliński (1612–1662), a prominent Polish politician and political thinker, published the second of his two influential political treatises, *Polonia Defensa*.[1] This work must be one of the most dyspeptic book reviews ever penned. It was directed at the unfortunate John Barclay (1582–1621), whose wry look at the peoples of Europe had helped make his quietly ironic *Icon Animorum* hugely popular: one estimate suggests that 30,000 copies were printed in a host of editions and translations.[2] Barclay had been dead for over quarter of a century by 1648; it may therefore have been the Polish translation, published in 1647, which galvanised Opaliński.[3] A leading critic of the Polish political system in his vernacular writings, in *Polonia Defensa* Opaliński nevertheless defended it in elegant Latin to an international audience. If Barclay's work was meant to be a joke – it is often regarded as the fourth part of his *Satyricon* cycle – Opaliński clearly did not get it. He reprinted verbatim the short section in which Barclay discussed Poland, which took up just over six pages, and then proceeded to demolish it line by sarcastic line in the remaining 131 pages, spitting vitriol from the first sentence of the preface.[4]

Polonia Defensa was a lively addition to the copious literature of *Descriptio Gentium* that was so popular in Renaissance and Baroque Europe. Opaliński's critique of Barclay was not so much *ad hominem*, in the time-honoured way of outraged reviewers, as *ad gentem*. For although Barclay had been born in exile of a French mother, probably never visited Scotland, and was referred to as French in contemporary British records,[5] it was his Scottishness, inherited from his renowned Royalist father William, that seized Opaliński's attention and gave him a target for his indignation. While his response was undoubtedly disproportionate, he did perhaps have a point. Barclay had portrayed the Poles as a barbarous and primitive people from the frozen North, who shivered on wide open plains with no mountains to protect them from the snell septentrional winds. He primly stated that their cruel and licentious character meant that Poles fell some way short of modern standards of civilisation.[6] Opaliński mocked Barclay's observations, claiming that someone who, though *gente Caledonius*, had been born in France, should nevertheless have known that his geographical musings bore more relation to Scotland than to Poland, most of which, as Opaliński tartly pointed out, lay considerably to the south of Scotland.[7] To Barclay's contention that Poland lacked commerce, Opaliński retorted that the great cities of Royal Prussia were thriving mercantile centres, attracting the Dutch, who bought all sorts of goods, many of them brought from India, while the English sought only bread. As for the Scots:

> This nation, ashamed of its miserable and barren fatherland, flees over the seas and seeks its fortune in Poland [. . .] At one time they sold only needles, knives, brooches and other trifles of that sort; carrying their wares on their backs in chests and boxes; now, (because they do not know Barclay's lies about the bad state of our roads), they travel in waggons and sell their wares at our village markets. *Mercatura autem* (as Cicero says) *si tenuis est, sordida est.*[8]

Opaliński closes his diatribe by observing that in Poland the Scots were considered to be on a level with the Jews, adding that the Poles regarded the Scots as thieves and the Jews as outcasts; given Barclay's less than favourable view of the Jews, this gibe would undoubtedly have stung had he been alive to read it.[9] To Barclay's perfectly reasonable observation that Polish houses outside the cities were largely constructed of wood, as Poland was short of stone for building, Opaliński retorted that this meant that the Scots, wandering from village to village, had nowhere to hide from the dogs.[10]

This bout of educated Billingsgate is undoubtedly entertaining, and suggests that we should not project too rose-tinted an image of Polish–Scottish interaction across the ages. Undoubtedly, as is clear from studies by Waldemar Kowalski, Arthur Williamson, and the paper from David Worthington in this volume, the large number of poor Scottish pedlars in Poland meant that relations between Scots and their Polish hosts were often tense.[11] It was by no means only Opaliński who bracketed them with the Jews; numerous ordinances of the Polish Sejm (Diet) and of local authorities singled out Scots alongside Jews as targets for exclusion, extra taxation, or the other unsavoury regulations which are so often applied to impoverished immigrants.[12] Not all migrant Scots, however, were forced to hide from the dogs; considerable numbers of them chose to settle in Poland, and the ease with which many of them integrated into Polish burgher and, to a lesser extent, noble society, suggests that relations were not as black as Opaliński paints them.[13] It might also be pointed out that in Poland–Lithuania the Jews were treated with a degree of toleration remarkable in early modern Europe and had substantial privileges of their own: both Jews and Scots had their own parliamentary bodies which settled matters internal to the two communities. Few migrant groups elsewhere in early modern Europe were allowed such latitude.

For all his fulminating about Scots, Opaliński was no snorting xenophobe. He was a sophisticated political thinker with a substantial library which showed that he was by no means ignorant of matters Scottish and British. He owned copies of Buchanan's *Rerum Scoticarum Historia*, Camden's *Anglica, Normanica, Hibernica, Cambrica a veteribus scripta*, and Dodsworth and Dugdale's *Monasticon Anglicanum*. Although he does not seem to have owned *Icon Animorum* or its Polish translation, he did have a copy of *Argenis*, Barclay's celebrated *roman-à-clef*. Perhaps some of his animosity against Barclay derived from the fact that he also owned a copy of William Barclay's *De regno et regali potestate contra monarchomachos*. He had certainly read it: his copy is heavily annotated in his own hand.[14] Indeed, Opaliński cites the elder Barclay on two occasions: once in his 1641 *Rozmowa plebana z ziemianinem* and once in *Polonia Defensa*. Although he broadly approved of William Barclay's attack on the monarchomachs, he felt that the Scot 'concerned himself too much with the fate of kings'.[15] He strongly rejected, however, John Barclay's implicit claim that the Poles themselves were monarchomachs. He pointed out that the elective nature of the Polish monarchy meant that their kings were kept firmly in check, congratulating his native land for ensuring that its monarchs were not above the law but were subject to it, and asserting that they never-theless realised that this fact in no way detracted from their majesty. Thus the Poles did not need to keep their kings in line by force of arms.[16] He contrasted this orderly system with the bloody civil wars in contemporary Britain, observing that Barclay's Scottish compatriots had behaved scandalously towards their own monarch, first treating him 'wickedly and shamelessly' after he had flung himself on their mercy, and then selling him to the English after protracted negotiations.[17] Even in their politics, apparently, the Scots were merchants.

Polonia Defensa, published the year before Charles I's execution – the ulti-mate outcome of this sordid transaction – was to scandalise political opinion in Poland, where the phrase 'the English axe' (*topór angielski* or *siekierka angielska*) soon entered everyday political parlance, reminding the Commonwealth's citizens of the dangers of mob rule. It proved, however, an unfortunate year for a Pole to express such satisfaction with the Commonwealth's political system. Opaliński could not have known it when he was composing the work, but Poland–Lithuania stood on the brink of its own period of political turbulence, as the Cossack revolt which began in the Ukraine in 1648 provoked a full-blown crisis of state and royal power, in the early stages of which he was to be heavily involved.

Yet Opaliński probably knew rather more about British politics than his educated Scottish counterparts knew of Poland–Lithuania. For, despite the extent of the Scottish migration to the Commonwealth, this substantial movement of people across the Baltic seems not to have spread much awareness of Polish–Lithuanian politics back home in Scotland. In many respects, Scottish views of Poland remained broadly ill-informed and stereotypical; in this sense, Opaliński's anger was justified: Barclay clearly did not know very much at all about Poland. What did he and other learned Scots know, and how did they know it?

It seems that, beyond the spheres of religion and science, two areas that I have no space to consider here, the answer is 'very little'; indeed, Opaliński's diatribe is one of very few examples of any sustained engagement between the two political cultures at the learned level. This fact might, at first sight, seem surprising, for, to the modern historian, there appear to be striking parallels between the two countries. As Opaliński implicitly recognised, Scotland, like Poland, suffered from the fact that, in a Renaissance Europe obsessed with the writings of the Ancients, both were seen as remote, cold, northern lands – Tacitus has much to answer for – whose barbarian peoples had remained largely untouched by the glorious civilisation that was Rome. Both Poland and Scotland came to the Renaissance relatively late, and this meant that sixteenth-century scholars in both countries felt compelled to justify their place in European culture. Thus Polish and Scottish historians sought to create elaborate historical lineages to display their national worth and to establish both the ancient foundations of their kingdoms and their independence from neighbouring powers; in Scotland this had to be maintained against English claims, while the Poles went to great lengths to demonstrate that they had never been subject to the Holy Roman Empire. If the Scots dubiously traced their royal lineage back to 330 BC, the Poles sought, just as unconvincingly, to demonstrate that the line of Polish kings and princes ran back far beyond Mieszko I at the end of the tenth century, when a Polish state first definitively emerges in written records, to the mythical founder Lech, and to the equally legendary Piast, a simple peasant invited to ascend the throne, mentioned in the twelfth-century *Chronicle of the Anonymous Gaul*, the first historical work to be written on Polish soil. Like the Scots, the Poles took pride in the fact that they had not been conquered by Rome; historians debated fiercely whether they were descended from the Goths, the Vandals, or the Sarmatians, who emerged as the favourite progenitors among Poles themselves, who rejected western claims that they were descended from the barbaric Scythians.[18]

To the modern historian, however, it is the political and constitutional parallels between the two countries which seem most striking, rather than these misty-eyed exercises in historical credulity.[19] In both Poland–Lithuania and Scotland, the Renaissance brought a close interest in the classical notion of the *forma mixta*, which influenced political writers deep into the seventeenth century; Opaliński was himself a noted proponent of the idea.[20] Consequently, in both Scotland and Poland during that first century of the

Renaissance, radical critiques of monarchical systems of government were developed under the influence of classical republicanism. Scots and Poles formed sophisticated doctrines of the sovereignty of the citizen body that saw monarchy as both limited and elective, and which claimed the right for the citizen body to depose a tyrant or a monarch who broke their coronation oaths. If in some ways the most radical version of this credo was expressed in Scotland in the works of John Knox and, in a more secular vein, by George Buchanan, in particular in his *De Jure Regni apud Scotos* (1579), it was in Poland–Lithuania in 1572 that the fully elective nature of monarchy – of which Buchanan was an advocate – was institutionalised in the constitutional revolution which followed the death of Sigismund August, last of the Jagiellon dynasty. If Buchanan's treatise was clearly written *post factum* to justify the deposition of Mary Queen of Scots in 1567, and if his royal pupil, Mary's son James VI, was to react strongly against Buchanan's vision of republican monarchy, in Poland–Lithuania the formal depostion of Henry of Valois, the first elected monarch, after he fled Poland to take up the French throne in 1573, took place explicitly on the basis of his breach of the articles and the *pacta conventa* he had sworn to uphold at his coronation.[21]

Thus Poland–Lithuania embarked in 1569–72 on a republican path from which Scotland turned away in the seventeenth century: when Andrew Fletcher of Saltoun claimed in 1703 that before the Union of the Crowns 'no monarchy in Europe was more limited, nor any people more jealous of liberty than the Scots', he was implicitly suggesting that it was no longer so.[22] Yet there was an even more significant parallel between the two polities. For Britain and Poland–Lithuania were also the two great union states of early modern Europe. In both cases separate political entities came together in political unions in which the consent of the citizens expressed through parliamentary bodies played a central role in defining those unions, and in which the political trajectory was remarkably similar, even if Scotland's position in the British union was more directly comparable to that of Lithuania than that of Poland, which was the dominant cultural and political partner. Both Britain and Poland–Lithuania moved from a dynastic or personal union to a real or parliamentary union in this period, with Poland leading the way: the personal union with Lithuania began in 1386, while the parliamentary union was forged at Lublin in 1569, nearly half a century before James VI started on his way south. No other states in Europe in the early modern period developed in this way, and few had such lasting unions: it will not be until 2013 that the Anglo–Scottish union surpasses that of Poland and Lithuania for longevity.

Thus, as both Benedict Wagner-Rundell and Allan Macinnes have pointed out, there were many similarities between the development of the republican tradition, and in practical republican politics, between Scotland and

Poland–Lithuania in the seventeenth and eighteenth centuries, yet even if, as Macinnes suggests, through figures such as John Durie the Polish institution of confederation may have had an impact on Scottish political practice of the 1630s and 1640s, at least in its religious aspects,[23] actual knowledge of the Polish–Lithuanian constitution and its operation was limited. For all the similarities, these parallels do not seem to have struck contemporaries with such force, at least after the sixteenth century. Some attention was indeed paid to the Polish–Lithuanian union in the fierce debates before and after the Anglo–Scottish union of 1603, but knowledge of the Polish system was limited. The Englishman Sir Henry Savile may have devoted an entire chapter of his treatise on union to the Commonwealth, and mentioned the Poles at several other points in his text, but the Scot Sir William Craig more or less ignored them, beyond claiming, as many writers did, that Lithuania had been incorporated into Poland. While this was certainly the Polish view of what had happened in 1386, Lithuanians had resisted this interpretation of the various union documents signed down to 1501. When the Poles tried to press for the execution of this incorporation in the debate over closer union in the 1550s and 1560s, continued Lithuanian resistance eventually brought about the more confederal arrangements agreed at Lublin in 1569, with the Grand Duchy retaining its own government, currency, legal system and army. Thus it was not just learned English commentators such as Savile who displayed scant knowledge or interest in Poland–Lithuania in the union debates before and after 1603, as Macinnes suggests; Scottish writers were little better, and David Hume of Godscroft, in his more practical treatise, ignored the Poles completely.[24] Yet this relative lack of interest is hardly surprising. There were many examples in early seventeenth-century Europe of unions of crowns. Examples of parliamentary unions in Europe were singularly lacking, however, yet there was remarkably little interest in the Commonwealth in the union debates in Scotland in the years before 1707, despite the fact that Poland–Lithuania had resolved many of the issues facing the Scots: it had opted for an elective monarchy to solve a succession crisis in 1572; it had created a common parliament to preserve the union; it had maintained separate legal systems, armies and governments; and it had, largely successfully, dealt with the myriad problems of office-holding, noble status and property ownership which provoked so much discussion in pre-union Scotland.

Yet the Commonwealth was largely absent from the debate. Fletcher of Saltoun made one fleeting reference to Poland–Lithuania in his treatise on the Spanish monarchy, before recommending in his *An Account of a Conversation Concerning the Right Regulation of Governments* that Poland and Lithuania might well be united under one government with the southern part of European Muscovy; the northern part of Muscovy, Fletcher suggested, should be partitioned off to be ruled alongside Sweden, Norway, Finland and

Livonia, a plan which suggests scant acquaintance with the realities of east-European power politics during the Great Northern War.[25] Macinnes suggests that it was Fletcher of Saltoun and his adherents who raised the anonymous protest against the third clause of the proposed treaty of union in the Scottish parliament on 18 November 1706, which claimed that this clause failed to respect the sovereignties and privileges of the two nations, unlike the union of Poland and Lithuania; if he is correct, then this suggests that Fletcher was well aware of the nature of the Union of Lublin, which had finally buried the issue of incorporation.[26] Given that so much of the debate leading up to 1707 was not so much about whether there should be closer union, as about the form it was to take, one might have expected rather more discussion of the closest European parallel to the union being proposed by Queen Anne's ministers.

What explains this apparent lack of appreciation by the Scottish political and cultural elite of the relevance of the Polish–Lithuanian system to the British debate? Members of the Scottish diaspora in Poland–Lithuania who did write about Poland–Lithuania were often highly informed and thoughtful in their judgements on Polish politics. Whether or not the Caithness-born William Bruce, in 1596–7 Professor of Roman Law at Jan Zamoyski's new university at Zamość, wrote the extensive and anonymous 1598 manuscript *Relation of the State of Polonia* as Stanisław Kot claimed, in his later capacity as an agent of the Stuart government, Bruce wrote detailed and highly informed accounts of Polish politics for Robert Cecil.[27] His successors in this role, Patrick Gordon, and then Gordon's nephew Francis, who died in Aberdeen in 1644, were equally well-informed. The diary of the more famous Patrick Gordon of Auchleuchries, shows a shrewd understanding of Polish conditions, reflecting the fact that he moved in high circles, being particularly associated with Crown Grand Marshal and Field Hetman Jerzy Sebastian Lubomirski.[28]

Yet Gordon's diary was unpublished, as were diplomatic reports, including the *Relation*. It was in fact difficult for educated Scots to gain a firm under-standing of the Polish–Lithuanian constitution. The debates surrounding the 1603 Union of the Crowns coincided with the first phase of the fracturing of the common Latinate culture of the high Renaissance. As was the case else-where in Europe, political debate in Poland–Lithuania had long been conducted largely in the vernacular, and writers on Polish history were increasingly turning to Polish to feed the burgeoning internal market for their works, rather than writing in Latin for the Republic of Letters. Scottish and English political writers seeking information about the Polish political system had, therefore, few up-to-date sources after the turn of the sixteenth century. To a very great extent they based themselves on chapters on Poland in general works, such as the influential histories of Botero and de Thou, or, where they did cite a native Polish account, on the great history of Poland *De origine et rebus gestis Polonorum* by Marcin Kromer (1512–1589), Bishop of Warmia (Ermland), the first edition of which was published in Basel in 1555, or his shorter *Polonia, sive situ populis, moribus, magistratibus, et respublica Regni Poloniæ libri duo*, the first authorised edition of which was published in 1577.[29]

De origine is the sole source cited by Savile for his chapter on Poland in his *Historical Collections*, and these two works, supplemented by general histories of Europe, seem to have been the main source of Scottish knowledge of Poland for well over a century after their publication. This can be gauged by the frequency of citation, and by the number of surviving copies in Scottish libraries, whose holdings of sixteenth- and seventeenth-century Polish materials are relatively scanty. Thus the National Library of Scotland and the university libraries of Aberdeen and St Andrews possess copies of the 1555 first edition of *De origine*; while Aberdeen also possesses the second edition of 1558. Both the National Library and St Andrews have copies of the 1568 edition.[30] Aberdeen has a copy of the 1578 Cologne edition of the *Polonia*. The *Polonia* was also reproduced in a 1627 compilation of works on Poland, published in Leiden; Aberdeen has two copies; Glasgow University library has three; while the National Library has a copy of the 1641 edition. Even at the end of the seventeenth century, Kromer was still influential: Fletcher of Saltoun owned a copy of the 1589 Cologne edition of the *Polonia*, one of several polonica in his library.[31]

Kromer's *De Origine* was, at the time of its publication and for a considerable period thereafter, the most extensive and best-grounded history of Poland in print, since Jan Długosz's massive fifteenth-century chronicle covering Polish history down to 1478 was not published until the early eighteenth century. Kromer was well-informed: in the early 1550s he had been given the task of organising and cataloguing the royal archives at Wawel Castle in Cracow, which took eighteen months, and was conducted with exemplary efficiency. His work drew on some 135 original documents from these archives, and Kromer was always careful to submit his sources to evaluation and criticism. These virtues – and the fact that it was published outside Poland itself – ensured that *De Origine* deservedly secured a wide international readership; this in turn meant that its influence was even greater than can be appreciated merely from counting the number of copies in libraries: until deep into the seventeenth century, Kromer remained the leading source for European historians incorporating Poland into their general histories.[32]

Yet for all his many virtues as a historian, Kromer's dominance in the market meant that European readers who relied on him secured a picture of Poland which was increasingly out of date. Moreover, there were particular features of Kromer's account which meant that the relevance of Polish history for Scotland at this period was obscured. Both *De Origine* (1555) and *Polonia* (1577) were written before the Union of Lublin launched the constitutional revolution of 1569–72.[33] Kromer covered the dynastic union of 1386 and the extracts from the relevant documents he printed in his account were drawn on by Savile.[34] Yet Kromer's *De Origine* ended in 1506, well short of the Union of Lublin, and he accorded Lithuanian history very little attention, covering the various stages of the developing relationship with Poland in scant detail. Długosz's chronicle was one of Kromer's major sources, and he echoed much of Długosz's negative portrayal of many members of the Jagiellonian dynasty: when *De Origine* was published, Mikołaj Radziwiłł the Black, the leading Calvinist magnate in Lithuania, formally protested about its negative portrayal of the Grand Duchy.[35] In hurriedly updating the *Polonia* for publication after an unauthorised edition appeared in 1575, Kromer merely added a few vague lines on the new relationship with Lithuania. Finally, Kromer, who was of relatively humble, non-noble origins, owed his controversial nomination to the prestigious see of Warmia to his long years of service to the king; if he was far from being a supporter of absolute monarchy, his work was broadly supportive of the monarchy, and did not reflect the more radical take on Polish politics of chroniclers such as his older contemporary Marcin Bielski (1495–1575), who was close to the noble reform movement that, influenced by classical republicanism, sought to limit the powers of the Crown. Bielski's chronicle, with its emphasis on citizenship and its use of the newly coined term *Rzeczpospolita* (Commonwealth), the Polonised form of the Latin *Res Publica*, did much to help embed in the consciousness of the *szlachta* an alternative version of Polish history to the chronicle of reigns to be found in Kromer.[36] Since it was published in Polish, however, the republican glories of Bielski's chronicle were unavailable to educated Scottish readers. There are no copies of Bielski in the major Scottish collections, which possess only the odd copy of the more republican versions of Polish history published in Latin.[37]

Thus the very real parallels between Polish and Scottish political history remained largely veiled from the Scottish elites at the time of the unions of 1603 and 1707. The turn of Polish writers to the vernacular meant that Scots were largely dependent on general accounts in foreign works. As Macinnes points out, they did read newsletters, in which Poland–Lithuania featured prominently in the seventeenth and early eighteenth centuries.[38] Yet these newsletters covered day-to-day politics, and were not very informative on the Commonwealth's constitution or the nature of its political system, while their accounts of the sufferings of Poland–Lithuania in the long cycle of wars between 1648 and 1721 did little to promote the idea that its system was worth emulating. Indeed, the political consequences of the disasters unleashed on the Commonwealth after 1648 meant that the increasingly disparaging works of foreign authors had turned the Commonwealth into an object of satire within British politics by the time of the 1707 union debates. Literary Scottish exiles in Poland did little to counter the increasingly negative publicity. William Bruce's published work concentrated on his hobby horse: the need for a new European crusade against the Ottoman Empire,[39] while if Jan or John Johnston, born in Szamotuły of Scottish parents and a graduate of St Andrews University, included extensive passages on Polish history in his historical works, apart from the National Library of Scotland, they do not seem to have reached other major Scottish collections, where the scientific and medical works for which he was renowned across Europe are strongly represented.[40]

By the end of the seventeenth century, interest in the Polish political system among learned Scots had withered. Fletcher of Saltoun actually had an impressive selection of books on Poland–Lithuania in his library: as well as Kromer, he owned Beauplan's description of the Ukraine, Chwałkowski's *Regni Poloniae ius publicum*, a 1672 edition of Heidenstein's *Rerum polonicarum*, a 1608 edition of Jan Zamoyski's 1563 *De senatu romano*, Kobierzycki's history of Władysław IV, Hartknoch's *Respublica Polonica* and works on military affairs by Jakub Sobieski, Andrzej Maksymilian Fredro, Gustav Freitag and Szymon Starowolski.[41] He did not, however, seem to draw on them in his political writings. Sir George Mackenzie of Rosehaugh discussed the French, the Spanish, the Swiss, the Dutch and the Portuguese in his *Ius Regium*, in which he attacked Buchanan and other supporters of elective monarchy in favour of the hereditary succession. By that time, the Poles would have provided an excellent example to support Mackenzie's case, but he ignored them completely. Twenty years later, in his *Parainesis Pacifica*, Mackenzie surveyed a number of unions, but only mentioned Poland in the context of its failed medieval union with Hungary.[42] Similarly, the Polish–Lithuanian Union warranted not a single mention in the 1703 pamphlet by the Englishman James Hodges, *The Rights and Interests of the Two British Monarchies*, which did examine a number of European examples of unions, including Spain, France, England, the United Provinces and the Swiss.[43] Despite the many close ties between the north-east of Scotland and Poland, Sir William Seton of Pitmedden also failed to mention Poland–Lithuania in his two pamphlets on the Union, *The Interest of Scotland*, and *Scotland's Great Advantages by an Union with England*, though he did in his famous speech in the Scottish Parliament on 18 November 1706, where he showed that he did have some knowledge of the Polish constitution when he claimed that the government of Scotland was not 'a Polish aristocracy, founded on *Pacta Conventa*, whereby all the Gentry are Impowered in their particular meetings to prescribe rules to their representatives in a General Dyet'.[44]

Pitmedden did not, however, use the Commonwealth's political decline to bolster his case for an incorporating rather than a federative union.[45] It seems that, like so many educated Scots in the early eighteenth century, his knowledge of the Commonwealth was derived largely from newsletters: unlike Fletcher of Saltoun, Pitmedden seems not to have had any great access to books on Poland–Lithuania, judging by the contents of his father's library, sold at auction in 1720: it contained the English edition of *Icon Animorum* and histories of Bohemia and Hungary, but none of Poland; the only Polish works mentioned were the 1584 Cologne edition of Stanisław Sokołowski's *De verae et falsae ecclesiae discrimine* and a work by the noted Arian Stanisław Lubieniecki on comets.[46]

The ignorance of contemporary Scottish politicians is perhaps best summed up by the case of George Ridpath, who was a supporter of a federative union in so far as he supported union at all. Ridpath did mention Poland on a couple of occasions in his *Considerations upon the Union of the Two Kingdoms*, but simply quoted from Sir William Craig's account, already a century old, which was in any case based on Kromer, and therefore showed no knowledge of the arrangements established at Lublin in 1569.[47] This was entirely characteristic of the debates over the royal succession and the parliamentary union: by the early eighteenth century, a 'Polish Diet' was the last thing that the Scottish Parliament wished to become. Perhaps the most frequent mention of Poland in the union debates was with reference to the Duke of Hamilton, whose claims to the throne were lampooned by his being dubbed 'Stanislas, king of Poland', a direct reference to Stanisław Leszczyński, who mounted the Polish throne in 1704 in a farcical and legally dubious election carried out at the behest of Charles XII and carefully marshalled by Swedish troops.[48]

In any case, Scots had always shown rather more interest in Polish religion – for the most part in its Protestant varieties – and Scottish libraries, including that of Fletcher of Saltoun, have considerably larger holdings of contemporary works by or about Poland–Lithuania's Protestant community, in particular by Polish Arian followers of Faustus Socinius. There was also considerable interest in the Polish toleration for religious dissenters which so impressed John Durie.[49] Yet the seventeenth century saw the steady erosion of the attraction of Protestantism, which had been considerable down to the end of the sixteenth century, for the noble elites of Poland–Lithuania. As the Catholic Reformation took hold and Poland–Lithuania settled down as one of Europe's Catholic states, the barriers to any engagement with its political culture on the part of the Scottish elites became insurmountable, not least because of the steady erosion of the tolerant political environment of Renaissance Poland during the long wars against Sweden, Russia and the Ottoman Empire after 1600. Within two decades of the Anglo–Scottish Union of 1707, the 1724 Tumult of Thorn [Toruń], following which the Lutheran burgomeister of the city, which had long been a centre of the Scottish community in Poland, and nine others were executed after anti-Jesuit riots, sealed the Commonwealth's reputation among educated Britons as a centre of intolerant baroque Catholic superstition.[50] On the other hand, for the increasingly Catholic elites of Poland–Lithuania, Scotland remained a Calvinist country subject to what they saw as the pernicious and subversive political mores of that creed: 'One sees what disturbances and disasters the Calvinist religion in England has established and stirred into life', as Wojciech Tolibowski, Bishop of Poznań, put it in a speech at the 1658 Sejm.[51]

Thus, for learned Scots, from the early seventeenth century, Poland was classed among the Catholic powers, and linked therefore to a stereotype of absolute monarchy and arbitrary power, despite the fact that the Catholic hierarchy in Poland, while broadly monarchical in its sympathies, was by no means a supporter of absolute royal power; ironically Catholic Poland–Lithuania had remained true to the Roman republican and Ciceronian tradition which had so influenced Scottish Calvinist political discourse in the sixteenth century. After 1603, however, the political cultures of the two powers diverged, as Poland largely missed the turn from Cicero to Tacitus which, in Scotland as elsewhere in Europe, drew attention to the inglorious end of the Roman Republic.[52] Opaliński's *Defensa Polonia* marked in many ways the end of an era in which the two political cultures, had they had access to the right literature, might have entered constructive political dialogue. Yet Opaliński's bilious pamphlet, as far as I know, was fired into a void, and attracted no attention in Scotland: the National Library possesses a copy, but it was only purchased in 2005. It is absent from the collections of the ancient universities. With Barclay long dead by 1648, there was in any case nobody to shout back. It was not until later in the eighteenth century that Scots once more began to pay attention to a Commonwealth by then in its death-throes.

Notes

1 Łukasz Opaliński, *Polonia defensa contra Ioan. Barclaivm, ubi, occasione ista, de regno genteque polona multa narrantur, hactenus litteris non tradita.* (Danzig, 1648). For Opaliński's career see Stanisław Grzeszczuk, 'Łukasz Opaliński (1612–1662)', *Polski Słownik Biograficzny* (hereafter *PSB*) 24, pp. 93–6.
2 John Barclay, *Icon Animorum* (London, 1613). There were new editions in 1614, 1616, 1617, 1619, 1628, 1629, 1637, 1655, 1658, 1664 and 1674. It was published in France (1628, 1637, 1674); and was translated into French (1625), English (1631), and German (1660), with some thirty editions overall: Hans-Jürgen Bömelburg, *Frühneuzeitliche Nationen im östlichen Europa. Das polnische Geschichtsdenken und die Reichweite einer humanistischen Nationalgeschichte (1500–1700)* (Wiesbaden, 2006), p. 272.

3 John Barclay, *Opisanie animuszów piąci co naprzednieyszych narodow w Europie* (1647).

4 '*Indignanti mihi sæpius, tam contumeliose descriptam, aut traductam potius gentem nostram à Ioanne Barclaio, in libro, cui nomen ICON ANIMORVM; Deinde vero accusanti incuriam non vindicantium hucusque patriam calumnia tanta atque impostura.*' Opaliński, *Polonia Defensa*, A2. The preface covered an additional four pages. For Barclay's section on Poland, see John Barclay, *Icon Animorum* (London, 1614), ch. VIII, pp. 164–9.

5 Nicola Royan, 'Barclay, John (1582–1621)'. *Oxford Dictionary of National Biography* [http://www.oxforddnb.com/view/article/1342, accessed 11 Sept 2009].

6 '*Nec populi [. . .] moribus factis ad nostri seculi venustatem*', quoted by Opaliński, *Polonia Defensa*, p. 57, '*Gens ad ferociam & licentiam nata, quam vocant libertatem*', ibid., p. 79. Barclay, *Icon Animorum*, pp. 167, 168.

7 Opaliński, *Polonia Defensa*, pp. 33, 46.

8 'For if trade is meagre, it is sordid.' ibid., p. 45. The passage in Cicero makes it clear that trade is a worthy pursuit if carried out on a large scale: '*Mercatura autem, si tenuis est, sordida putanda est; sin magna et copiosa, multa undique apportans multisque sine vanitate inpertiens, non est admodum vituperanda; atque etiam si satiata quæstu vel contenta potius, ut sæpe ex alto in portum, ex ipso se portu in agros possessionesque contulit, videtur iure optimo posse laudari.*' Cicero, *De officiis* 1, 42, 151. Thus the Polish *szlachta*, exporting large quantities of grain through the Royal Prussian ports, could look down with impunity on Scottish tinkers.

9 For Barclay's views on the Jews, see *Icon Animorum*, ch. IX, pp. 208–10.

10 Opaliński, *Polonia Defensa*, pp. 46, 53.

11 Waldemar Kowalski, 'The placement of urbanized Scots in the sixteenth and seventeenth centuries', in Alexia Grosjean and Steve Murdoch, eds, *Scottish Communities Abroad in the Early Modern Period* (Leiden, 2005), pp. 53–103; Arthur H. Williamson, 'The nation epidemical: Scoto-Britannus to Scoto-Polonus', in *Britain and Poland–Lithuania. Contact and Comparison from the Middle Ages to 1795*, ed. Richard Unger (Leiden and Boston, 2008), pp. 287–304.

12 See Zenon Guldon, ed., *Żydzi i Szkoci w Polsce w XVI–XVIII wieku, Studia i Materiały* (Kielce, 1990).

13 Waldemar Kowalski, 'Kraków citizenship and the local Scots, 1509–1655', in Unger, ed., *Britain and Poland–Lithuania*, pp. 263–85; Peter Paul Bajer, 'Scotsmen and the Polish nobility from the sixteenth to the eighteenth century', in Unger, ed., *Britain and Poland–Lithuania*, pp. 329–53.

14 William Barclay, *De regno et regali potestate adversus Buchananum, Brutum, Boucherium & reliquos monarchomachos, libri sex* (Paris, 1600); Kamila Schuster, *Biblioteka Łukasza Opalińskiego marszałka nadwornego koronnego (1612–1662)* (Wrocław, 1971), pp. 206, 210, 220, 229, 249.

15 '*nimiumque de fortuna Regum solicito*', Opaliński, *Polonia Defensa*, p. 101. Łukasz Opaliński, *Rozmowa plebana z ziemianinem, albo dyszkurs o postanowieniu terazniejszym Rzeczypospolitej y o sposobie zawierania seymow* (1641). See Stanisław

Grzeszczuk, 'Wstęp', Łukasz Opaliński, *Wybór pism*, ed. Stanisław Grzeszczuk (Wrocław-Cracow, 1959), p. lxxxi.

16 '*Quinimmo gratulor Patriæ meæ, tales Principes hactenus ei contigisse, qui non se supra leges esse, sed leges supra se rati, nihilque detrahi hinc majestati suæ merito reputantes, vi & armis ad observationem illarum nusquam fuerunt adigendi.*' Opaliński, *Polonia Defensa*, p. 101.

17 '*& vel maxime tua, ô Barclai, Britannia Symplegadum more colliditur, cum tot furias facesque belli intestini nuper accendit: tamque longo, tam cruento dissidio evertit imperium, & Regem omni jure ac potestate spoliavit. Maxime autem populares tui Scoti, qui Principem, se ultro illis permittentem, scelere turpissimo ac perfidia, post longam licitationem, vendidere Anglis, postquam multis injuriis & contumeliis prius captivum affecerunt*', ibid., p. 105.

18 The best account of Polish history writing in this period is Bömelburg's excellent *Frühneuzeitliche Nationen* (see note 2). For Scotland see Roger Mason, 'Usable pasts: history and identity in Reformation Scotland', in Roger Mason, *Kingship and the Commonweal. Political Thought in Renaissance and Reformation Scotland* (East Linton, 1998), pp. 165–86.

19 Paweł Gorzelski, 'The Commonwealth and *Monarchia Mixta* in Polish and English political thought in the later sixteenth century', in Unger, ed., *Britain and Poland–Lithuania*, pp. 167–81, and Benedict Wagner-Rundell, 'Liberty, virtue and the chosen people: British and Polish republicanism in the early eighteenth century', in Unger, ed., *Britain and Poland–Lithuania*, pp. 197–214.

20 Maria Pryshlak, *Państwo w filozofii politicznej Łukasza Opalińskiego* (Cracow, 2000).

21 For Buchanan, see Roger Mason, 'George Buchanan, James VI and the Presbyterians', in Mason, *Kingship and the Commonweal*, pp. 187–214; Mason, '*Rex stoicus*: George Buchanan, James VI and the Scottish polity', in John Dwyer *et al.*, eds, *New Perspectives on the Politics and Culture of Early Modern Scotland* (Edinburgh, 1982), pp. 9–33, and James H. Burns, 'The political ideas of George Buchanan', *Scottish Historical Review* 30 (1951), pp. 60–8.

22 Andrew Fletcher of Saltoun, 'Speeches by a member of the Parliament which began at Edinburgh the 6th of May, 1703', in John Robertson, ed., *Andrew Fletcher. Political Works* (Cambridge, 1997), p. 135.

23 Benedict Wagner-Rundell, 'Republicanism in early modern Poland–Lithuania: the politics of virtue in the reign of August II', unpublished D.Phil. thesis, University of Oxford (2008), ch. 6, pp. 244–77; Allan Macinnes, 'The Hidden Commonwealth: Poland–Lithuania and Scottish political discourse in the seventeenth century', in Karin Friedrich and Barbara Pendich, eds, *Citizenship and Identity in a Multinational Commonwealth. Poland–Lithuania in Context, 1550–1772* (Leiden, 2009), pp. 233–60.

24 Sir Henry Savile, *Historical Collections left to be considered of, for the better perfecting of this intended union between England and Scotland*, ch. 22 'The articles of union between Lituania and Poland', in Bruce Galloway and Brian Levack, eds, *The Jacobean Union. Six Tracts of 1604* (Edinburgh, 1985), pp. 218–22; Sir Thomas Craig, *De Unione Regnorum Britanniæ Tractatus*, ed. C. Sanford Terry (Edinburgh,

1909), pp. 283, 300–1, 391, 408, 469; *The British Union. A Critical Edition and Translation of David Hume of Godscrofts* De Unione Insulae Britannicae, Paul J. McGinnis and Arthur H. Williamson, trans. and ed. (London, 2002). Macinnes, 'The Hidden Commonwealth', p. 238. For an overview of the development of the Polish–Lithuanian union, see Robert Frost, 'Union as process: Confused sovereignty and the Polish–Lithuanian Commonwealth, 1500–1795', in Micheál O'Siochrú and Andrew Mackillop, eds, *Forging the State. European State Formation and the Anglo–Scottish Union of 1707* (Dundee, 2009), pp. 67–85.

25 Fletcher, *Political Works*, pp. 100, 203.

26 Macinnes, 'The Hidden Commonwealth', p. 260.

27 William Bruce merits an entry in the Polish Biographical Dictionary *Polski Słownik Biograficzny*, but not in the *Oxford Dictonary of National Biography*: Stanisław Kot, 'William Bruce', *PSB* 3 (Cracow, 1937), pp. 3–4; see also Stanisław Kot, 'Nationum Proprietates', *Oxford Slavonic Papers* VII (1957), p. 99. Charles Talbot, who edited the *Relation* for publication, rejects Kot's contention that Bruce was its author: *Res Polonica ex Archivo Musei Britannici I Pars. 'Relation of the State of Polonia and the United Provinces of that Crown anno 1598'*, Charles Talbot ed., *Elementa ad Fontium Editiones* 13 (Rome, 1965), pp. xii–xiii. This conclusion is echoed by Sebastian Sobecki, 'The Authorship of *A Relation of the State of Polonia, 1598*', *The Seventeenth Century*, 18 (2003), pp. 172–9. Another scholar, despite his highly dubious enlistment of modern graphologists to show that the *Relation* could not have been written by Sir George Carew, who served as ambassador to Poland–Lithuania in 1598 and who is frequently suggested as its author, makes a strong case for Bruce having at least played a part in its composition: Edward Mierzwa, 'William Bruce, professor Akademii Zamojskiej i agent handlowy The Eastland Company, in Henryk Gmiterek, ed., *W Kręgu Akademickiego Zamościa* (Lublin, 1996), pp. 207–23. It may or may not be significant that George Carew's signature appears on the title page of the National Library of Scotland's copy of Alexander Guagnini's *Sarmatiae Europeae descriptio* (Speyer, 1581): A. M. Graham, ed., *Poland. An Exhibition Mainly of Printed Books* (Edinburgh, 1965), p. 3.

28 Anna Biegańska, 'The learned Scots in Poland (from the mid-sixteenth to the close of the eighteenth century)', *Canadian Slavonic Papers* 43 (2001) pp. 18–23. *Diary of General Patrick Gordon of Auchleuchries 1635–1699*, vol. 1, *1634–1659*, ed. Dmitry Fedosov (Aberdeen, 2009).

29 *Martini Cromeri de origine et rebus gestis Polonorum libri XXX* (Basel, 1555); Marcin Kromer, *Polonia: sive de situ, populis, moribus magistratibus et respublica Regni Polonicae, libri duo* (Frankfurt am Main, 1577).

30 Aberdeen's copy of the 1558 edition was part of Thomas Reid's bequest to Marischal College (1624), while the St Andrews' copy was owned by Sir Thomas Henryson, Lord Chesters, who died in 1638, and then William Guild, Principal of King's College, Aberdeen, who left his library to the University of St Andrews. Many of the relatively scanty holdings of sixteenth- and seventeenth-century polonica in the National Library of Scotland were in fact part of a donation to the Library of the Writers to the Signet by Count Konstanty Zamoyski and other

Polish exiles in 1820, and a further donation by Count Jan Tarnowski in 1964: Graham, *Poland. An Exhibition*, preface. The Library's copy of *De Origine* was not part of these donations.

31 P. J. M. Willems, *Bibliotheca Fletcheriana: or, the Extraordinary Library of Andrew Fletcher of Saltoun* (Wassenaar, 1999).

32 There is, alas, no comprehensive modern study of this crucial figure. See Henryk Barycz, 'Kromer, Marcin h. Własnego (1512–1589)', *PSB* 15 (Cracow, 1970), pp. 219–25. Bömelburg, *Frühneuzeitliche Nationen*, p. 112. For the way in which Kromer was filtered through other sources, and the misunderstandings that thereby arose, see Teresa Bałuk, 'Sir Robert Filmer's description of the Polish constitutional system in the seventeenth century', *Slavonic and East European Review* 62 (1984), 246–9.

33 For the making of the Union of Lublin, see Harry E. Dembkowski, *The Union of Lublin. Polish Federalism in the Golden Age* (Boulder, CA, 1982); Frost, 'Union as process'.

34 Savile, *Historical Collections*, p. 219. Savile was using the Basel edition of 1568.

35 Bömelburg, *Frühneuzeitliche Nationen*, p. 121.

36 Marcin Bielski, *Kronika wszystkiego świata, na ssesc wyekow, Monarchie cztery rozdzielona, s Kosmográphią nową [. . .] po polsku pisána, s figurami [. . .] Między ktorémi też nászá Polska ná ostátku zosobná yest wypisána*. (Cracow, 1551). For Bielski, see Bömelburg, *Frühneuzeitliche Nationen*, pp. 101–10.

37 Aberdeen University library has a copy of Stanisław Orzechowski's *Annales Stanislai Orichovii Okszii* (Dobromile, 1611), while Glasgow University library possesses Szymon Starowolski's *Polonia, nunc denuo recognita et aucta* (Danzig, 1652). The National Library's copy of the same work was part of a reprint of several works of Starowolski published in 1733.

38 Macinnes, 'The Hidden Commonwealth', p. 238.

39 William Bruce, *Ad principes populumque Christianum de bello adversus Turcos gerendo [. . .] consilium* (Cracow, 1594) and *De Tataribus diarium Guilielmi Brusci Scoti* (Frankfurt am Main, 1598).

40 The National Library of Scotland has four copies of Johnston's *Historia universalis civilis et ecclesiastica, res præcipuas ab orbe condito ad annum MDCXXXIII gestas brevissimi exhibens*: the second edition (Leiden, 1638), the third edition (Amsterdam, 1641), the amended third edition (Amsterdam, 1644), and the extended and augmented fourth edition (Frankfurt am Main, 1672). It has two copies of his *Polyhistor, seu rerum ab exorto universi as nostra usque tempora, per Asiam, Africam, Europam & Americam, in sacris & profanis gestarum succincta & methodica series*. (Jena, 1660) and the augmented second edition (Jena, 1667). Johnston was, however, a much better scientist than a historian, and the passages on Poland–Lithuania are rather general and generic, adding little to what was available in other works.

41 Willems, *Bibliotheca Fletcheriana*. N. Chwalkovius [Mikołaj Chwałkowski], *Regni Poloniae ius publicum* (Königsberg, 1684; Guillaume le Vasseur de Beauplan, *Description d'Ukraine* (Rouen, 1673) (first edition 1660); R. Heidenstenius [Reinhold Heidenstein], *Rerum Polonicarum [. . .] libri XII* (Frankfurt, 1672);

S. Kobierzyczko [Stanisław Kobierzycki], *Historia Vladislai Poloniæ et Sueciæ prinipis, ejus Natales et Infantiam, Electionem in Magnum Moscoviæ Ducem, Bellum Moscovitica, Turcica, cæterasque res gesta continens, usque ad excessum Sigismundi III* (Danzig, 1655); Christoph Hartknoch, *Respublica Polonica libri II* (Leipzig, 1698).

42 Sir George Mackenzie, *Ius Regium, Or the Just and Solid Foundation of Monarchy in general, and more especially of the Monarchy of Scotland, Maintain'd against Buchanan, Naphthali, Dolman, Milton &c.* (London, 1684) and *Parainesis Pacifica; Or, a Perswasive to the Union of Britain* (Edinburgh, 1702), p. vi.

43 James Hodges, *The Rights and Interests of the Two British Monarchies Inquir'd into, and Clear'd; With a Special Respect to an United or Separate State* (Edinburgh and London, 1703).

44 Sir William Seton of Pitmedden, *The Interest of Scotland in Three Essays* (London, 1700), and *Scotland's great advantages by an union with England: showen in a letter from the country. To a member of Parliament.* (Edinburgh?, 1706). 'A Speech in Parliament spoken by Mr Seton junior of Pitmedden, 18 November 1706, on the subject of the third Article then being in Debate in the House', printed in Daniel Defoe, *The History of the Union of Great Britain* (Edinburgh, 1709), p. 76.

45 Sir William Seton of Pitmedden, *A Speech in Parliament the second day of November 1706 by William Seton of Pitmedden Junior, on the First Article of the Treaty of Union* (Edinburgh, 1706).

46 Stanislaus Socolovius [Stanisław Sokołowski], *De verae et falsae Ecclesiae discrimine [. . .] libri tres* (Cologne, 1584); Stanislaus Lubieniecius [Stanisław Lubieniecki], *Theatrum Cometicum* 2 vols (Amsterdam, 1657); *A catalogue of valuable books, in several languages and faculties, viz. divinity, law, medicine, history, [. . .] being the library which belong'd to Sir Alexander Seton of Pitmedden Baronet, lately deceased. To be sold by way of auction on Munday the 11 day of January 1720, [. . .] Catalogues {. . .] at Mr James McEuen's [. . .]*, National Library of Scotland, MS.3802, pp. 26, 57. My thanks to Professor Colin Kidd for his help in locating this source.

47 George Ridpath, *Considerations upon the Union of the Two Kingdoms: with an Account of the Methods taken by Ancient and Modern Governments, to effect an Union, without endangering the Fundamental Constitutions of the United Countries* (Edinburgh?, 1706), p. 23.

48 See, for example, *The Right of Succession to the Crown and Sovereignty of Scotland Argued* (London, 1705).

49 Macinnes, 'The Hidden Commonwealth', pp. 243–5, 249.

50 See, for example, *A faithful and exact narative of the horrid tragedy; lately acted at Thorn, in Polish Prussia; by the contrivances and instigation of the Jesuits* (London,1725?).

51 'Mann sehe waß die Calvinische Religion in Engellandt für Unruhe undt Unheil angerichtet undt Erwekhet habe', Archiwum Państwowe w Gdańsku, 300/29/146 f. 10v.

52 Tacitus was not a part of school curricula in Poland–Lithuania in the first half of the seventeenth century: Bömelburg, *Frühneuzeitliche Nationen*, pp. 194–5.

4   The Reasons for the Immigration of Scots to the Polish Commonwealth in the Early Modern Period as Outlined in Contemporary Opinions and Historiography

Waldemar Kowalski

As is widely known, the state of Poland and Lithuania, united in 1569, was a state multi-ethnic and multi-denominational in character. The influx of peoples ethnically foreign, first and foremost Jewish and German, lasted for the entire Middle Ages. Jews were a relatively numerous ethnic group in Poland, and possessed a separate legal status as well as self-government. Self-government was also enjoyed by Scots, present in numbers from the turn of the sixteenth century, as well as Armenians, Tartars and Wallachians.[1]

Around 1500, the number of inhabitants of Poland, which covered an area of 265,000 km², was close to 4,000,000, of which ethnic Poles constituted around 70 per cent. The remaining 30 per cent were: Ruthenians – around 15 per cent, Germans – above 10 per cent, and other ethnic groups – chiefly Jews and Wallachians.[2] In the first half of the seventeenth century, the area covered by the Polish–Lithuanian state increased to 990,000 km², with its inhabitants numbering no more than 9,000,000. The percentage of Poles, however, had reduced in size to around 50 per cent; 40 per cent of the population were Lithuanians and Ruthenians, while the remaining 10 per cent was composed of the ethnic minorities already mentioned together with Italians and Hungarians. Only about 23 per cent of the population lived in towns, 10 per cent was the chiefly rural-based nobility and gentry, with the remaining population comprising peasants estimated to number 67 per cent of the total inhabitants.[3]

The relations between the Polish population and those incomers, as well as between the inhabitants that were ethnically not Polish, are a complicated and extensive subject. For these relations were shaped differently in different areas of the Commonwealth; the situation looked different in the countryside and in small towns, and different again in the large towns. Undoubtedly, the generalisation that economic inter-relations influenced these relationships would be a valid one. One may recall a vista that the competitors to Polish merchants and artisans were the Jews, the Italians and the Scots. Thus this explains the propaganda action directed against them by the burghers. In the defence of the urban corporation stood clerical publicists coming from urban circles,[4] who attacked also with their pen, among others, Jewish doctors. On the other hand, the gentry and clergy willingly took advantage of the trade intermediary of Jews, with whom they also invested capital. The representatives of both the estates mentioned, as well as the peasantry, often stocked up from foreign traders. Simultaneously, however, they accused them of becoming rich contrary to the law in force. These accusations were motivated by gentry disdain for urban trades, i.e. craft and commerce, as well as envy inflamed by the view of urban tenements of shops.[5]

Besides the economic factor, a significant influence on the mutual perception of ethnic groups was played by denominational affiliation. The dislike, or hostility, that derived hence was expressed during the polemics of theologians, and moreover through attacks on Protestant chapels and their parishioners. Generally, the Catholic majority perceived Germans as Luther's henchmen, while Scots were associated with being adherents of Calvin. Such mistaken generalisations linking particular ethnic groupings with the typical confessional adherence associated with them became increasingly often the case with the Catholic Counter-Reformation reaction, resulting in the subsequent marginalising of Protestants within public life, a process that had its origins at the end of the sixteenth century.[6]

The Polish gentry viewed foreign nations from the heights of the national megalomania fostered by this estate. This megalomania was based particularly on three dogmas. The 'granary dogma' was the conviction that Polish grain was a necessity on foreign markets and the analysis of the economy in its entirety in relation to its export. The second dogma proclaimed the Commonwealth 'the bulwark of Christianity' for it had seemed to defend Europe from the flood of Islam. The Polish–Lithuanian state occupied a unique position within the Catholic world. The gentry, in its opinion, were to act as the guard of the true faith as threatened by the attacks of the schismatic and heretical neighbours of the Commonwealth. The third dogma was the myth of the ideal republican state order harking back to Roman traditions. It is not surprising therefore that mistrust dominated relations with other nations, even manifesting itself at times in hostility, and that this xenophobia did not spare the foreign traders, soldiers, and even clergymen who happened to settle within the borders of the Commonwealth.[7]

Wandering stall-keepers, including Scots, supplied the peasants with goods which they otherwise would have had to have found at town markets. In this sense, from the viewpoint of the owners of villages, these traders played a positive role. For their activities upheld the gentry's policy of limiting the peasantry's access to towns.[8] On the other hand, in the concerted opinion of the gentry estate expressed systematically at Diet, dietines and in publications, the Scots and other arrivals involved in trade enriched the Crown's coffers at a level far below their possibilities.[9] These self-same authors accused

the Scots of enriching themselves quickly, often against the law in force. This
wealth was exhibited, contrasting it with the poverty experienced by the Scots
in their homeland. It is Łukasz Opaliński in his *Polonia defensa contra Ioannem
Barclaium* (1648) who has devoted the most space to the reasons for Scottish
emigration. This was a reply to John Barclay's *Icon animorum* (1611), which
presented unfavourably the national traits of Poles.[10] Opaliński, one of the
most influential politicians of his day as well as being a publicist, refuted the
charges made by the Scottish poet. He wrote thus about the Scottish immigrants in the Commonwealth:

> This nation, sickened by their poor and infertile homeland, escapes over
> the sea from indigence and seeks a livelihood in us. Formerly the most
> inferior pedlars whose equipment was only baskets and hay, they sold mere
> trinkets of the ilk of needles, buckles and blades carrying on their backs
> crates and boxes. While now . . . they transport in wagons their goods and
> travel around town fairs.[11]

One may note that this view as to the poverty that forced the Scots to migrate
is in accordance with the reasons outlined by Fynes Moryson in 1593.[12]

In answering Barclay's charge concerning the lack of stone for the construction of houses, Opaliński harshly replies:

> In sum to such a degree that the Scots wandering around villages have
> nowhere to shelter from dogs. They would have more wisely acted if they
> had demanded from their homeland that treasure that constitutes their
> greatest riches.[13]

This is only one of a chorus of voices describing the collective career from rags
to riches of Scots for whom Poland was 'the America of the day'.[14] In 1638,
Władysław Stanisław Jeżowski recalled with sentiment the formerly good
times for the gentry:

> Our forefathers previously loved the clay
> Of false contracts never was there say
> Which in Poland of this day abundance sway
> For as a village before Scots and Jews could not be bought
> Forced is a nobleman to town for what rurally he would have sought
> Better such favours be enacted by noble blood
> Than by the Jewish, Scottish or German flood.[15]

A year later Adam Grodziecki, Międzyrzecz Castellan, recalls that in his
youth, twenty years before:

genus inutile . . . on foot from village to village they tramped, with boxes on shoulders and in the box soap, crochet hooks, hooks and eyes, needles, dice, blades, cards etc. while yet from such trade under the sacred memory of the father of Your Most Regal Majesty, as well as under King Stephen they had always been driven off to war. Now you have no longer such a pauper that would not send goods and materials to fairs with four nags on wagoner carts to several different towns at the same time with intermediaries from his people, they even trade in oxen [and] furs, and only a cottage *propter indigenatum* purchased in any place for a few coins, gravely they collect money and transport it to Scotland, while they send other hungry *sangui suas* to Poland to their homes. That it follows to impose on them something greater, for with our disgrace they have a judge of their nation in Elbląg under the rule of Your Most Regal Majesty.[16]

Foreign merchants were blamed for the economic collapse of towns. This was formulated *expressis verbis* by Jan Herburt, a historian and humanist connected with the royal Court: 'Through the work of Italians, Scots and other foreigners our towns are experiencing great damage.'[17] Stanisław Cikowski, Cracow Chamberlain, complained that: 'Italians, Germans, Scots, and even Jews, under the cloak of town law, bought for three score, want more prerogatives than do the gentry.'[18]

This author emphasises the incomers' getting rich quick by means of trickery to the detriment of the Royal Treasury:

> Foreign merchants who try the hardest for warehouses in their towns in order for them to be transferred from Poland to their own, what their brethren here invoice and with the destruction of age-old families in towns and then the gentry estate, they enrich themselves, take all the money from Poland, or they buy villages, frontal tenements and castles.[19]

Łukasz Opaliński was also against the settlement in Poland of foreign merchants – competition for the gentry. He cited a constantly repeated argument – 'for such prosperity and riches is *nil conferunt* for the Homeland, for what they take here, they transport to foreign realms'.[20]

Scots were commonly accused of participating in customs fiddles. On 12 March 1623, Sigismund III Vasa obliged merchants to prove by oath to the customs secretary that they traded in their own goods. They were also to report to one of the main chambers, either the Cracow or Poznań chamber, '"alone" in person and not through an intermediary or agent'. These decrees were directed first of all to the merchants of the largest towns, of which the issuer included: Cracow, Poznań, Zamość, Tarnów, Opatów and Lelów. The king also pointed to the abuse in the trading of oxen carried out 'under the pretext of gentry freedoms'.[21] The execution of such decrees was certainly not effective. After a quarter of a century, the historian and publicist Szymon Starowolski complained about the gentry that 'many people of trade, both ours and foreign, Italians, Germans, Armenians, Scots, Jews, in return for a gift take goods free of duty'.[22] In another of his works *Polonia sive status Regni Poloniæ descriptio* (1632), directed towards a foreign reader, he cites the presence in Lublin and Vilnius of English and Scottish merchants as one of the reasons for the successful development of these towns.[23]

The views expressed above resulted from protectionist attempts motivated by the ideas of mercantilism. The reform of duties, the encouragement of foreign merchants to purchase local goods as well as the ban on the export of coinage were to be a part of an effective economic policy which would allow the crisis which had been intensifying from the end of the sixteenth century to be overcome.[24]

Aleksander Wejnert (1804–1879) was the first Polish historian of Scottish immigrants to perceive the question in a wider sense. He saw the genesis of their emigration in the growing interest in the Reformation under the rule of James V. He explained the emigration as the necessity to escape religious and political persecution, and the search for 'freedoms of conscience and property'. He did add, however, that the majority of the emigrants were poor.[25]

The eminent Cracovian art historian Stanisław Tomkowicz (1850–1933) in describing the customs of the burghers of the Commonwealth's capital at the turn of the seventeenth century takes note, in an article published in 1898, of the incomers from a distant country of interest to us: 'The political and religious revolutions in distant England are driving to us a new wave of hitherto unknown Scots, who are employed in the cloth and spice trade, and also found numerous brotherhoods, even running an interesting and long lasting law suit with the English king.'[26]

Tomkowicz is moreover the author of a work published a year later and devoted first and foremost to the Scots in Cracow. This is the best-documented work presenting the place of Scottish merchants in the Commonwealth to be published before World War II. The author describes at length the causes for immigration, emphasising the absence of wider research for the question: what persuaded Scots to abandon their homeland? The answer to this question is unlocked by the following assessment of the internal state of the Stuart monarchy:

> Scotland from the mid-sixteenth century had fallen into a chronic state of political and religious unrest, conflicts with England and civil war. This constant ferment triggering off commotion of conscience and the economic ruin of Scotland's inhabitants had reached such a stage that it had become simply impossible for many of them to live and stay within its borders.

When one mixes matters of religion with politics then passions usually take on a great force; while finally the two races from which the population of that country is comprised – both the Anglo-Saxon and the Celtic – are hard, unscrupulous, and ruthless in battle.[27]

Further on the author depicts the denominational changes beginning from around 1550 up until the occupation of Scotland by Cromwell, paying especial attention to the relationship of subsequent monarchs to the Evangelical Church. He seeks the main cause of emigration in the religious conflicts of subsequent generations. He does note, however, that:

> The Scots had been for a long time an industrious and commercial people. These emigrants consequently turned to countries where there were open and favourable fields for their activities. Such were found first and foremost in Gdańsk and the eastern lands of Prussia, and further in Poland. Here and there they threw themselves into trade, in a way similar to the Jews. Hence has derived for sure the certain commonality within their lot in the new homeland and that of the Jews.[28]

Also Jerzy Sadownik, the author of the work on Scots in Lublin in the seventeenth century, sees as the main causes for their emigration the religious persecution 'of Calvinists by the Anglican Church' although he also perceives 'economic considerations'.[29]

More cautious in his evaluations was Wacław Borowy (1890–1950), a literary historian connected with the University of Warsaw and the School of Slavonic Studies in London. In a paper, 'Scots in Old Poland', delivered first in 1938 in the *Warsaw Weekly*, and subsequently reprinted in Edinburgh in 1941, he writes:

> The reasons for this emigration might have been various. The most important of them was certainly that Scotland's resources were not sufficient for its population. The principle of primogeniture forced younger sons even of more prosperous families to look for a career abroad and whetted in them the taste for adventure.
>
> Another important reason came with the persecution of the Catholics and of the Presbyterians: the very dates of their developments seem to mark larger waves of the Scottish influx in Poland.[30]

The authors who explained the causes of immigration in works that were written in the period immediately after World War II connected themselves to the historiographic tradition outlined above. Aleksander Kossowski (1886–1965) perceived these causes in the civil wars and the persecutions that were denominationally motivated. This author of numerous valuable works on the period of the Reformation in Little Poland (Małopolska) explained among other things the successive consequences of the adoption by the Scots of the Protestant religion: 'Catholicism maintained itself only in inaccessible mountain regions. Denominational antagonisms were intertwined with national ones, for England supported the Anglican Church.'[31] Janina Bieniarzówna (1916–1997), an economic historian, also mentioned 'religious persecutions' as the reasons behind the Scottish settlement in seventeenth-century Cracow.[32]

Stanisław Seliga (1895–1991) and Leon Koczy (1900–1981), the authors of the work *Scotland and Poland. A Chapter of Forgotten History*, published in 1968, point, however, to 'poverty, periods of famine . . .', and subsequently to 'religious persecution either by the Roman Catholics or the Presbyterians'. They also enumerate 'civil disorders' evoked by 'a young Scot in a lawsuit in Wrocław at the end of the fifteenth century', and moreover the 'lack of good prospects in their native country for the younger sons of noble families'. The wider context for emigration displayed by these authors as well as the priority given to economic factors must have resulted from the fact that these historians were themselves emigrants in Great Britain and had access to the appropriate literature. The already mentioned context also covered 'the Scottish propensity to seek a life of adventure in the world at large'.[33]

Almost twenty years later, Stanisław Gierszewski (1929–1993), the urban and Pomerania historian, again explained the causes of the discussed migration as 'chiefly religious conflicts'.[34]

It was Anna Biegańska, a highly-regarded researcher into the history of Scots in Poland, in her work *Scottish Soldiers in the Commonwealth* of 1984, who for the first time clearly pointed to economic reasons as the fundamental cause for the emigration. She also did not dismiss 'denominational and political factors', i.e. 'the tension between Catholics and Protestants [and] subsequently between the adherents of Presbyterianism and the Episcopal Church'.[35] In another article published in 1991 and devoted to Scottish Catholics and Presbyterians in Poland, Dr Biegańska claims that 'among the reasons behind the emigration of the Scots in the second half of the sixteenth and in the seventeenth centuries religious factors ranked among the most important'.[36] While in the work *The Learned Scots in Poland (From the Mid-Sixteenth to the Close of the Eighteenth Century)* she notes that generally: 'Drawn from their homeland by economic, political and religious causes, the Scottish emigrants and refugees were attracted by advantageous conditions in Poland.'[37] Such a position has been adopted equally by Maria Bogucka, who characterised Scottish circles in Gdańsk of the early modern epoch,[38] as well as by Zenon Guldon in his work on the Scots in the palatinate of Sandomierz.[39]

In the work *The English and Scottish Population in Poland in the Mid Seventeenth Century*, published in 1982, Zenon Guldon and Lech Stępkowski, linking themselves to the earlier research cited here, note that: 'Scottish immigration has been consistently explained by chiefly religious considerations forcing the Scottish Presbyterians to leave their homeland.' They do not leave out economic factors, however, and to give weight to their argument cite the view of Łukasz Opaliński quoted above.[40]

To sum up the above observations: twentieth-century Polish historians writing about Scottish immigration to Poland in general view its causes to lie in denominational and political conflicts. Economic considerations advanced as primary reasons by the Polish polemicists of the early modern epoch, are rated by only a few nineteenth- and twentieth-century researchers. As recently as the year 2000, an art historian describing late-medieval goldsmiths and their circles in Cracow refers to 'a small group of Protestants from France and Scotland in search of protection from the barbarity of the religious wars in their countries'.[41] While at the same time in the opinion of British historians it is economic considerations, i.e. the repeated famine of the sixteenth and seventeenth centuries as well as the limited possibilities for professional development in the fields of craft and trade, that forced chiefly young people to search for better conditions abroad, including in Poland.[42] This obviously does not mean that we must exclude denominational and political reasons. But it was not these, however, that were responsible for the mass exodus from Scotland during the period of interest to us.

The exposure of political and religious conflicts has a complex origin. It results, first and foremost, from the domination of those aspects of general history in the said pieces of research and in university education itself. Such a perception of the past is the sum of the political actions of eminent individuals. In such an approach there was no room for the observation of wider social processes, consequently economic problems gained with difficulty at most a marginalised place within academic textbooks.[43] A good example of the historiography presented here, one that overtly combines political history with biographical study, is the entry for 'Scotland' in the most important Polish encyclopaedia of the nineteenth century and early twentieth century. The encyclopaedia, edited by the famous Warsaw publisher Samuel Orgelbrand, had as its aim the 'quality' popularisation of the historical study of the day.[44]

Also not without significance was the extremely limited contact with Western historiography enjoyed by Polish historical studies following the end of World War II. The absence of a widespread and permanent exchange of research experiences and subject literature must have limited the interpretational possibilities of facts from Poland's past.[45]

Another reason that is clear in the works of certain older Polish researchers is the interpretation of events in Scotland, chiefly the origins and development of the Reformation, through the prism of the better known political-denominational history of England. Now such a false examination belongs in principle to the past. Removing oneself from such an approach is not made any easier though by the appearance of syntheses of the history of the nations of the British Isles, an example of which is *The Oxford History of Britain*.[46] The late medieval and early modern chapters of this volume in fact present exclusively the history of England. The authors of these chapters treat Scotland as merely one of the neighbours of the Tudor kingdom, on a par with France, Spain, or the Netherlands. Such works are obviously not a source of knowledge for historians researching the history of emigration from Scotland. Historical syntheses do, however, convey in the best way, or at least should convey, the range of events from the past, as well as form a wider knowledge about it.

Notes

1 See Z. Guldon, W. Kowalski, 'Between Tolerance and Abomination: Jews in Sixteenth-Century Poland,' in *The Expulsion of the Jews. 1492 and After*, eds R. B. Waddington and A. H. Williamson (New York–London, 1994), pp. 161–2; T. C. Smout, N. C. Landsman, T. M. Devine, 'Scottish Emigration in the Seventeenth and Eighteenth Centuries', in *Europeans on the Move. Studies on European Migration, 1500–1800*, ed. N. Canny (Oxford, 1994), pp. 76–112; W. Kowalski, 'From the "Land of Diverse Sects" to National Religion: Converts to Catholicism and Reformed Franciscans in Early Modern Poland', *Church History* 70.3 (2001), pp. 482–526; W. Kowalski, 'The Placement of Urbanised Scots in the Polish Crown during the Sixteenth and Seventeenth Centuries', in *Scottish Communities Abroad in the Early Modern Period*, eds A. Grosjean, S. Murdoch (Leiden–Boston, 2005), pp. 53–103; W. Kowalski 'Robert Spens i szkocka gmina w Krakowie u schyłku XVI stulecia', in *Między Lwowem a Wrocławiem. Księga jubileuszowa Profesora Krystyna Matwijowskiego*, eds B. Rok and J. Maroń (Toruń, 2006), pp. 409–17.

2 H. Samsonowicz, 'Grupy etniczne w Polsce XV wieku', in *Ojczyzna bliższa i dalsza. Studia historyczne ofiarowane Feliksowi Kirykowi w sześćdziesiątą rocznicę urodzin*, eds J. Chrobaczyński, A. Jureczko and M. Śliwa (Kraków, 1993), p. 469.

3 S. Litak, *Od Reformacji do Oświecenia. Kościół katolicki w Polsce nowożytnej* (Lublin, 1994), p. 29.

4 A good example is M. Bembus SI, *Kometa to jest pogróżka z nieba na postrach, przestrogę i upomnienie ludzkie* (Kraków, 1619).

5 About which broadly J. Tazbir, 'L'attitude envers les étrangers dans la Pologne au XVIIe siècle', *Il Pensiero Politico* 6.2 (1973), p. 169–87, as well as the Polish version of this article 'Stosunek do obcych w dobie baroku', in J. Tazbir, *Szlaki kultury polskiej* (Warszawa, 1986), pp. 186–202.

6 The advances of the Catholic reaction have been characterised by Kowalski, 'From the "Land of Diverse Sects"', pp. 488–96. Mutual interdenominational relations, and first of all the policy of the Roman Catholic Church, have been

dealt with in detail also by M. Teter, *Jews and Heretics in Catholic Poland. A Beleaguered Church in the Post-Reformation Era* (Cambridge–New York, 2006).

7 Quoted after Tazbir, 'Stosunek do obcych', pp. 192–3 and *passim*. See also Teter, *Jews and Heretics, passim*.

8 For more see M. Małowist, *Wschód a Zachód Europy w XIII–XVI wieku. Konfrontacja struktur społeczno-gospodarczych* (Warszawa, 2006), pp. 280–1; W. Rusiński, *Gospodarka i społeczeństwo w Polsce w okresie późnofeudalnym (XVI–XVIII w.)* (Poznań, 2008), pp. 138–41; A. Nowak, 'Przeobrażenia struktury społecznej ludności wiejskiej w Polsce w okresie panowania systemu folwarczno-pańszczyźnianego (XV–XVIII wieku). Próba ujęcia modelowego', in *Badania nad historią gospodarczo-społeczną w Polsce (Problemy i metody)*, eds J. Topolski *et al.* (Warszawa–Poznań, 1978), pp. 136–46; M. North, 'Die Entstehung der Gutswirtschaft im südlichen Ostseeraum', *Zeitschrift für Historische Forschung* 26.1 (1999), pp. 43–59.

9 Statements defending foreign merchants were the exception; see E. Lipiński, *Studia nad historią polskiej myśli ekonomicznej* (Warszawa, 1956), pp. 256–7; E. Lipiński, *Historia polskiej myśli społeczno-ekonomicznej do końca XVIII wieku* (Gdańsk, 1975), pp. 192–3.

10 See W. Ostrowski, 'Angielsko-polskie związki literackie', in *Słownik literatury staropolskiej: Średniowiecze – Renesans – Barok*, ed. T. Michałowska (Wrocław, 1998), p. 32; cf. M. Fumaroli, M. Slater, 'A Scottish Voltaire', *Times Literary Supplement* 4842 (19 January 1996), pp. 16–17.

11 'Naród ów, zbrzydziwszy sobie swą ubogą i nieurodzajną ojczyznę za morze ucieka przed biedą i u nas szuka zarobku. Dawniej najpośledniejsi przekupnie, których sprzętem kosze i siano, rozprzedawali tylko igły, nożyki, sprzączki i inne drobiazgi tego rodzaju, nosząc na plecach skrzynie i pudła. Teraz zaś [. . .] wozami rozwożą towary i jeżdżą po jarmarkach miejskich'; Ł. Opaliński, 'Obrona Polski', in his *Wybór pism*, S. Grzeszczuk, ed., (Wrocław, 1959), p. 158. This quote is mentioned by Guldon and Stępkowski, 'Ludność szkocka', p. 202.

12 A. F. Steuart ed., *Papers Relating to the Scots in Poland 1576–1793* (Edinburgh, 1915), xiii. His peregrinations are presented by D. R. Holeton, 'Fynes Moryson's Itinerary: A Sixteenth Century English Traveller's Observations on Bohemia, its Reformation, and its Liturgy', in *Bohemian Reformation and Religious Practice*, ed. D. R. Holeton, vol. 5, pt. 2 (Prague, 2005), pp. 379–84.

13 'W ogóle do tego stopnia, iż Szkoci po wsiach wędrujący nie mają się gdzie schować przed psami. Przezorniej by uczynili, gdyby zażądali z ojczyzny tego skarbu, który stanowi największe ich bogactwo'; Opaliński, 'Obrona Polski', p. 164.

14 This view was repeated after Thomas Fischer by Borowy, *Scots*, p. 6.

15 'Przodkowie naszy przedtym w rolej się kochali
   O fałszywych kontraktach nigdy nie słyszęli
   Których tych czasów w Polszcze po dostatku wszędzie
   Bo przed Szoty, Żydami wioski nie nabędzie
   Szlachcic, musi do miasta, bo na wsi nie może
   Lepiejby tę życzliwość czynić krwi szlacheckiej

Nie żydowskiej, nie szkockiej, ani też niemieckiej'; W. S. Jeżowski, 'Ekonomia abo Porządek zabaw ziemiańskich', in *Staropolska poezja ziemiańska*, eds J. S. Gruchała and S. Grzeszczuk (Warszawa, 1988), p. 247; the same source quoted in *Biblioteka starożytna pisarzy polskich* (Warszawa, 1843), pp. 218–19.

16 '[g]enus inutile [. . .] piechotą od wsi do wsi się wałęsali, z krobkami na ramieniu, a w krobce bywało mydełko, szydełko, awtki, igły, kostki, nożyki, karty etc., a przecie od tego towaru za śp. ojca WKM, u króla Stefana zawsze ich na wojnę wyganiano. Teraz ni masz tak ubogiego, co by czterema szkapami na furmańskich wozach do kilku miast różnych razem nie wysyłał na jarmarki, z faktorami swego narodu, towarów i materyj, nawet wołami [i] futrami kupczą, a tylko chałupkę propter indigenatum kupiwszy w lada miejscu za kilka grzywien, srodze zbierają pieniądze i do Szkocyjej wywożą, a inszych głodnych sangui suas przysyłają do Polski do onych domków. Owa na nich trzeba co większego założyć, bo i z hańbą naszą mają swego narodu sędziego w Elblągu pod panowaniem WKM'; This Diet *votum* is quoted by W. Guldon, Z. Guldon, 'Saga szkockiego rodu Russellów w Szydłowcu w pierwszej połowie XVII wieku', in *Szydłowiec. Z dziejów miasta*, ed. J. Wijaczka (Szydłowiec, 1999), p. 36.

17 'Przez Włochów, Szotów i innych cudzoziemców miasta nasze wielką szkodę biorą'; J. Herburt, *Statuta i przywileje koronne* (Kraków, 1570), p. 309.

18 'Włosi, Niemcy, Szoci, ale i Żydowie nawet, pod płaszczykiem prawa miejskiego, za kopę dostanego, większej prerogatywy być chcą niż stan szlachecki'; S. Cikowski, *W sprawach celnych odpis*, pt. 1 (Kraków, 1602), pp. 10, 18, 20, 31–2.

19 'Kupcy cudzoziemscy, którzy się o składy w mieściech swych nabarziej starają, aby je z Polski do swych przenieść mogli, czego ich szwagrowie, bracia w Polsce tu faktorując i z zniszczeniem starożytnych familij w mieściech, a potym stanu szlacheckiego, sami się bogacą, pieniądze z Polski wywożąc wszytkie, albo wsi, kamienice przednie i zamki skupując'; ibid., pt. 2, p. 2.

20 '[b]o taki dostatki i zbogacenie nil conferunt Ojczyźnie, gdyż co tu zbiorą, w obce kraje wywożą'; [Ł. Opaliński], *Dyszkurs o pomnożeniu miast w Polszcze* (Kraków, 1648), p. unnumbered; see also A. Wyrobisz, 'Attitude of the Polish Nobility towards Towns in the First Half of the Seventeenth Century', *Acta Poloniæ Historica* 48 (1983), p. 86.

21 AmKr, Consularia, sygn. 460, s. 451–3.

22 '[w]ielu kupieckich ludzi, i swoich i cudzoziemskich, Włochów, Niemców, Ormian, Szotów, Żydów za podarunkiem z towary wolno od ceł wyprowadzają'; S. Starowolski, *Reformacja obyczajów polskich* (c. 1650, no publication data available), p. 175.

23 S. Starowolski, *Polska albo opisanie położenia Królestwa Polskiego*, ed. A. Piskadło (Kraków, 1976), pp. 84, 87.

24 For more detail see Lipiński, *Historia polskiej myśli społeczno-ekonomicznej*, pp. 155–160.

25 A. Wejnert, 'Prawa i swobody Szkotów w Polscedo końca XVIII wieku,' *Gazeta Polska* 20 (1877), p. 1.

26 'Przewroty polityczne i religijne w dalekiej Anglii napędzają nam nową falę

nieznanych dotąd Szkotów, którzy trudnią się handlem bławatnym i korzennym, i również zakładają liczne bractwa, prowadzące nawet proces ciekawy a długotrwały z królem angielskim'; S. Tomkowicz, 'Z dziejów obyczajów mieszczaństwa krakowskiego na początku XVII–go wieku', *Biblioteka Warszawska* 2 (1898), p. 250.

27 'Szkocja od połowy XVI wieku popadła w chroniczny stan niepokojów politycznych i religijnych, walki z Anglią i wojny domowej. Ferment ten ciągły, wywołujący zamieszanie sumień i ruinę ekonomiczną mieszkańców, dochodził do takie stopnia, że czynił życie i pobyt wielu z nich w ojczyźnie zupełnie niemożliwymi. Gdzie z polityką miesza się sprawa religii, tam zwykle namiętności występują z wielką siłą, a zresztą dwie rasy, z których składa się ludność tej ziemi: tak anglosaska, jak celtycka, należą do twardych, nie przebierających w środkach, w walce bezwzględnych'; S. Tomkowicz, 'Przyczynek do historyi Szkotów w Krakowie i w Polsce', *Rocznik Krakowski* 2 (1899), p. 158.

28 'Szkoci byli od dawna ludem przemyślnym i handlowym. Emigranci więc zwracali się w kraje, gdzie dla działalności ich przedstawiało się otwarte i korzystne pole. Takie znalazło się przede wszystkim w Gdańsku i Prusiech wschodnich, a dalej – w Polsce. Tu i tam rzucali się na kupiectwo, podobni w tem do Żydów. Stąd to zapewne pochodzi także niejaka wspólność ich kolei w nowej ojczyźnie z losami Żydów'; ibid., pp. 159–160.

29 J. Sadownik, 'Szkoci w Lublinie XVII wieku', *Historia* (June 1937) 1.

30 W. B[orowy], *Scots in Old Poland. Scottish Society Publications*, no. 2 (Edinburgh– London, [1941]), p. 7; A. Biegańska, 'Żołnierze szkoccy w dawnej Rzeczypospolitej', *Studia i Materiały do Historii Wojskowości* 27 (1984), pp. 83–4; See also J. Maślanka, ed., *Wacław Borowy (1890–1950): uczony humanista* (Kraków, 2008).

31 A. Kossowski, 'Przyczynek do dziejów Szkotów w Polsce', *Roczniki Humanistyczne* 2–3 (1950–51), p. 381.

32 J. Bieniarzówna, K. Kubysz, *400 lat reformacji pod Wawelem* (Warszawa, 1958), p. 27.

33 S. Seliga, L. Koczy, *Scotland and Poland. A Chapter of Forgotten History* (Glasgow, 1969), p. 2.

34 S. Gierszewski, 'Szkoci w mniejszych miastach Pomorza Gdańskiego (XVI–XVIII w.)', *Zeszyty Naukowe Wyższej Szkoły Pedagogicznej im. Powastańców Śląskich w Opolu. Historia* 26 (1988), p. 49.

35 Biegańska, 'Żołnierze szkoccy', p. 85.

36 A. Biegańska, 'In Search of Tolerance. Scottish Catholics and Presbyterians in Poland', *Scottish Slavonic Review* 17 (1991), p. 37.

37 *Canadian Slavonic Papers* 43 (2001), p. 2.

38 M. Bogucka, 'Scots in Gdańsk (Danzig) in the Seventeenth Century', in *Ships, Guns and Bibles in the North Sea and Baltic States, c.1350–c.1700*, eds A. I. Macinnes, T. Riis, F. Pedersen (East Linton, 2000), p. 39.

39 Z. Guldon, *Żydzi i Szkoci w Polsce w XVI-XVIII wieku* (Kielce, 1990), p. 7.

40 *Kwartalnik Historii Kultury Materialnej* 2 (1982), p. 202.

41 '[g]rupkę protestantów z Francji i Szkocji, szukających schronienia przed

okrucieństwem wojen religijnych w ich krajach'; J. Pietrusiński, *Złotnicy krakowscy XIV–XVI w. i ich cech* (Warszawa, 2000), p. 150.

42 Such a position is held by, among others, M. Flinn *et al.*, *Scottish Population History from the 17th Century to the 1930s* (Cambridge–New York, 1977), pp. 7–8; A. J. S. Gibson, T. C. Smout, *Prices, Food and Wages in Scotland 1550–1780* (Cambridge–New York, 1995), p. 12 and *passim.*

43 See for more H. Wójcik-Łagan, *Nauczyciele historii szkół średnich i powszechnych w latach 1918–1939* (Kielce: Wydawnictwo WSP im. J. Kochanowskiego, 1999).

44 *Encyklopedia powszechna*, vol. 24 (Warszawa: S. Orgelbrand, 1867), pp. 652–7.

45 Cf. R. Frost, 'Scottish Soldiers, Poland–Lithuania and the Thirty Years' War', in *Scotland and the Thirty Years' War, 1618–1648*, ed. S. Murdoch (Leiden–Boston, 2001), p. 193.

46 K. O. Morgan, ed., *The Oxford History of Britain* (Oxford, 2001); cf. J. G. A. Pocock, 'The Limits and Divisions of British History: In Search of the Unknown Subject', *American Historical Review* 87.2 (1982), pp. 311–36.

5 'Pardon me my Lord, that I wrytte to your honor in Scottish . . .'

William Bruce as the first Stuart diplomatic agent in the Polish–Lithuanian Commonwealth

Anna Kalinowska

In the autumn of 1606, Robert Cecil, Earl of Salisbury and James I's Secretary of State received a letter from one of many diplomats working for him abroad. It contained the latest news from Poland–Lithuania, Transylvania and Brandenburg. The report also included information about some suspicious actions of the Hansa towns which were intending to plot against England as well as some complaints concerning the diplomat's pay. The letter was in many ways very similar to dozens of reports delivered to him every month. There was, however, one difference, as it ended with a rather unusual apology: 'Pardon me my Lord, that I wrytte to your honor in Scottish. I had not ane that I might truste quha culde wrytte Inglisse at this tyme. Iffe your honor be not weille acquainted with this sorte of wryttinge, sall in tymes cumme wrytte either in Latine, frenche or Italiens . . .'[1] Cecil's reaction to the letter is unknown, but it appears he did not care too much about the writer's lack of fluency in English since the man, Doctor William Bruce, kept his post and for the next few years continued his work as a Stuart diplomatic agent in the Polish–Lithuanian Commonwealth.[2]

The whole story seems to be nothing more than an anecdote but in fact it gives us an important insight into both relations between Stuart monarchy and Polish–Lithuanian Commonwealth and the work of a new British diplomatic service formed after 1603. Accession of James VI to the English throne brought a key change in London's foreign policy. Not only did the new monarch end the war with Spain, he also decided to pursue a more active policy in the Scandinavian and Baltic countries like Denmark, Sweden and Poland–Lithuania. As in many points it was a continuation of James's previous diplomatic agenda, it was the Scots who were given a crucial part in its execution, especially as they usually had an important advantage of being familiar with the region and local languages and having already some contacts necessary to succeed as efficient diplomats.[3]

This transformation can be easily seen in the case of contacts with the Polish–Lithuanian Commonwealth. Under Elizabeth I (r. 1558–1603) they were dominated almost exclusively by the commercial issues and English

diplomacy operated by sending *ad hoc* missions when it seemed to be necessary, while within a year of the new reign it was decided that there should be
a permanent diplomatic representation of the Stuart monarchy, though of
lower rank, established in Poland, that was to keep London informed about
the situation in the Polish–Lithuanian state, react promptly to the latest
events, and protect the English and Scottish merchants' interests. There was
also a Scot, the same William Bruce who two years later troubled Secretary
Cecil with his linguistic problems, named as an official diplomatic agent of
James I to the Polish Court and city of Gdańsk's Senate. He was the first of
the three diplomatic agents of Scottish origins who worked in Poland–
Lithuania in the first half of the seventeenth century. Since his diplomatic
career serves as a perfect illustration of some problems that the British diplomacy dealt with after 1603, he himself and his work as a diplomat definitely
deserve some more attention.

Bruce was born probably around 1560 in Stanstill in Caithness to a
Catholic family. In the late 1570s or early 1580s, he left Scotland for the
Continent where he completed his education and started an academic career:
he studied in France where he was awarded a doctorate in Roman Law in
Cahors in 1584[4] and then in the late 1580s he became a lecturer in Toulouse
and Cahors; next he lived in Italy before moving in around 1590 to Würzburg,
where he worked as a lecturer.[5] In 1594, Bruce gave up this position and
joined Christian forces fighting against the Turks in Hungary. This adventure
ended quite quickly, however. Within months he moved to Poland where he
stayed in Żywiec as a guest of the local landlord and in 1595 published the
first of his books, *Ad principes populumque Christianum de bello adversus ad
Turcos gerendo*, printed in Cracow – where he presented the idea of a universal
crusade against the Ottoman Empire.[6]

In 1595 or early 1596, Bruce made contact with the Polish Chancellor Jan
Zamoyski, who offered him a position as professor of Roman Law in the
newly founded Academy in Zamość. He worked there in December 1596
when, requested by the Chancellor, he escorted papal diplomat Boniface
Vanozzi. Vanozzi's account of their meeting sheds some light on Bruce's past.
It presents the Scot as accomplished and well-acquainted with the world,
especially Italy (we learn that he lived for several years in Rome) and gives us
some details of his life in Poland, like the information that he was paid 400
thalers per annum and was enthusiastic about the idea of being introduced to
papal nuncio Cardinal Gaetani.[7]

In spite of the substantial salary and excellent conditions offered by the
Academy, Bruce did not stay in Zamość. In 1598, he left for Bohemia and
took up the position of chancellor to the Bishop of Olomouc and commander
of his military units, but soon he was back in Poland. In the same year he
published in Frankfurt his second book, *De Tartaribus diarium Guilelemi*

Brusci Scoti, being the aftermath of his meeting with the diplomats of the Tartar khan. For the next two years he was travelling in search of a new employment only to end up again in Zamoyski's service.

In the late summer of 1600, Bruce visited London, where on behalf of the Chancellor he attempted to secure the queen's protection for Prince Stephan Bathory, nephew of the late king of Poland. We do not know if during his stay in England he met Cecil, but he was in contact with Christopher Parkins, a former Jesuit and English Ambassador to Sigismund III, who dealt with him on behalf of the English Government.[8]

A few months later, he can be traced in Livonia where he was taking part in Zamoyski's campaign against the Swedes as a commander of a cavalry unit and in Kowel where in early July 1601 he was detained for reasons that are unclear but released almost instantly.[9] In the autumn of 1601, he went back to Scotland, probably for the first time in twenty years. In 1603, he was in Poland again, but his stay did not last.[10] After the accession of James VI to the English throne, Sigismund III made a decision to appoint Stanisław Cikowski as his special ambassador to the new king and Bruce was to accompany him.

It seems that in England Bruce, apart from assisting the Polish diplomat, worked hard either to get the patronage of some influential people at the Court or to renew old contacts. Some of his letters written a few years later suggest that he had some links with Edward Bruce, Lord of Kinloss, but we cannot say how close they were and when exactly they started.[11] It is likely that he hoped it would help him find a new employment, preferably again in Poland, but this time as a representative of the British Government. Therefore he tried also to secure the support of Sigismund III who was to recommend him to James I as an excellent candidate for a diplomatic post in the Polish–Lithuanian Commonwealth.[12]

Bruce's attempts proved a success as in early 1604 the king and Cecil decided that he was to take care of the business of the English merchants, but it was a few more months before he was officially employed as an agent with the salary of 100 pounds per annum[13] (although it seems that he waited for his letters of credence or 'patent' until at least 1607).[14]

One cannot be certain when exactly Bruce left his post. By the autumn of 1610 there was a new agent appointed, another Scot, Patrick Gordon, working for the British Government in Poland and Gdańsk.[15] Bruce can be traced again three years later, this time in Prussia where he tried to prevent the expulsion of the Scots from the city of Königsberg, but his whereabouts after 1613 remain unknown.[16]

Bruce's life and activities have attracted historians' attention for many years – as early as the 1930s his biographical entry was printed in *Polski Słownik Biograficzny* (Polish Biographical Dictionary), followed by some other publications, although their authors focused chiefly on his alleged authorship of the anonymous work *A Relation of the State of Polonia and . . . in Anno 1598*, a unique account of Poland and its economic, political and social life in the late 1590s.[17]

Despite many arguments adduced both by the opponents and the supporters of the idea that it was Bruce who had written this text, his authorship seems to be still a matter for debate.[18] The fact that Bruce had been living in Poland for some time before 1598 and had an intimate knowledge of the Polish–Lithuanian state, as well as his relationship with Zamoyski, suggest that he could have prepared the *Relation*. The only contender, Sir George Carew, Elizabeth's Ambassador to Poland, had hardly an opportunity to become so familiar with the country during the few months he spent there as to be able to write such a detailed work.[19] On the other hand, *A Relation . . .* shows no signs of Scots or northern spelling or vocabulary which makes Bruce's authorship problematic, but this can be explained away as he could have had the text anglicised, just as was later done with his letters to Cecil. It is still difficult to explain why the text supposedly written by Bruce presents such a strong Protestant bias that it makes it very unlikely that its author could have been a member of the Church of Rome. There is so far no proof to believe that Bruce had chosen to convert to Protestantism.

Although we are unable to prove Bruce's authorship, his close links with Poland, including the fact that he had spent some time in Zamoyski's service, make it possible to argue that even if he did not write the *Relation* himself, he could have been involved in its composition.[20] Certainly these were also the factors that made Bruce a perfect candidate for the post of diplomatic representative in Poland–Lithuania. There is also no doubt that he was eager to accept the appointment as he had already tried to get the job.

Almost all we know about Bruce's life and activities after 1604 derives from his letters to King James and Salisbury and his papers preserved in Gdańsk. The letters present a complex picture of his activities of all kinds, from typical diplomatic duties to his involvement as a lawyer in various court cases.[21] They may give us also, at least to some extent, an explanation of why, despite promising prospects, Bruce's diplomatic career came to an abrupt end after only few years.

Like any other diplomatic agent, Bruce was supposed to do mainly two things – to inform his supervisors about the situation in the state he resided in and, when necessary, to intervene on behalf of his Government. It appears that he dealt reasonably well with the first of these duties. His elaborate reports show that he did try and managed to collect all kinds of information he believed to be useful or interesting for the Secretary of State and the king, as well as for Queen Anne.[22] Apart from providing Cecil and James with detailed information on the internal situation in Poland–Lithuania, especially the differences between Sigismund III and the opposition that in 1606 evolved into a civil conflict and then the pacification of the country, Bruce regularly reported on Poland's contacts with its neighbours. In his letters he focused on the two most important elements of Polish foreign policy of this period – the involvement of the king and some noblemen in Moscow who were actively supporting some pretenders to the Russian throne as well as confrontation between Sigismund and his uncle Charles and his Swedish subjects. From time to time he also gave information about the situation in Brandenburg, Hungary, or Turkey.[23] There is no doubt he sought information directly connected with the interest of the British Government – for instance, in 1606, he mentioned the Venetians' attempts to get some commercial privileges in Poland, suggesting that if they were to succeed it would be dangerous for the English merchants, and regularly warned of the actions of the Hansa towns and of the activities of the Swedish fleet in the Baltic. Sometimes he also attached some documents circulating in Poland and Gdańsk, such as copies of correspondence between the king of France and the Jesuits, proclamations by the Polish Parliament, or articles of agreement between Sigismund III and the opposition.[24]

The accuracy of Bruce's information concerning Polish political life suggests he had some reliable sources of news and must have stayed in touch with someone very well informed about the current events. Interestingly, his reports are rather impartial – he condemned the fact that the Polish nobility threatened to depose their king, but he also fairly presented their reasons for starting the rebellion. He was also clearly determined to get the information he believed would be important for his work by trying out other methods. When he suspected Gdańsk's Senate to be involved in some anti-English activities and was unable to get the details, he considered going to Nürnberg or Limburg, where he was not known, to work for the British Government. Unfortunately, he was stopped by the lack of money to pay for the trip.[25]

We do not know if the Secretary of State was satisfied with the quality of Bruce's reports, but he did criticise the agent for not writing as often as he should. In answer, the diplomat tried to excuse himself by stressing the distance, the high costs of postal services (although in most cases his letters were carried by merchants going back to England) and their unreliability, but also assured Cecil that he wrote at every opportunity.[26] In fact, it was rather Bruce who had reasons to complain as he hardly ever received new instructions and consequently very often was forced to act on his own initiative.[27]

Not all his efforts, however, were received with appreciation in London. When, in 1606 or 1607, Bruce suggested to Cecil that James I should write to Sigismund III and the Polish nobility and act as a mediator and even prepared the Latin drafts of the letters, the king demanded explanation.[28] James was also annoyed by 'the unreverent form of [Bruce's] writing . . .

which indeed is without all good fashion, beginning it with commendations to his Majesty, and ending with a subscription of his name so close to the lines of his letter as there is almost no distance between'.[29] Nonetheless, the agent had not changed his attitude. He continued to make new suggestions and present his actions as highly successful even if in fact he had to deal with some serious failures. In his letters he stressed his extraordinary position due to the fact that he represented James, who was supposed to be 'generally respected heir abowe al other Christiane princes'.[30] For example, in 1608, he boasted that he would help the merchants as he could 'beside this King . . . obtain any favour necessary for them, if they would demand it in time'.[31] Bruce's supervisors seemed to hope that this could be used not only to their advantage, as they ordered him to assist the chancellor of the Danish king, Mr Ramelius, with his contacts with the Polish court, but we do not know what exactly he was to do to help the Dane and what was the outcome of the whole business.[32]

Similarly, nothing can be said about the methods Bruce wanted to employ to achieve his goals. We do not know for example if he tried to secure the support of any influential courtiers. Unlike other diplomats, including Ambassadors of Elizabeth I John Herbert or Christopher Parkins, who often reported on their efforts to approach the high-rank state officers, there is nothing about such attempts to be found in Bruce's papers. The only people who did appear in his correspondence with Cecil and James I in a similar context were young Tomasz Zamoyski, the son of Bruce's late patron, and Prince Janusz Radziwiłł, but, as the first was not even a teenager and the other played an important role in the anti-royal opposition, it would be rather naïve to expect that they would be able to help him with his proceedings at the court.[33]

Instead he suggested that the Eastland Company should provide him with enough money to bribe people who could be helpful in furthering its business, but it seems that either the merchants did not do it or the scheme did not work, since in the following years he still had to struggle to secure their commercial privileges. The task became even more difficult when a former Company member, Richard Lewis, supported by Gdańsk's authorities, accused the organisation of selling outstretched cloth in Poland, of abusing the Polish judicial system through the English court in Elbing, and serious duty frauds. Additionally, Lewis hoped to bring his personal complaints against the Company to the Polish court, which would be a very dangerous precedent harming the Company's position. As always, Bruce tried to persuade Cecil that he had the situation under control, but in fact it was going from bad to worse as Sigismund III decided to establish a special committee to investigate the allegations and in 1608 examined Lewis's case himself. However, the legal battle was not over. It lasted for some more years as we know that in 1616 the case was being reviewed by the English Privy Council.[34]

The fact that Bruce did not manage to prevent the intervention of the Polish king subverted the independence of the Company court in Elbing. The outcome of the whole case resulted in him being accused of negligence. He tried, of course, to defend himself, mainly stressing that he had done even more than could have been expected, especially as he never had enough money to finance his activities. In his letters to Cecil he mentioned that his 'provisioune fromme his Majestie is not correspondante to my greatte chairges' and asked for a rise, but it was mostly the Company's tight-fistedness that he blamed for his difficult situation[35]. 'I may justly complain of this Company,' he wrote in June 1606, 'who know that this year I have done more for them than anyone employed with public authority to assist them, at their great charges, and have yet been gratified so much by them as the paper allnost [almost] I write for them' and tried to move Cecil to intervene and make the merchants reimburse his expenses.[36] From their point of view Bruce was probably paid more than he deserved as they blamed him for the increasing costs of the legal battle against Lewis. They could also have been suspicious of his intentions as he did not disguise his negative attitude towards their attempts to force the Scottish merchants active in Poland–Lithuania to sell and buy their goods exclusively at the Company's staple port at Elbing. Contrary to their intentions, Bruce advised Cecil and Lord Kinloss that the Company's plan should be abandoned, and stressed how advantageous it would be if all James's subjects could trade 'without restricting to any place and company and that will be most thankful and acceptable to this king [Sigismund]'. He argued also that it would help to avoid some serious conflict between 'our new united nations' as the Scots did not intend to give up their freedoms.[37] All this was in direct contradiction to the arguments Bruce should present to the Polish Government, so one can suspect that merchants might have lost their trust in Bruce's integrity and complained to the Government. He himself claimed they treated him badly as they were simply 'evil affectionate to us all who are born northward', and that there was nothing that he had neglected or mishandled.[38] The conflict dragged on for some time, as the Company was not able to dismiss him because he was employed by the king, but also because Bruce probably enjoyed the patronage of Cecil and Kinloss. The fact that in 1609 or in early 1610 he finally lost his job suggests that they might have given up their support for him. It seems that the agent did not expect the dismissal as in late October he asked for royal letters he believed to be useful in his efforts to protect the Scottish community in Prussia.[39]

Bruce's diplomatic career, and maybe even more the way it ended, shows how complex his position was – he was a Scot, but he was supposed to assist all subjects of James VI and I and was responsible to the English Secretary of State who ordered him to act on behalf of the organisation whose actions were quite often to his countrymen's disadvantage. As a result, he had to face the problem of divided loyalties that made his work as a diplomat more difficult and finally might have been the cause of him being dismissed. Nonetheless, both Bruce's successors working as Stuart agents in the Polish–Lithuanian Commonwealth were also Scottish, which may suggest two things. Firstly, that they became much more aware – which was not easily accepted by Bruce – that they had to balance their personal feelings with the fact they were now to represent the two nations united under the Stuart rule. And secondly, that, despite the initial complications, it was the London Government's belief that as far as Poland–Lithuania was concerned it was the Scottish diplomats who, due to their experience and familiarity with the country, were best prepared to handle the British interests there.

Notes

1   C. H. Talbot, ed., *Elementa ad Fontium Editiones*, vol. 6, *Res Poloniacae Iacobo I Angliae Regnante Conscriptae ex Archivi Publicis Londoniarum* (Rome, 1962) (hereafter *EFE* 6), p. 18.

2   William Bruce's biographical entries can be found in *Polski Słownik Biograficzny* (hereafter *PSB*), vol. 3, pp. 3–4, and in *The Scotland, Scandinavia and Northern European Biographical Database (SSNE)*, A. Grosjean and S. Murdoch. http://www. st-andrews.ac.uk/history/ssne Date accessed 12 February 2010. William Bruce, *SSNE* no. 4348. For more information on him see: S. Kot, *Dwaj profesorowie Anglicy w Polsce XVI w.*, in *Polska złotego wieku a Europa. Studia i szkice* (Warszawa, 1987), pp. 642–6; J. K. Fedorowicz, *England's Baltic Trade in the Early Seventeenth Century. A study in Anglo-Polish commercial diplomacy* (Cambridge, 1980), pp. 134–8.

3   S. Murdoch, *Diplomacy in Transition: Stuart–British Diplomacy in Northern Europe, 1603–1618*, in *Ships, Guns and Bibles in the North Sea and the Baltic States, c.1350–c.1700*, eds A. I. Macinnes, R. Riis and F. G. Pedersen (East Linton 2000), p. 93.

4   Archiwum Państwowe w Gdańsku (State Archives in Gdańsk – hereafter APG), Bibliotheca Archivi, 300 R/Bb, 32, f. 11.

5   Ibid., f. 137.

6   Within months of the first book being published, Bruce produced another text dealing with this problem. It was written as an answer to an anonymous tract that ridiculed his arguments presented in *A Principes . . .* and was entitled *Epistola ad Illustrem Dominum Iohannem Gostomium a Leżenice . . .* (Gorlicii, 1596).

7   J. U. Niemcewicz, ed., *Zbiór pamiętników o dawnej Polszcze*, vol. 2 (Warszawa, 1822), p. 261.

8   *Calendar of the Manuscripts of the Marquis of Salisbury Preserved at Hatfield House* (Historical Manuscripts Commission), vol. 10 (London, 1904) (hereafter HMC Salisbury 10), pp. 289–90. 'Concerning the Scotsman came from the Chancellor of Poland', ed. C. H. Talbot, *Elementa ad Fontium Editiones*, vol. 17, *Res Poloniacae*

ex *Archivo Musei Britannici, II Pars* (Romae, 1967) (hereafter *EFE* 17), p. 174: 'Some other particulars I have understood of his messenger not incredible, fitter for speech then letters which I will declare at my next being with you . . .'

9 APG, 300R/Bb, 32, f. 134.

10 APG, 300R/Bb, 32, f. 131, 135.

11 *EFE* 6, p. 22; It seems unlikely however (contrary to Stanisław Kot's suggestion in PSB) that Bruce met Kinloss in London in the summer of 1600 as Kinloss was not sent there by James until early February of 1601, cf. G. P. V. Akrigg, ed. *Letters of King James VI & I* (Berkeley, 1984), p. 168.

12 *PSB*, vol. 3, pp. 3–4.

13 F. Devon, ed., *Pell Records of the Exchequer: being payments made out of His Majesty's revenue during the reign of king James I* (London, 1836), p. 12: '5 June, – By order, 28th May, 1604. To Doctor William Bruce, sent to the King of Poland, there to remain for a time, the sum of 25l., parcel of his yearly allowance of 100l. upon his diets and other charges, by way of advance, for the space of 3 months 25l.'

14 *Calendar of the Manuscripts of the Marquis of Salisbury Preserved at Hatfield House*, vol. 19 (London 1965) (hereafter HMC Salisbury 19), p. 189; *EFE* 6, p. 32. It seems necessary to comment on Bruce's status at the time, as he happened to be described by some historians as 'a commercial agent of the Eastland Company' or 'a royal commercial agent'. It suggests that he was employed not by the Government, but either by the Eastland Company or by the king as his commercial factor and had nothing to do with diplomatic service which is not true, as proved by J. K. Fedorowicz, cf. B. Krysztopa-Czupryńska, *Kompania Wschodnia (Eastland Company) a Rzeczpospolita w latach 1579–1673* (Olsztyn, 2003), p. 54; E. A. Mierzwa, *'William Bruce, profesor Akademii Zamojskiej i agent handlowy The Eastland Company',* in *W kręgu akademickiego Zamościa*, red. H. Gmiterek, (Lublin, 1996), pp. 207–23.

15 Devon, ed., *Pell Records of the Exchequer . . .*, p. 108: 'to Gordon, gentleman, appointed to be sent into Poland, there to reside, for his Majesty's service, in the place of Doctor Bruce, lately departed, the sum of 121l. 13s. 4d., by way of imprest upon his allowance of 6s. 8d. per day, for one whole year beforehand, to begin from the 1st of May last past, 1610, and so from year to year the like allowance, by way of imprest, for so long time as he shall be employed in that service. By writ, dated 2nd of June, 1610 . . . 121l 13s 4d.'

16 *PSB*, vol.3, p. 4

17 C. H. Talbot, ed., *Elementa ad Fontium Editiones*, vol. 13, *Res Poloniacae ex Archivo Musei Britannici, I Pars, Relation of the state of Polonia and the United Provinces of that Crown Anno 1598* (Romae, 1965).

18 E. A. Mierzwa, *Angielska relacja o Polsce z roku 1598*, Annales Universitatis Mariae Curie-Skłodowska, Sectio F, Nauki filozoficzne i humanistyczne, vol. 17 (1962), pp. 87–118; E. A. Mierzwa, *Na marginesie wydania angielskiej relacji o Polsce z 1598 roku*, Przegląd Historyczny, t. LVIII (1967), pp. 664–7; S. Sobecki, 'The Authorship of *A Relation of the State of Polonia, 1598*', *Seventeenth Century* 18 (2003), pp. 172–9; J. K. Fedorowicz, *England's Baltic trade . . .*, pp. 20–1.

19 The only part of the Polish–Lithuanian Commonwealth that Carew had an opportunity to visit was Prussia, as upon his arrival in Gdańsk he was informed that Sigismund III had left for Sweden. He followed the king and after few weeks came back to Gdańsk and Elbląg where he stayed at least for two months, cf. C. H. Talbot, ed., *Elementa ad Fontium Editiones,* vol. 4, *Res Poloniacae Elisabetha I Angliae Regnante Conscriptae ex Archivi Publicis Londoniarum* (Romae, 1961), pp. 222, 239. He was put forward as a possible author of the *Relations* by G. Warner and J. Gilson in their *Catalogue of Western Manuscripts in the Old Royal and King's Collections,* vol. 2 (London, 1921), p. 279, mainly as he was the only English diplomat in Poland in 1598, but also an author of a similar text on France, where he served as an ambassador between 1604 and 1609, cf. T. Birch, ed., *An Historical view of the Negociations between the Courts of England, France and Brussels, from the year 1592 to 1617 . . . To which is added A Relation of State of France, with the characters of Henry IV and the principal persons of thet Court. Drawn up by Sir George Carew upon his return from his embassy there in 1609. Never before printed* (London, 1749), pp. 415–528.

20 A. Mączak, 'Poland', in *The Renaissance in National Context,* R. Porter, M. Treich eds, (Cambridge, 1992), p. 188. The theory is supported by the fact that Bruce can be traced in Prussia in 1598, which means that he could have met Carew or other member of the English mission, cf. the list of members of St Martin's Brotherhood of Elbing in 1598, APG, Elbląg Rks. III/255.185 quoted by J. K. Fedorowicz in *England's Baltic trade . . .* , p. 267.

21 Bruce's correspondence with James I and Cecil has been preserved in the National Archives, Public Record Office (in State Papers) and in the Cecil Papers in Hatfield House (these letters were printed in *EFE* 6 and *EFE* 17 and HMC Salisbury, vols. 16, 18, 19 and 20) and in the State Archives in Gdańsk (Bibliotheca Archivi, 300R/Bb, 32). For his non-diplomatic activities see, for example: APG, 300R/Bb, 32, ff. 144–53, 155–6v.

22 APG, 300R/Bb, 32, ff. 19, 53–53v. Among the people to whom he wrote during his stay in Poland were also James Sandilands, Sir John Hume, Sir James Murray and John Murray, as well as Lady Barbara Autherby, ibid., f. 27.

23 *EFE* 6, pp. 15–16.

24 Ibid., pp. 13–18, 20–2, 36–8, 43–5.

25 Ibid., p. 17.

26 HMC Salisbury 19, p. 189.

27 *EFE* 6, p. 20. In December of 1606 Bruce complained that he had not been sent 'anie adverteisement fromme your honor [Cecil] sen my parting', i.e. since the spring of 1604.

28 HMC Salisbury 19, p. 189–90.

29 Ibid., p. 11.

30 *EFE* 6, p. 43.

31 HMC Salisbury 20, p. 107.

32 *EFE* 6, pp. 38, 43.

33 HMC Salisbury 19, p. 189.

34 Fedorowicz, *England's Baltic Trade . . .* , pp. 134–9.

35 HMC Salisbury 19, p. 129.
36 HMC Salisbury 18, p. 181, *EFE* 6, p. 22.
37 HMC Salisbury 18, p. 180.
38 Ibid.
39 *EFE* 6, pp. 68–9. He wrote that in Poland–Lithuania 'nowe at his present al our countreymen treffecquinge heire ar at quyetnes abydinge this kinge his retourney back againe into this kingdome'. The hostile attitude to Scots in Prussia was actually the reaction to the behaviour of some German mercenaries led by Scottish officers.

6   Scots in the Cracow Reformed Parish in the Seventeenth Century

Peter P. Bajer

*Being arrived in Cracow, the capital city of Poland (though but of small impor-
tance) I met with divers Scottish merchants, who were wonderful glad of mine
arrival there, especially the two brothers Dickson, men of singular note for
honesty and wealth.*

William Lithgow, a Scottish traveller and author, penned the above account
in 1615 in a chronicle of his famous peregrinations.[1] Although his narrative
is doubtlessly exaggerated in a typically aureate baroque style, there is no
doubt, however, that the traveller indeed made acquaintance with 'divers
Scottish merchants' in Cracow.[2]

The Scots had lived in the then capital of the Polish–Lithuanian
Commonwealth, at least since the first decade of the sixteenth century. James
Morrison (Morrisen von Dondey ex Scocia), the first Scot admitted to
burgher rights, acquired this entitlement in 1509.[3] The steady growth of this
ethnic group, particularly since the middle of the sixteenth century, is reflected
by an account of another famous Scottish traveller, Sir John Skene of
Curriehill, who visited the city in 1569.[4] Skene was so impressed by the
number of his compatriots encountered there that in his famous dictionary
De Verborum Significatione, while describing pedlars, he wrote that he saw
'great multitude [of them] in the town of Cracovia'.[5]

Perhaps because of this alleged size, the group attracted the attention of
several historians who explored various aspects of its existence. Employing
primarily the documents of the civic authorities and the toll records, the
researchers investigated the geographical origins of the migrants, their
socio-economic situation, participation in local trade and their social
advancement.[6] Although as Kowalski rightly observed, apart from language
and customs, the creed was the one particular feature that distinguished this
minority group from the others – the vast majority of Scots were either
Presbyterians or Episcopalians – the relatively well-preserved records of the
Reformed brethren of Cracow hitherto have been insufficiently examined.[7]
Yet, as will be revealed, the records of this congregation provide a wealth of
information about the Scots in the parish: their demography, mobility,
social make-up, ratio between sexes, the situation of the Scottish women,

and the role of the Kirk in retaining and maintaining ethnic identity. When cross-checked with other documents, the data offers a broadly consistent snapshot of the Scottish presence at its peak in the 1640s and the 1650s at the heart of the Commonwealth.

The Protestants in Cracow and the Scottish co-religionists in the sixteenth century

In the opinion of its prominent chronicler Rev. Węgierski, the Cracow parish was regarded in times past as one of the most influential centres of the Polish Reformation, grouping nobles, burghers, academics, intellectual élite and visitors, often refugees fleeing persecution in their own countries. Although the first Reformed church service was held there in 1557, the brethren did not have a permanent place of worship until 1570/1572 when a chapel, shared with other Protestants, known as *Bróg*, was formally established in a house at St John Street.[8] However, by this time, the Reformation in Poland had decidedly slowed down and the Roman Catholic Church marked the beginnings of its resurgence. The religious upheavals that followed brought destruction of many Protestant places of worship and had a detrimental effect on their membership. Furthermore, the discriminatory practices applied against the Protestant nobility by both the staunchly Catholic King Sigismund III Vasa and, from the beginning of the seventeenth century, by the guilds and town courts, pushed the Protestants on to the defensive.[9]

No parish records survived to assess the Scottish presence in Cracow's evangelical brethren in its early period, although Scots documented as 'heretics' and living in the Catholic parish of St Mary's were recorded as early as 1568.[10] A note on the financial organisation of the Cracow parish written by Rev. Węgierski mentions a set of rules compiled in 1567 obliging Scottish merchants to collect alms amongst themselves during the numerous fairs they attended. The money raised was to be forwarded to the parish coffers for the benefit of the entire brethren.[11] By the 1580s, it seems, the Scots already formed a sizeable congregation within the larger Reformed assembly. In his last will of 1584 Robert Spens, a Catholic, bequested a sum of fifty thalers to the poor compatriots belonging to the parish.[12] By the 1590s, the number of Scots must have increased considerably. This is corroborated by a diary entry describing a skirmish between the Catholics and the Protestants on 23 May 1591. According to one account, during the attack on *Bróg*, the Protestants, among them the Scots, not only withstood the mob's advance, but also subsequently counter-attacked.[13] When the royal troops separated the two parties, as retaliation the mob rushed to set the stalls belonging to Scots on fire. After this was prevented, and on the following day, the Scottish merchants were commanded to shut down their booths and because of their involvement, were summoned at the court. According to the same document, rather than attend the trial, many Scots simply left the town.[14]

Strong Scottish presence in the parish is also confirmed by findings of a royal inquest set up in 1603 to expose organisation of Scots in Poland. The document shows not only strong anti-Catholic sentiment among the members of the brethren, but also informs of the existence of clergymen among them, possibly deacons.[15] Other documents from the turn of the century, such as Andrew Duncan's last will (1606), suggest that the Scots most likely followed the Presbyterian creed. This, as Kowalski observed, could have been a feature which distinguished them from other ethnic groups, as well as from other Calvinists.[16]

The ramifications of the previously mentioned third and final attack on *Bróg* were not just felt by the Scots, but also affected the other Protestants of Cracow. The chapel and its record books have been destroyed and the brethren were effectively driven away from the city. In 1591, the Reformed brethren relocated their place of worship to a nearby country estate, Aleksandrowice. The congregation used it only for a couple of years, until its destruction in 1613.[17]

Undeterred by the series of setbacks, the Scots alongside their host co-religionists adapted well to this increasingly difficult situation. The parish elders acquired two chapels located on the private estates of the local nobility, in Lucianowice (today Łuczanowice) and in Wielkanoc, which they decided to use concurrently as places of worship. Lucianowice, because of its close proximity to Cracow, was selected to cater for the elderly, infirm and those unable to take longer trips, and the church in Wielkanoc, established in 1614, was chosen to become the main seat of the congregation. Since it was located further away from the city, the elders felt it would be safer to relocate its minister there, to establish a burial ground and to hold services during religious feasts.[18] The church records confirm that, indeed, both churches were used by the assembly and were attended by the same group of worshippers.[19]

The well-preserved church books kept in the parish since the late 1630s show a continuous Scottish presence in both places of worship over the next hundred years.[20] The documents are second to none as a source of information on Scottish urban congregations, their worship in rural parishes, and specifically on Scottish settlement in Cracow since the 1630s, and as such deserve closer inspection.

The records

The parish records consist of two books: *Księga Wtóra* ('The Second Book'), established in 1637, and *Księga Trzecia* ('The Third Book'), containing records from 1664 to 1716. The titles of the books suggest that there once must have also been 'The First Book', containing possibly the oldest records of the congregation. The two books that survived are much more than just registers of vital records. 'The Second Book' contains, among other things: an inventory of possessions belonging to the Wielkanoc parish; information about the parish ministers; a list of Cracow parishioners attending the chapels in Wielkanoc and Lucianowice; a register of baptisms 1610–57; a roll of parishioners in 1637; a list of converts 1631–56; as well as a partially damaged register of the excommunicated and those making penance; lists of communicants 1636–53 and 1651–3; a short chronicle of the congregation including descriptions of various persecutions committed against it; a register of marriages 1631–56; a register of the deceased in the parish based on the information taken from tombstones 1631–56; records of visitations; minutes of the parish sessions; and collections records. 'The Third Book' contains corresponding data but for the 1692–1734 period.

Since the Scots appear in almost all parts of the books, the data obtained from them offers not only material for statistical analysis of the demographics and the size of the group, but also provides an insight into customs and practices of the Scottish Protestant community of Cracow, their interaction with the hosts, ways of maintaining their ethnic identity, as well as their integration. Moreover, the records do not discriminate on the base of age, sex or social standing unlike, for example, poll tax records or the rolls of individuals admitted to the burgher rights. The significance of the books lies also in the fact that the registers of baptisms, marriages and deaths which they contain are supplemented by the registers of communicants. Of all the Reformed congregations in the Polish–Lithuanian Commonwealth which were attended by larger groups of Scots and for which records survived until present, apart from Cracow, only registers of the Kiejdany parish hold an equally complete set of data.[21] However, the pre-1637 Cracow entries have been recorded retrospectively, for example the list of the deceased in the parish, as its author has indicated, has been based on the details taken from the tombstones. As a result, the register for the 1610–37 period cannot be viewed as entirely accurate.

Important observations about the Scottish Protestants of Cracow can also be formed based on information obtainable through several tombstones from the burial ground at Wielkanoc.[22]

The size of the Scottish congregation according to the parish records

The baptismal, marriage and death records, as well as communicant lists kept by the Reformed congregation since 1637, reveal the continuous Scottish presence in the parish till the late eighteenth century, and also demographic changes over time (table 6.1). The growth of this ethnic group in the first half of the seventeenth century can be illustrated more precisely through the baptismal records kept since 1610. In that particular year, only one baptism was performed that concerned Scots, that of Peter Orem son of Thomas, citizen of Cracow, and Susanne Orem née Hewitt. Until the end of this decade an estimated seven baptisms of children whose father, at least, was of Scottish origin, were recorded in the parish. This number grew slightly in the following decade when eight baptisms were recorded. In the 1630s, the number had risen to 22, and in the 1640s, when the group was numerically at its peak, it reached 30. In the 1650s, the numbers probably dropped due to the smallpox epidemic in 1651 and 1652 which decimated the town's population. The Swedish invasion and two-year occupation of the city (1655–7) may have further affected its population. The decrease could also be related to the fact that the 1650s marked the end of Cracow's economic success. Although the decline in the city's importance began in 1596 when King Sigismund III Vasa moved the capital of Poland–Lithuania from Cracow to Warsaw, it was not until the late 1650s that its prosperity ceased altogether.[23]

It is impossible to present a precise account of the next three decades, as no records were kept from 1656 until 1691. It is clear, however, that the numbers decreased dramatically in the following decades. Only three baptisms were held in the 1690s and the same number was recorded in the 1700s. Moreover, the baptisms undoubtedly involved a higher percentage of second- and third-generation migrants, settled families with multiple offspring. The same trend was reflected in the number of worshippers attending communion, as well as in the marriages and deaths records.

The first and the only official roll of parishioners of 1637 reveals that among 303 worshippers, some of whom were of German, French and Dutch origin, the Scots were numerically the second largest group after the Poles. The circa 75 people of Scottish origin – 50 men and 25 women – constituted nearly a quarter of the parishioners (24.9 per cent).[24] The group was certainly larger than the register may suggest, as the document did not include children and the elderly.[25] A close examination of the records reveals that among the 73 Scots listed, there were at least 9–10 couples, and that each of them had on average 3–4 children. Using this information, it is possible to establish that in that particular year the group must have consisted of at least 100–110 more permanent members of the parish.

The partially complete list of the communicants for the entire 1630s shows 115 Scots (78 men and 37 women), among them 13 couples. Of those, 47 people (42 men and 5 women) could be classified as irregular visitors, i.e. appearing in the records less than three times during the period.[26] Using this information as a basis for computation, it is possible to speculate that in the 1630s the group may have comprised around 170 Scots. The Scottish congregation grew in size in the following decade. Based on the register of

Table 6.1: Number of religious ceremonies involving Scots and number of Scottish communicants at Lucianowice and Wielkanoc parishes between the 1610s and 1710s according to the church registers

	1610s	1620s	1630s	1640s	1650s	1660s	1670s	1680s	1690s	1700s	1710s
Baptisms	7	8	22	30	10	1	1		3	3	
Marriages	3	6	8	9	5				3	4	5
Deaths		1	15	24	11	5	2	6	7	8	11
Communicants			115	190	75	33	46	43	47	110	66

Source: 'Księga Wtóra Kościoła Ewangel[icko] Reformowanego w Wielkanocy', Archiwum Parafii Ewangelicko-Augsburskiej Św. Marcina w Krakowie, no signature, folios 43–149

communicants for the 1640–9 period, it is possible to identify 190 individuals of Scottish extraction – 134 men and 56 women – who took communion. Of those, 61 males and 18 females appeared in the records no more than twice. The nearly 1:1 (63:61) ratio between men residing in the parish and the infrequent visitors reveals much about the make-up and dynamics of the parish. Furthermore, the data shows that women were less mobile than males, and that more than two-thirds of them resided in the parish (38:18). Among them, in the 1640s, there were at least 21 couples. Several more individuals appearing in the list of communicants give the impression that they were married, but this cannot be confirmed beyond doubt. Nevertheless, it would be safe to assume that the number of Scottish families in Lucianowice and Wielkanoc in the fourth decade of the seventeenth-century parish could possibly have been as high as 25.[27] The data obtained from the baptismal lists show that each couple had on average 3–4 children. Such families, the more permanent members of the congregation, would account easily for around 125–30 individuals. This could be conservatively converted to a 200- to 250-person-strong community, if the elderly and the more infrequent visitors were to be included in the computation (the lists of communicants clearly indicates a presence of not 50 but 190 Scottish adults who received the communion during the 1640s).

Figure 6.1: Scots admitted to civic rights in Cracow (1570s–1650s)

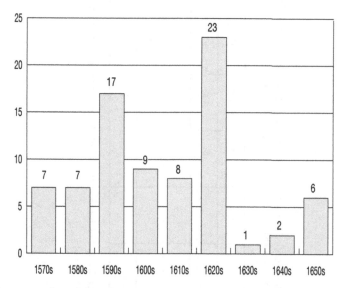

Source: *Księgi przyjęć do prawa miejskiego w Krakowie 1507–1572, Libri iuris civilis Cracoviensis 1507–1572*, eds A. Kiełbicka and Z. Wojas (Kraków, 1993); *Księgi przyjęć do prawa miejskiego w Krakowie 1573–1611, Libri iuris Civilis Cracoviensis 1573–1611*, eds A. Kiełbicka and Z. Wojas (Kraków, 1994); W. Kowalski, 'Kraków Citizenship and the Local Scots, 1509–1655', in *Britain and Poland–Lithuania: Contact and comparison from the Middle Ages to 1795*, ed. R. Unger (Leiden 2008), tables I and II.

The growth of the Scottish community affected the ethnic make-up of the Reformed brethren. If in the 1630s the Scots accounted for nearly a quarter of the parishioners, this ratio rose to above 30 per cent in the 1640s. The Palm Sunday services during this decade attracted on average 118 parishioners – among them 38 Scots (32.2 per cent).[28] A similarly high ratio continued into the 1650s, but fell to around 22 during the next decade. The overall number of adult parishioners fell sharply too. If during the 1650s the communion at Palm Sunday was being taken on average by about 120 adults (among them 25 Scots), in the 1660s on average there were only about 50 communicants (among them 15 Scots). The whole congregation shrunk by a staggering 60 per cent – the number of Scots diminished by around 40 per cent. In the 1670s, the overall numbers plummeted further to about 30 communicants per record (among them 10 Scots), before rising again towards the end of the seventeenth century. The last three lists of communicants recorded at Wielkanoc in 1713, 1714 and 1715 showed 57, 55 and 49 communicants (among them 21, 14 and 12 worshippers of Scottish origin) respectively. At this stage, parishioners of Scottish descent made up nearly a quarter of the congregation.

The formidable Scottish presence, particularly in the 1640s and 1650s, illustrates the importance the Scottish Protestants had in this and possibly some other Reformed parishes of Poland–Lithuania. While the Counter-Reformation and the war against Sweden resulted in decreasing numbers of parishioners, the data shows that the Scottish community was losing supporters more slowly than its Polish coreligionists. However, overall, the Scottish membership in the assembly was falling. This was reflected in both a decreasing number of communicants and fewer religious ceremonies held in the parish (figure 6.1). An analogous trend was observed in other Reformed parishes across the Commonwealth attended by Scots with the exception of Kiejdany where the number of Scottish settlers continued to rise throughout the second half of the seventeenth century until the late 1690s.[29] The strength of the Cracow community may have attracted compatriots belonging to different confessions. The 1631–56 conversions inventory lists several Scots who renounced *Papiestwo* (popery). Unfortunately, the creed of several other Scots such as Peter Gordon (1640) was not recorded. It is probable, however, that among them there were also Episcopalians.[30]

Overall, during the period under the investigation, i.e. from 1610 until 1734, over 500 Scots appeared in the records either as regular parishioners or one-off visitors.

The make-up of the Scottish congregation

Much information about the composition of the Scottish congregation of the Cracow Reformed parish can be gained by cross-referencing parish records against other sources, most importantly burgher rolls and tax records.

The citizenship record books for Cracow indicate that between 1509 and 1703, some 84 Scots or people of Scottish descent obtained civic rights there.[31] The great majority of grants were issued between 1590 and 1630. Of these, 17 Scots received citizenship in the 1590s, 9 in the 1600s, and 8 in the 1610s. The numbers peaked in the 1620s when 23 Scots became burghers. In the two following decades, only three grants were issued to the Caledonians. This number grew slightly in the 1650s when 6 Scots acquired citizenship (figure 6.1).[32]

When cross-referenced against the parish records, the data suggests that among the Scottish citizens of Cracow, a large number belonged to the Reformed brethren. For instance, of the 9 Scots admitted to the burger estate between 1630 and 1650, at least 7, i.e. 78 per cent, belonged to the parish. Although the incomplete pre-1637 records prevent establishing more accurate statistics for the 1610s and 1620s, nevertheless, the records demonstrate that of the 23 men elevated to burghership in the second decade of the seventeenth century, at least 11 men, i.e. 47.8 per cent, belonged to the Reformed congregation. While Nathaniel Keith (Kieyth) and Peter Wood (Odt), admitted to a civic right in 1525, can be identified as Roman Catholics, the denomination of the other 11 Scots cannot be presently verified.[33] It seems that of the latter group, some simply left Cracow. The worsening economic situation in the city, the growing tensions between the Protestants and the Catholics, and the relocation of the royal Court to Warsaw, swayed some of the Scots to seek prosperity elsewhere. Although we cannot be certain which motive influenced John Monkhaus's decision to resign the citizenship conferred upon him in Cracow, it is evident that he subsequently moved to Gdańsk.[34]

A great deal of information concerning the Scots of the Cracow congregation during the 1650–55 period can be also gauged by comparing its records with the 1651 register of subsidy to Charles II, which placed a 10 per cent property tax on all Scots and English living in the realm (table 6.2).[35] In light of that document, the Scots from the parish appear as an affluent group of people. Of the 16 people listed in the register in Cracow, 14 contributed altogether a sum of 7,766 zł, that is, they estimated the value of their possessions at around 4,850 zł per head, while the other two were exempt from the tithe. Of these 14 contributors, 10 belonged to the Reformed congregation.[36] The magnitude of the wealth of the Scottish congregation can be fully appreciated, when compared with contemporary prices. A horse in the 1650s was worth around 30 zł and 1 zł could purchase around one *korzec* (about 120–5 kg) of wheat.[37] A selection of nine epitaphs belonging to the Scottish Protestants of Cracow further attests to the affluence of its owners and that particular community.[38]

Table 6.2: Religious background of the Scots who contributed to the 1651 tithe in Cracow

Surname	First name	Amount	Member of the Reformed parish
Blackhall (Blakal)	Albert (Albertus)	2,038 zł 24 gr	yes
Carmichael (Karmichell) [Snr.]	James (Iacobus)	1,800 zł	yes
Carmichael (Karmichel) [Jnr.]	James (Iacobo)	960 zł (they paid together)	yes
Blackhall (Bladzkal)	Albert (Alberto)		no
Corbet or Corbett (Korbet)	James (Iacobus)	50 zł	yes
Cruickshank (Kruckszang)	George (Georgius)	600 zł	yes
Cruickshank (Krukessian)	George (Georgio)	240 zł (they paid together)	no
Fraser (Frazer)	Andrew (Andrea)		no
Dixon, version of Dickson	Alexander (Alexandro)	840 zł	yes
Fraiter (Frede)	Abraham (Abrahamus)	60 zł	yes
Fraser (Frasser)	Andrew (Andreas)	870 zł	yes
Hewison née unknown (Huysen)	Anna	exempt from tax	yes
Hewison (Huysen)	William (Wilhelm)	exempt from tax	yes
Hunter (Huntter)	Casper (Gaspar)	9 zł	yes
Torrie (Thore)	William (Wilhelmus)	300 zł	yes
Wall (Walls)	Peter (Piotr)	5 zł	no
Total:		**7,772 zł 24 gr**	

Source: 'Exactio decimae partis substantiarum a mercatoribus cateris/q/ue nationis Scothiae et Anglicanae hominibus in Regno Poloniae degentibus iuxta ordinationem constitutionis comitialis die mensis Decembris 1650 pro subsidio serenissimi magnae Britaniae regis laudatae. Expedita Radomii sub tempus tribunalis die 13 mensis Martii anno 1651', AGAD, Warsaw, sig. ASK I 134, fols 1–39; 'Księga Wtóra Kościoła Ewangel[icko] Reformowanego w Wielkanocy', Archiwum Parafii Ewangelicko-Augsburskiej Św. Marcina w Krakowie, no signature.

The parish documents indicate that among the wealthier members of the Scottish congregation, apart from the residents of Cracow – although they were in the majority – there were also Scottish inhabitants of nearby towns like Olkusz, Tarnów, Lublin, and Lubowla. For example, John Chiesley (Kieczle) and Thomas Murray (Morey), both of Lublin, and both steadfast supporters of the parish, estimated the value of their possessions at around 1,000 zł and 2000 zł respectively.[39]

Understandably, the tithe was not well received by some of the parishioners. Alexander Dickson voiced his objection to the tithe by declaring in Polish: 'I was born here; I have lived in Kraków for 57 years and continue to live here; and as to this tax, I am ready to swear that I took no inheritance whatsoever after my parents, and ought not to pay this tith . . .' His protestation, referred later to the royal Court, brought no positive result. The prosecutor 'produced Letters Universal of His Royal Majesty, whereby he showed that the heirs of Scots were likewise bound to pay the same tithe' with which he rejected the plaintiff's arguments.[40] Dickson was forced to pay 840 zł. Yet, another very similar appeal was more successful.[41] After stating that she was born in Cracow and did not inherit anything after the death of her husband, Ursula Elmslie née Orem (Urszula Elmsle'owa), was exempted from paying the tithe. Moreover, unlike William and Anna Hewison, she was not listed on the tithe register.[42]

Elmslie was not the only person omitted from the roll. Using Cracow's parish records, it is possible to establish that out of all 33 regular Scottish worshippers who did not pay the tax, about half managed to avoid the subsidy.[43]

By cross-referencing the tithe roll with the parish registers, it was possible to determine that all the contributors who belonged to the parish were either first- or second-generation Scots, all were accomplished merchants and that a majority enjoyed the civic rights of Cracow. Furthermore, the data shows that apart from Abraham Fraiter, John Chiesley and Thomas Murray, who appear to have been single, all the other contributors to the tithe and the members of the congregation were married and most likely had offspring. In total, during the 1650–5 period, 15 Scottish families frequented the chapels in Lucianowice and Wielkanoc. The heads of five of them somehow avoided contributing to the 1651 subsidy altogether (table 6.3).[44]

The parish records reveal much about the ratio between men and women within the congregation. The evidence suggests an imbalance between the sexes in favour of men. The aforementioned register of parishioners of 1637 lists, in total, the names of 73 Scots, 49 men and 24 women. Although the total number of women in the parish (125) also seems to be smaller than the total number of men (178), it is quite clear that the ratio of men to women amongst the other parishioners is more equal than that amongst the Scots.

While Scottish women were outnumbered by their male counterparts nearly two to one, at a parish level women made up about 44 per cent of the congregation.[45] A scrupulously detailed analysis of the lists of communicants, encompassing the period from 1636 to 1716, allowed the identification of 556 individuals who could be described as being of Scottish origin and who appeared at least once in the records. Only around 30 per cent of those registered, that is 165 individuals, were women. This proportion of men to women appears to be constant throughout the seventeenth-century period. Of note is the fact that of these 165 women, 62 (37.6 per cent) received communion in the parish not more than twice. The ratio of women permanently residing in the parish to those who appear on the lists of communicants sporadically could be even higher as it is difficult to trace women after they married (marriage records seldom contained maiden names). The motives for moving between parishes were varied, and women had different reasons from men. While some of them were possibly travelling alongside their husbands or visited parishes to become godmothers or witnesses, others – especially maidens – were moving elsewhere to join their new husbands.

Moreover, it appears that many marriages were conducted among Scots not only in the first, but also in second, third or later generations. The family histories indicate that this practice was taking place throughout the period. An interesting example is that of Thomas Orem, burgher and merchant of Cracow, and his wife Susanne Hewitt (Zuzanna Heidówna) who married in Wielkanoc in 1606.[46] Their eldest daughter Susanne (Zuzanna) (b. 1612) was married in Lucianowice in 1629 to her countryman William Torrie (Thory), merchant and burgher of Cracow.[47] Orem's second daughter, Elisabeth (Helszka) (b. 1620), was wed in 1641 in the same parish to another influential Scot of Cracow, James Chambers.[48] Of their children, daughter Anna Constantia Chambers (Ciamerówna, Czamer, Forbesowa) (b. c. 1652) married in Lucianowice in 1668 a first-generation Scot, Peter Forbes, originally from Mowney in Aberdeenshire.[49] Their child, Thomas Orem's great-grand-daughter, Anna Constantia (Lowa, Lowowa, Louwa) (b. c. 1678), married yet another Scot, Robert Low (Lau, Laul, Leow, Loow, Löo, Loöw, Louw, Low, Lowe, Löv) who was Royal Postmaster (fl. 1695–1718) and later a Royal Secretary (fl. 1713–1718).[50]

Parishioners' profiles

Much information about the character of the Scottish congregation can be obtained by examining the careers and lives of individual parishioners. Among its most successful and affluent members were Robert Blackhall, James Carmichael the Elder [Snr.] and James Carmichael [Jnr.], and Robert Forbes.

Table 6.3: The Scottish families of the Cracow congregation in the 1650s

Husband	Wife	Citizenship	Subsidy	Generation	Number of children
Blackhall Robert	Burnet Ewa	1622	2,038 zł 24 gr	1st	13
Burnet Bartholomew	Rait Agnes	–	not listed	2nd	2
Carmichael James [Snr.]	Dickson Anna	1625	1,800 zł	1st	2
Carmichael James [Jnr.]	Burnet Sarah	1654	c. 480 zł	2nd	8
Chambers James	Orem Elisabeth	1655	not listed	1st	7
Corbet James	unknown Susanne	–	50 zł	?	0
Cruickshank George	Jäger Susanne	1646	600 zł	1st	0
Dickson Alexander	Krauze Elisabeth	1623	840 zł	2nd	8
Fraser Andrew	Hewitt Susanne, married name Orem	1625	870 zł	1st	0
Gordon Richard	Torrie Elisabeth	Lwów	not listed	?	1
Hewison William [II]	Dickson Elisabeth	?	not listed	2nd?	5
Hunter Casper	unknown Catherina	1651	9 zł	2nd	1
Murray [Mohr] Jan	Frier (Frajerówna) Zuzanna	?	500 zł	?	0
Torrie William	Orem Susanne	1626	300 zł	1st	6
Wishart Abraham	Fiddes Madeline	Lubowla 1651	not listed	?	0
					Total: 53

Source: 'Księga Wtóra Kościoła Ewangel[icko] Reformowanego w Wielkanocy', Archiwum Parafii Ewangelicko-Augsburskiej Św. Marcina w Krakowie, no signature.

Robert Blackhall, who first appears in the parish records in 1636, was an active member of the congregation for the next twenty years. Born in 1586, Blackhall travelled to Poland from Aberdeen and settled in Cracow where he became a citizen in 1622.[51] Not much is known about his early years, although he must have been involved in commerce from a young age. It is likely that his arrival was not coincidental, but rather was a part of chain migration. Between 1649 and 1650 Blackhall traded with Leipzig. In 1649, together with other prominent Cracovian Scots, Alexander Dickson and George Elmslie, and James Chalmer (Jakub Czamer) and Robert (Wojciech) Farquhar, both of Poznań, he was involved in importing merchandise into Cracow: fustian, cotton yarn, silk, tapestry, knives and other goods. In 1653, Blackhall imported from Leipzig knives, candlesticks, pistols, mirrors, combs, glasses, brushes, strings, playing cards, scissors, and powder-horns.[52] His activities made him one of the most affluent Scottish merchants of the first half of the seventeenth century. As mentioned earlier, in 1651 Blackhall's estate was valued at over 20,000 zł.[53] However, his good fortune came to an end soon after. In 1652, Blackhall lost his son and two of his servants to the plague.[54] Moreover, services rendered to Swedes during their occupation of Cracow in 1655–6, is likely to have made him many enemies among the supporters of the Polish cause. Despite that, when he died in 1656, according to Węgierski, the funeral of this 'pious merchant' was well attended by the Reformed and the Roman Catholics alike.[55]

James Carmichael [Snr.], son of Robert Carmichael of Dundee and Margaret née unknown, acquired burgher's rights of Cracow in 1625. He was recommended by the Honest James Leslie from Dundee and the Honest Robert Auchinleck (Aucstenleg) from Gostyń who gave true testimony concerning his lawful birth. The witnesses confirmed under oath that they knew his parents well and that Carmichael was begotten in the state of holy matrimony according to the rites of the Roman Catholic Church. It is unknown if he himself was a Catholic, and if so, when he converted. The evidence indicates that he was a member of the Reformed congregation between 1637 and 1655, when his name appears frequently in the records. Carmichael's commercial expertise helped him to amass a considerable wealth. In 1651 his estate was valued at 18,000 zł. Moreover, Carmichael also gained the acclaim of his co-religionists and his compatriots. He was elected Elder of the Cracow Reformed brethren in 1642 and 1644, and Elder of the Scottish Brotherhood of Cracow in 1639, 1642 and 1644. As an active merchant Carmichael was often away and the previously mentioned Robert Blackhall was chosen to be his assistant. According to Węgierski, Carmichael died during the siege of Cracow (by Swedes) in 1655. Of his two known sons, James [the Younger] and Alexander, it is the former whose career deserves a closer look.[56] James the Younger, born around 1627, was granted citizen's rights on 25 September 1654. A merchant in his own right, in 1649/50 he imported goods from Royal Prussia. In 1650, he organised five transports, among them 'Dutch wares'. In the same year, he also imported two transports of goods from Breslau (Wrocław). In addition, his commercial interests extended to Leipzig.

Similarly to Blackhall and many other Scots of the Reformed parish, he supported Swedes during their occupation in 1655–6. He faced an uncertain future after the Swedish rule was over. Listed on the register of collaborators (1657), Carmichael was subsequently incarcerated. However, his stay in prison was cut short, thanks to a royal pardon. It is possible that this lenient treatment was due to the fact that together with Kasper Hunter (who was also guilty of collaboration and arrested), they had the capacity to provide a large loan (6,000 zł) to the Polish monarch who was strapped for cash. Carmichael fell victim to the outbreak of smallpox in 1678. This dedicated supporter of the Reformed congregation (his name appears in the parish records continuously from 1641) was laid to rest at Wielkanoc. According to Węgierski, Carmichael's funeral was frequented by church elders and some of the council members of Cracow.[57]

Another prominent parishioner, a second-generation Scot, was Robert Forbes, son of William of Tarnów and Ursula Dickson. Forbes acquired a civic right in 1679 and in 1692 he was nominated a king's secretary. The nomination letter patent issued by the Royal Chancellery described Forbes's ability to import fine-quality foreign goods and supply provisions for the royal artillery.[58] Forbes was also involved in banking. From his head office in Cracow he conducted business in all the bigger cities of the Polish–Lithuanian Commonwealth and all major fairs. Through commission agents, Forbes acquired goods from other merchants using receipts signed with his name. Jewish merchants of Cracow often used his network. Among other transactions, Forbes was lending substantial amounts of money to the Jewish assembly of elders in Cracow, while he himself borrowed from the nobility and the clergy. His company collapsed when his debt reached the sum of 133,621 zł. The 478-page report of a special commission set up in 1699 by King August II to investigate the workings of the company shows that among his debtors were 187 Jews. Like many other well-off Scots, Forbes conducted philanthropic activities, financially supporting the Reformed parish.[59]

Among the successful parishioners there were at least three Cracow-based female merchants, one active in the 1610s and two in the 1650s: Eva Forbes (Forbess), Ursula Elmslie (Emslowa Jurkowa, Emzle, Emzlowa, Hamsle, Hendzlowa) née Orem (b. 1588; d. 1651) and Anna Hewison (Huison) who was importing goods from Prussia.[60] Forbes, recorded in the 1617 and 1618 toll registers, specialised in wine. She was importing it from Sopron (Ödenburg) in Hungary, and from Nový Jičín and Levoča in Slovakia.[61]

Elmslie, who had been a widow since about 1625, was involved in trade until her death. In 1650, she imported two loads of goods from Breslau into Silesia. In the same year, she also brought in goods from Royal Prussia: spices and Dutch wares – three separate shipments.[62] Elmslie was described as *pobożna* (devout) in her death certificate.[63] Indeed she was heavily involved with the life of her community. She appears continuously in the list of communicants in Lucianowice and Wielkanoc from 1636 to 1651, and in Wiatowice parish from 1649 to 50.[64] She was recorded as a godmother to numerous children in the parish (mostly Scots), in 1614, 1616, 1617, 1618, 1621, 1622, 1624, 1627 – twice, 1628 – twice, 1629, 1630, 1631, 1632, 1633, 1634, 1635 – three times, 1637. Moreover, Elmslie also contributed generously to several parish collections.[65]

Not all parishioners were as successful. Samuel Cheyne, a 'youth' from Nowopole near Tarnów, who frequented the parish between 1650 and 1653 while studying at the Cracow Academy, was employed as a tutor of Wilhelm Torrie's children.[66] The death record of William Chambers of 1666 indicates that he was a servant of yet another affluent merchant of Cracow, James Chambers.[67] Similarly, Robert Lamb (in 1684) and John Livingstone (in 1694) were recorded as servants of Robert Forbes. William Clelland, a youth who died in Wielkanoc in 1651, was recorded as a factor of several unnamed, but most likely Scottish, merchants from Ukraine. A death of a certain *Ubogi Wilhelm nationi Scotus* was noted, for example, in 1642.[68] Apart from being described as *ubogi* (impoverished), of note is the fact that he was simply recorded by his Christian name William. Deaths of several other less wealthy Scots, like a certain Paul, glover, who died in 1648, have been recorded in a similar style.[69]

Scottish women in the parish

As the statistical data and the example of Ursula Elmslie show, many Scottish women were actively involved in the life of their parish. Although they were not allowed among the elders, their involvement included, among other things, looking after less fortunate members of their communities. Catherine née King, wife of the late William Paterson, was noted for such deeds. Before her death in 1637, she left a 60 florin bequest to the poor of the Cracow parish.[70]

Although some women were involved in trade, the usually elaborate inscriptions on epitaphs dedicated to the deceased Scottish women imply that the great majority of them were charged with many different responsibilities and were expected to display particular qualities. Suzanne Chambers née Sommer has been described as 'a living model of virtues, a true exemplar of kindness'.[71] The inscriptions, like the one on the epitaph of Catherine

Paterson, reflect the fate of many women of those times: early marriage, followed by premature death.[72]

It has been established that such epitaphs were also used to propagate a certain model of pious life to create specific role models for women.[73] The good wife was to be pious, prudent, dutiful and modest, which would manifest itself in her clothing, rejection of luxury and in her willingness to look after the poor. Above all, a good wife was also to be a good mother, giving birth and raising offspring, fulfilling the basic role of a married woman. The iconographic material from the epitaphs seems to suggest that the ideal of a good wife held by the Scottish community was identical to that held by the wealthier strata of sixteenth- and seventeenth-century Poland–Lithuania. The epitaph of the already mentioned Catherine Paterson provides the best evidence to support such a view. In this instance, the ideals are represented through Catherine's sunken-relief portrait and the inscription on her epitaph. Paterson is depicted dressed modestly in a traditional female old-Polish costume consisting of a long and plain skirt, and a cloak. Her head is covered in a bonnet with a *rańtuch* (a kind of a shawl or scarf made from a wide cloth) falling on to her shoulders. Her piety is indicated by a prayer book or the Bible held in her right hand just over her heart. A number of entries in the parish registers describing charitable work of the deceased female members of the congregation provide proof that many Scottish women upheld such ideals.

Life in the parish and within a wider community

The organisation of the Scottish congregation was in many respects analogous to the organisation of Scots elsewhere. Although the baptismal registers do not provide the most accurate data, names of godparents were sometimes left out; nevertheless, they show that the Scots formed a distinct community within the larger Reformed assembly. The records demonstrate that, as a rule, a new child of Scottish parents would have first- or second- generation Scottish godparents presenting him/her at baptism. Such practice was true of even mixed marriages, where only the father was of Scottish extraction.[74] Table 6.4 shows that between 1610 and 1656, 240 out of 374 godparents (i.e. 64.1 per cent) were of Scottish descent. In reality, this ratio was probably higher, as in the computations only godparents whose ethnic origins could be verified, that is who bore Scottish surnames, were considered to be bona fide Scots. Consequently, the tally excluded women married to Scots, like Agnes Burnet née unknown (Agnieszka Bornatowa), or wife of Daniel Forbes (listed simply as Danielowa Forbesowa), and women who appear in the baptismal records under the German, French, or Polish surnames of their husbands, but who may have been in fact of Scottish descent. The ethnicity of godfathers was much easier to establish. Of the 211 godfathers listed in the register, 163, i.e. 77.2 per cent, have been identified as Scots.[75]

Correspondingly, Scots dominated amongst witnesses at Scottish weddings. Furthermore, the marriage records confirm that the Scots showed a preference for marrying their own compatriots. Of the 15 Scottish families frequenting the parish during the 1650 to 1655 period, 11 spouses were of Scottish descent, two of Polish or German, while the origins of the remaining two were unknown. As previously indicated, the majority of the families were connected with each other through marriage, if not in the preceding or their own generation, then through marriage of their children. Such families of first- and second-generation Scots and their children formed the core of this particular, close-knit community (table 6.4).

Differentiation from the local followers of Calvinism was not necessarily caused by ethnic or language dissimilarities alone. Dogmatic divergence played possibly a considerable role in separating the migrants from their hosts, and especially during church feasts. The records show that despite living abroad, the Scots in Poland–Lithuania were still adhering to their much stricter brand of Calvinism. This, for example, had an effect on church attendance. The Scottish presence in Lucianowice was nearly always the strongest on Palm Sunday, but relatively few of them, unlike their local co-religionists, attended services at Christmas.

Attempts to retain identity did not mean disconnection from the Protestant community. In fact, more than a few Scots became heavily involved in the life of the Cracow assembly as executives and financial supporters, godparents, or witnesses. As early as 1586, Robert King (Woyciech Kin) became its deacon. Later, in 1616, he became a senior of Alexandrowice, along with possibly another Scot, William Smith (Kilian Szmid).[76] Roughly at the same time (1614) Alexander Dickson and George Elmslie (Emsel) were elected as auditors of the accounts of the parish.[77] Andrew Fraser, a senior of Lucianowice in 1631, was elected to look after its poor-box a year later. Among the administrators there were also Thomas Forbes, a senior of Wielkanoc (1633, 1639), and of Lucianowice (1637), and Alexander Dickson, a senior of the latter parish (1637). In 1639, James Carmichael [Snr.] was elected an elder of Lucianowice.[78] This participation did not diminish due to the war with Sweden. Some thirty years later, Scottish involvement in the life of the parish was actually as strong as it had ever been. In 1677, three men of Scottish origin: James Carmichael, William Hewison, and Peter Forbes were elected as its elders. While Hewison was to look after the church records, Forbes was left in charge of the poor-box.[79] The latter was also known for his multiple donations; for example, in 1681, he provided cloth for the altar, velvet, and a cover for the chalice. In 1682, he supported the renovations of the Wielkanoc church by providing nails and calcium hydroxide.[80] Finally, in 1704, another

Table 6.4: Ethnic origins of godparents to children born of Scottish parents in the Reformed parish in Cracow, 1610–5

Years	Number of baptisms	Godfathers			Godmothers			Total/ratio
		Scotsmen	Others	Sub-total	Scotswomen	Others	Sub-total	
1610–19	7	18	6	24	6	9	15	24 out of 39 (61.5%)
1620–9	8	11	6	17	4	12	16	15 out of 33 (45.4%)
1630–9	22	51	20	71	25	29	54	76 out of 125 (60.8%)
1640–9	30	68	10	78	33	29	62	101 out of 140 (72.1%)
1650–6	10	15	6	21	9	7	16	24 out of 37 (64.8%)
Total	77	163	48	211	77	86	163	240 out of 374 (64.1%)

Source: 'Reiestr Dziatek Ochrzczonych których imiona w księgach kościelnych przedtym nie były wpisane Rejestrzyk od samych ich Rodziców zebrany y do tych ksiąg podany (1610–1631)', Archiwum Parafii Ewangelicko-Augsburskiej Św. Marcina w Krakowie, folios 14–16v; 'Reiestr Ochrzczonych w Zborze Wielkanockim (1631–1657)', Archiwum Parafii Ewangelicko-Augsburskiej Św. Marcina w Krakowie, folios 17–27.

Scot, John Taylor, was elected as an elder at Wielkanoc.[81] Surprisingly, there were no ministers of Scottish descent in the parish until the eighteenth century. Only around 1709, Rev. Alexander Chambers, earlier a student of theology and tutor to the children of Daniel Davidson and Catharine née Aidy of Gdańsk, was assigned to the congregation and stayed in Wielkanoc till 1715.[82] In the 1740s, the assembly appointed to that post Rev. Bogusław Orem (Aram), who remained its minister until the 1760s.[83]

The acts of violence against the Dissenters of Cracow between 1569 and 1698, scrupulously documented in the parish books, may have also assisted the formation of closer ties between the Scots and the other parishioners. Attacks on churches, like the destruction of *Bróg* described above, and attacks on funeral processions and private homes, affected both communities alike. Among the Protestant merchants whose residences were attacked, there were several prominent, wealthy Scots. In 1631, in the early morning on the Feast of the Ascension, a gang of students plundered the house of the goldsmith, David Strachon. Later that morning, the same gang also broke into the house of Thomas Forbes. As Węgierski somewhat sarcastically observed, the looters, seeking 'heresy in his coffers', verbally assaulted Forbes and his wife and left with the booty.[84] Forbes's house was unsuccessfully attacked again during unspecified unrest (most likely unrelated to confessional issues), which took place in July–August 1640.[85] More serious assaults on the homes of William Torrie, James Carmichael and several other Protestant merchants took place in June 1647. While some of the assaults ended with full-scale looting, the mob, stopped by the city guards, did not break into the houses belonging to the two Scots.

The Scots, as staunch supporters of the Reformed cause, probably formed even stronger links with the native Protestant community during the war with Sweden (1655–6). Like many of their hosts, the Scots overwhelmingly sided with Karl X Gustav.[86] However, retributions that followed after the defeat of the Swedes and the change of attitude towards the nonconformist were not the ultimate causes of the demise of the Scottish community. By the mid-1600s, costly conflicts such as the Cossack Rebellion (1648–54), the Second Northern War (1655–60) and the Polish–Turkish Wars (1671–99) progressively ruined the once flourishing economy of Poland–Lithuania. From the late seventeenth century onwards, the decreased demand for Polish wheat in Western Europe, new military conflicts and destabilisation of the political system, made the state unattractive to potential investors. This coincided with the opening of new destinations for enterprising Scots, the late-seventeenth-century migration to Ulster and the later eighteenth-century migration to North America. Decline in the inflow of immigrants – a direct result of the changes in migratory patterns – led, in turn, to increased assimilation processes.

Conclusion

The records of the Reformed parish of Cracow allow for a much better understanding of the fortunes of the Scottish community there, and, more broadly,
the immigrants in seventeenth-century Poland–Lithuania. The information
allows for the questioning of the stereotypical representation of the migrants
in both historical documents and even more recent articles.[87] The Scottish
community that emerges from the registers looks like a complex, highly organised, sophisticated group of people, which evolved greatly over time. Whilst
the typical Scot arriving in Cracow in the second half of the sixteenth century
could be categorised as a petty trader desperately trying to support himself, the
church records from the 1630s, 1640s and early 1650s demonstrate few
persons who could fit such a description. Within this close-knit community
one can distinguish a clear hierarchical structure. The top layer consisted of the
wealthiest merchants, more often than not burghers of Cracow. These men,
possibly because of their social standing and commercial prowess, regularly
held positions of responsibility within the parish. Next on the ladder there
were their employees, merchant factors who conducted transactions on their
behalf. Below them, there seemed to be a group of apprentices, young men
and boys. Often employed as pedlars, such men were entrusted with distrib-
uting wares to more remote, smaller towns and villages. Finally, below them,
there were also servants. The family names of people of different strata suggest
that often they were somehow related to each other. As shown through various
social and commercial exchanges, these intricate family and professional
networks extended well beyond the congregation. This in turn helped the
Scots to sustain contacts not just with similar expatriate communities in
Poland but also to link them with their homeland. An important and thus far
underrated role in maintaining identity was played by the Scottish women.

The records suggest that although amongst the Scots in Cracow there were
those who declared themselves Roman Catholic, the majority formed lasting
affiliations with the Reformed Church. Their creed offered them unity and in
time became one of the main features that distinguished them from other
ethnic groups in the city. Moreover, many decided to hold on to their religious beliefs despite the fact that Calvinism placed them in a position of
disadvantage in seventeenth-century Cracow.

Although the Scots showed a preference for associating themselves with
their fellow countrymen, maintaining their identity did not stop them,
however, from immersing themselves in the life of the parish. Their contribution to Cracow's brethren, particularly throughout the seventeenth century,
was considerable. The Scots did not only bolster their meagre numbers, but
also supported them financially. Moreover, through participation in the positions of authority, they took part in shaping the future of the brethren.

Ultimately, the rise and fall of the Scottish congregation, closely entwined with the history of the Reformed assembly, reflects the situation of other Scots in Poland–Lithuania. After rapid growth in the early seventeenth century, the Scottish brethren achieved their highest number in the 1640s and remained a sizeable group within the congregation up until the mid-1650s. The aftermath of the war with Sweden marks the beginnings of their decline. It seems that, by the third and fourth decades of the eighteenth century, the Scots of Cracow, just like their compatriots in other locations, became integrated with the native population.

Notes

1 W. Lithgow, *The Totall Discourse of the Rare Adventures and Painefull Peregrinations of long Nineteene Yeares Travayles from Scotland to the most famous Kingdomes in Europe, Asia and Africa* (Glasgow, 1906), p. 243.

2 G. Phelps, ed., *The Rare Adventures and Painfull Peregrinations of William Lithgow* (London, 1974), pp. 7–21.

3 *Księgi przyjęć do prawa miejskiego w Krakowie 1507–1572, Libri Iuris Civilis Cracoviensis 1507–1572*, [hereafter *LICCr I*] eds A. Kiełbicka and Z. Wojas (Kraków, 1993), no. 148.

4 A. Murray, 'Skene, Sir John, of Curriehill (c.1540–1617)', in the *Oxford Dictionary of National Biography* (hereafter *ODNB*), http://www.oxforddnb.com/view/article/25669 (accessed September 28, 2006); cf. William Forbes Skene, ed., *Memorials of the Family Skene of Skene: From the Family Papers with Other Illustrative Documents* (Edinburgh, 1887), *passim*.

5 'Pedder', in J. Skene, *De verborum significatione the exposition of the termes and difficill wordes, conteined in the foure buikes of Regiam Majestatem, and uthers, in the Acts of Parliament, infestments, and used in the practique of this realme, with diverse rules, and common places, or principalles of the lawes. Collected and exponed be M. John Skene, clerke of our Soveraine Lordis register, councell and rolles* (London, 1641), pp. 104–5; cf. F. A. Steuart, ed., *Papers Relating to the Scots in Poland 1576–1593*, [hereafter *PRSP*], (Edinburgh, 1915), p. xiii.

6 One of the first historians who looked at Cracow's Scots was S. Tomkowicz, 'Przyczynek do historyi Szkotów w Krakowie i w Polsce', *Rocznik Krakowski*, ed. S. Krzyżanowski, 2 (1899), pp. 151–74. The most comprehensive and up-to-date accounts have been composed recently by Waldemar Kowalski. Cf. W. Kowalski, 'Scoti, cives Cracovienses: Their Ethnic and Social Identity, 1570–1660', in *British and Irish Emigrants and Exiles in Europe, 1603–1688*, ed. D. Worthington (Leiden–Boston, 2010), pp. 67–85; W. Kowalski, 'Robert Spens i szkocka gmina w Krakowie u schyłku XVI stulecia', in *Między Lwowem a Wrocławiem. Księga jubileuszowa Profesora Krystyna Matwijowskiego*, eds B. Rok and J. Maroń (Toruń, 2006), pp. 409–17; W. Kowalski, 'Kraków Citizenship and the Local Scots, 1509–1655', in *Britain and Poland–Lithuania: Contact and comparison from the Middle Ages to 1795*, ed. R. Unger (Leiden, 2008); W. Kowalski, 'Certificates of

legitimate birth (birth-brieves) in the practice of the city councils of Aberdeen and Cracow at the close of the sixteenth century and during the first half of the seventeenth century', in *Pragmatické písemnosti v kontextu právním a správním*, eds Z. Hojda and H. Pátková (Praha, 2008), pp. 187–201; W. Kowalski, 'Szkoci na rynku krakowskim w połowie XVII wieku', *Zeszyty Wszechnicy Świętokrzyskiej. Filologia angielska* 1, no. 23 (2006), pp. 15–38; W. Kowalski, 'The Scots at the Cracow Customs House in the first half of the 17th century', enlarged and corrected version of the paper presented to the Polish–Scottish Relations 15th–18th Centuries Conference, Institute of History, Polish Academy of Sciences, Warsaw, 20–23 September 2000. I am indebted to Professor Kowalski for providing an offprint of this paper.

7 Kowalski observed that the Scots in Little Poland did not attend their own churches or have their own clergy, choosing instead to worship within the local Reformed congregations. Moreover, Kowalski contended that the Scots were well aware of their brand of Calvinism: Kowalski, 'Scoti, cives Cracovienses', p. 85. Cf. W. Kowalski, 'The Scots at the Cracow Customs House', p. 1.

8 W. Węgierski, *Kronika Zboru Ewangelickiego Krakowskigo* (1651, reprinted Kraków, 1817), pp. i–iii, 16; cf. H. Kowalska, 'Z dziejów reformacji w Krakowie', in *Szkice z dziejów Krakowa od czasów najdawniejszych do pierwszej wojny światowej*, ed. J. Bieniarzówna (Kraków, 1968), pp. 193–5.

9 J. Tazbir, 'The fate of Polish Protestantism in the seventeenth century', in *A Republic of Nobles*, ed. J. K. Fedorowicz (Cambridge, 1982), pp. 203–4.

10 Urban suggests that Joannes *sarctor* listed in visitation records of 1565–70 is possibly the same as John Allan Scot from Aberdeen (Joannes Alanth de Abrodenor), admitted to the civic rights of Cracow in 1573: W. Urban, 'Heretycy parafii Mariackiej w Krakowie w 1568 roku', *Odrodzenie i Reformacja w Polsce* 32, (1987): p. 171.

11 Węgierski, *Kronika*, p. 11.

12 Kowalski, 'Robert Spens', pp. 410, 413.

13 H. Barycz, ed., *Kronika mieszczanina krakowskiego z lat 1575–1595* (Kraków, 1930), pp. 93–4.

14 Ibid., p. 94.

15 Tomkowicz, 'Przyczynek', p. 163; *PRSP*, p. 77; cf. Kowalski, 'Robert Spens', p. 413.

16 Duncan left a legacy 'pauperibus religionis suae, utpote Scoticae'. Archiwum Miasta Krakowa, Scabinalia, MS 26, 883, cited in Kowalski, 'Scoti, cives Cracovienses', p. 85.

17 'Extract Variorum Casuum Persequtionum Verum Gestarum in Eccla. (sia) Orth. Crac. (1569–1698)', in 'Księga Wtóra Kościoła Ewangel[icko] Reformowanego w Wielkanocy, zaczynająca się od roku 1637, Księga kościelna zboru Wielkanockiego y Lucianowskiego; sporządzona y spisana w roku 1637', Archiwum Parafii Ewangelicko-Augsburskiej Św. Marcina w Krakowie [hereafter *KW*], no signature, ff. 90–1; cf. Węgierski, *Kronika*, pp. 21, 43, 46, 59; Józef Łukaszewicz *Dzieje kościołów wyznania helweckiego w dawnej Małej Polsce* (Poznań, 1853), pp. 309–11.

18 'Extract Variorum Casuum', ff. 90–3; Węgierski, *Kronika*, pp. 21, 42–4; cf. W. Kriegseisen, *Ewangelicy polscy i litewscy w epoce saskiej 1696–1763: sytuacja prawna, organizacja i stosunki międzywyznaniowe* (Warszawa, 1996), pp. 60–5; Łukaszewicz, *Dzieje*, pp. 311, 371–2, 425–6.

19 'Reiestr Auditorów albo Słuchaczów Zboru Wielkanockiego y Lucianowskiego', in *KW*, ff. 7–9; 'Reiestr Communikantów w Zborze Wielkanocki[m] y Lucianowskim (1636–1651)', and 'Reiestr Communikantów w Zborze Wielkanocki[m] y Lucianowskim (1653–1657)', in *KW*, ff. 43–89a, 104–6a; 'Rejestr komunikantów (1657–1716)', in 'Księga Trzecia zboru w Wielkanocy od 1664–1716', Archiwum Parafii Ewangelicko-Augsburskiej Św. Marcina w Krakowie [hereafter *KT*], no signature, ff. 1–125v.

20 'Extract Variorum Casuum', ff. 90–3; 'Reiestr Auditorów', ff. 7–9; 'Reiestr Communikantów w Zborze Wielkanocki[m] y Lucianowskim (1636-1651)', and 'Reiestr Communikantów w Zborze Wielkanocki[m] y Lucianowskim (1653–1657)', ff. 43–89a, 104–6a; 'Rejestr komunikantów (1657–1716)', ff. 1–125v; Cf. Węgierski, *Kronika*, pp. 21, 42–4.

21 'Metryka Zboru Kieydańskiego w którey są zapisane chrzty y sluby w parafiey tey odprawowane od roku MDCXLI [1641] miesiaca Augusta', Lietuvos Valstybės Istorijos Archyvas, Vilnius, [hereafter LVIA], Fond 606, Ap. 1, bb. 144–50, 324, 336 – F. 1218, Ap. 1, b. 390a; 'Collecta Zboru Kiejdańskiego: To jest rachunek wszystkich recept i expens zborowych zaczęty roku 1628 dnia 20 novembra', unpublished print (Wilno, 1939). Lietuvos Mokslu Akademijos Biblioteka, RS F9-3040.

22 The epitaphs are no longer located in Wielkanoc. After the closure of the parish in the early nineteenth century, they were transported to a Reformed church in Sielec, near Staszów. This last Calvinist parish in Lesser Poland was closed in 1849, and the cemetery itself in 1945. It subsequently fell into ruin. In 1986, conservation work has been undertaken and the stones that survived years of neglect were indexed and moved to the lapidarium at the Calvinist Cemetery in Żychlin near Konin, where they are currently on display. Cf. W. Kriegseisen, 'Dokumentacja historyczna zespołu zabytkowego zboru i cmentarza ewangelicko-reformowanego (kalwińskiego) w Sielcu, gm. Staszów, woj. Tarnobrzeskie', Warszawa, 1988, unpublished manuscript held in Biblioteka Synodu Kościoła Ewangelicko-Reformowanego in Warsaw, sig. R-20; W. Kriegseisen, 'Sprawozdanie z prac inwentaryzacyjnych i poszukiwawczych na dawnym cmentarzu ewangielicko reformowanym (kalwińskim) w Sielcu, gm. Staszów, w latach 1986 i 1987', Warszawa, 1988, unpublished manuscript BSKER, sig. R-42.

23 J. Bieniarzówna, 'Stulecie upadku', in *Dzieje Krakowa. Kraków w wiekach XVI–XVIII*, eds J. Bieniarzówna and J. M. Małecki, (Kraków, 1984), pp. 357–61, 363–87; J. Bieniarzówna, 'Jewish Trade in the Century of Kraków's Decline', in *The Jews in Old Poland, 1000–1795*, eds A. Polonsky, J. Basista and A. Link-Lenczowski (London and New York, 1993), pp. 282–98.

24 'Reiestr Auditorów', *KW*, ff. 7–9.

25 There is also no assurance that the document is one hundred per cent accurate. An examination of a similar register constructed for the Reformed congregation

of Kiejdany in 1679 exposed evident omissions. A close examination of the roll which listed 76 parishioners of Scottish extraction did not include names of a further 18 individuals who most certainly belonged to the parish and appear in other church documents: P. P. Bajer, 'Scots in the Polish Lithuanian Commonwealth XVIth to XVIIIth Centuries: The Formation and Disappearance of an Ethnic Group' (PhD Thesis, Monash University, Melbourne, 2009), p. 234; cf. D. Mikołajewski, 'Rejestr Auditorów Zboru Kiejdańskiego (1679)', quoted in S. Tworek, 'Materiały do dziejów kalwinizmu w Wielkim Księstwie Litewskim w XVII wieku', *Odrodzenie i reformacja w Polsce* 14 (1969), pp. 213–15.

26 'Reiestr Communikantów', *KW*, ff. 43–51.

27 Ibid., ff. 52–85v.

28 The 1640 Palm Sunday celebrations in Lucianowice attracted 125 parishioners (38 Scots); in 1641, 132 (39); in 1642, 106 (29); in 1643, 119 (43); in 1644, 113 (42); in 1645, 122 (43); in 1648, 87 (25). Ibid.

29 Bajer, *Scots*, pp. 232–5; R. Žirgulis, 'The Scottish Community in Kėdainiai ca. 1630–ca.1750', in *Scottish Communities Abroad In The Early Modern Period*, eds A. Grosjean and S. Murdoch (Leiden, 2005), pp. 225–47.

30 Among the converts from Roman Catholicism were George Kinnaird (Jerzy Kenhart *Szot*) in 1632 and Anna, wife of Robert *Szot* of Lublin, in 1643: 'Reiestr do Słowa Bożego przyiętych y z błędów do Ewangeliey pozyskanych', *KW*, ff. 31, 32.

31 According to Kowalski, the official registration is far from complete, as other sources mention at least twenty Scots who acquired citizenship in Cracow but were not recorded in the *libris juris civilis Cracoviensis*: Kowalski, 'Scoti, cives Cracovienses', p. 68. Cf. Kowalski, 'Certificates of Legitimate Birth', p. 54.

32 *LICCr I*; *Księgi przyjęć do prawa miejskiego w Krakowie 1573–1611*, *Libri Iuris Civilis Cracoviensis 1573–1611*, [hereafter *LICCr II*], eds A. Kiełbicka and Z. Wojas (Kraków, 1994); cf. Kowalski, 'Cracow Citizenship', Tables I and II. Cf. 'Records of those Scots granted Citizenship in Cracow', quoted in *PRSP*, pp. 39–58.

33 Ibid., p. 50.

34 Ibid., p. 53.

35 'Exactio decimae partis substantiarum a mercatoribus cateris/q/ue nationis Scothiae et Anglicanae hominibus in Regno Poloniae degentibus iuxta ordinationem constitutionis comitialis die mensis Decembris 1650 pro subsidio serenissimi magnae Britaniae regis laudatae. Expedita Radomii sub tempus tribunalis die 13 mensis Martii anno 1651', [hereafter ASK I 134], Archiwum Główne Akt Dawnych, Warsaw, sig. ASK I 134, ff. 1–39.

36 ASK I 134, ff. 3, 33v.

37 A. Biegańska, 'Wielka emigracja Szkotów w Polsce druga połowa XVI – koniec XVII wieku' (PhD Thesis, Uniwersytet Śląski, Katowice, 1974), p. 195.

38 The stones presently are scattered in three different locations. Seven of the epitaphs are on display in the lapidarium at the Calvinist cemetery in Żychlin near Konin. They include the epitaphs of John (Yan) Taylor (d. 1716), Elisabeth Taylor née Forbes (2 Voto Lehnmann) (d. 1723), Catherine Paterson née Kin (d.

1637), George (Georg) Ross, Alexander Sommer, Susanne (Zuzanna) de Chambers née Sommer, Susanne (Zuzanna) Forbes née Von . . . en. The Epitaph of Wilhelm Ross can be found in Sielec and the last stone, the epitaph of Anna Forbes née Carmichael (Karmichell) (d. 1702), is at the St Martin Lutheran Church in Cracow.

39 Chiesley contributed 100 zł and Thomas Murray 200 zł: ASK I 134, ff. 20, 24.

40 'Admonition of the Alexander Dixon (3rd of March 1651)', quoted in *PRSP*, p. 82; 'Admonition of the Scots (28th of February 1651)', ibid., p. 83.

41 ASK I, MS 134, f. 3.

42 'Admonition of the Ursula Grużek (3rd of March 1651)', quoted in *PRSP*, p. 82. Steuart misread Ursula Elmslie's surname and transcribed it incorrectly as Grużek and Grule. Biegańska who cited the source, i.e. APKr 521, ff. 2566–7, corrected this mistake in her work: Biegańska, *Wielka emigracja Szkotów*, p. 190.

43 There were a further four Scots who on a regular basis visited the parishes. They resided permamently either in Lublin, Lubowla i Lwów, and paid their tithe there.

44 Bartholomew Burnet, James Chalmers, Richard Gordon, William Hewison and Abraham Wishart do not appear in the tax register: ASK I 134, ff. 1–39.

45 'Reiestr Auditorów', *KW*, ff. 7–9.

46 'LC 1606', *KW*, f. 131; cf. S. Kutrzeba and J. Ptaśnik, 'Dzieje handlu i kupiectwa krakowskiego', *Rocznik Krakowski* 14 (1911), p. 113 (Horain); *LICCr. II* no. 2337 (Horam); T. A. Fischer, *The Scots in Germany: being a contribution towards the history of the Scots abroad* (Edinburgh, 1902), p. 257; *PRSP*, pp. 39–40.

47 'LB 17 July 1612', 'LC 8 February 1629', *KW*, ff. 14, 132; cf. Guldon, 'Żydzi i Szkoci', p. 21; Kowalski, 'The Scotsmen', no. 70 (Torri); Kutrzeba and Ptaśnik, 'Dzieje handlu', p. 113; Fischer, *The Scots in Germany*, p. 257; *PRSP*, p. 56; Węgierski, *Kronika*, pp. 107, 110–2; J. Wijaczka, *Handel zagraniczny Krakowa w połowie XVII wieku* (Kraków, 2002), p. 166.

48 'LB 3 Jun 1620', 'LC 11 April 1641', *KW*, ff. 14, 133v; cf. Guldon, 'Żydzi i Szkoci', pp. 16, 67, 71; Kowalski, 'The Scotsmen', no. 78; Fischer, *The Scots in Germany*, p. 256; *PRSP*, p. 124; Węgierski, *Kronika*, p. 130.

49 'LB 1652' *KW*, f. 25; 'LC 1668', BUW 608, f. 92v.; cf. AP Kr. 469 ff. 539–40; AP Gd. 300, 60/5 k. 251; 'The birth brieve issued to Patrick Forbes by the City Council of Aberdeen on the 7th of June 1669', AP Gd, sig. 300R/Uu9, 01058; Sts. Peter and Paul, Gdańsk, S-B 1699 – EZAB, sig. 5462, f. 22.

50 Wiatowice LB 9 Aug 1678 – BUW 608, f. 100; 'LC 26 November 1696', *KT*, f. 134; cf. S. Uruski, *Rodzina: Herbarz szlachty polskiej*, 15 vols. (Warszawa, 1904–38), vol. 9, p. 146, vol. 10, p. 381; Fischer, *The Scots in Germany*, pp. 257, 268.

51 Robert Blackhall was recorded in sources as Albricht, Albert, Robert, Rubert, Woyciech. His surname was spelled as Bielak, Blak, Blakal, Blakał, Blakhal, and Blakhall: Bieniarzówna and Małecki, *Dzieje Krakowa*, vol. 2, p. 204; Kowalski, 'Cracow Citizenship', Table I, no. 55; Węgierski, *Kronika*, pp. 106, 121, 129–30; Cf. P. P. Bajer, 'Scots in the Polish-Lithuanian Commonwealth 1569–1795', (database) [hereafter SPLC], no. 111.

52 Wijaczka, *Handel zagraniczny*, pp. 15, 24, 26, 109, 138–40 Table I.

53 ASK I, MS 134, f. 3; *PRSP*, p. 81; Cf. Pernal and Gasse, 'The 1651 Polish Subsidy', no. 20.

54 Węgierski, *Kronika*, p. 121.

55 'LM 20 September 1656', *KW* AParEA Kraków, f. 149; Cf. His burial was noted in Węgierski's chronicle: 'In [. . .] 1656, on September 20th, we buried [. . .], in the seventieth year of his age, this old man, a pious merchant and a citizen of Cracow. [. . .] A beautiful attendance followed the dead man's body, people of the Reformed and Roman faiths singing even unto the grave itself, where there was a ceremony and where the usual funeral service was celebrated.' Węgierski, *Kronika*, pp. 129–30.

56 SPLC, no. 174; Kutrzeba and Ptaśnik, 'Dzieje handlu', p. 113; Pernal and Gasse, 'The 1651 Polish Subsidy', no. 1; Guldon and Stępkowski, 'Szkoci i Anglicy w Koronie', p. 57; Fischer, *The Scots in Germany*, p. 257; Węgierski, *Kronika*, pp. 106, 107, 111; Kowalski, 'The Scots at the Cracow Customs', Table 3, no. 8; Kowalski, 'Kraków Citizenship', pp. 281, 282; Wijaczka, *Handel zagraniczny*, pp. 24–5, Table 1.

57 SPLC no. 176. Wijaczka, *Handel zagraniczny*, pp. 97, 109, 138–40, and 216.

58 '. . . in conquirendis elegantioribus apud remotas gentes mercibus et in subminstranda pro artilleria Regni ammunitione . . .' APKr. Rel. Castr. Crac. 120 f. 469.

59 'COMM 1668–1703', *KT* AParEA Kraków, *passim*; 'LM Wiatowice 26th of January, 1711', BUW 608, f. 84v; APKr. Rel. Castr. Crac. 120, f. 469; 'Epitaph of Anna Forbes', sandstone, St Martin's Lutheran Church, Cracow; Bieniarzówna and Małecki, *Dzieje Krakowa*, pp. 438–9; Biegańska, *Wielka emigracja Szkotów*, Table X; Cf. SPLC no. 428.

60 It should be noted that the ethnic origins of two of these women cannot be satisfactorily verified. Wijaczka explicitly lists Anna Hewison (Huison, sometimes listed as Wojciechowa Huisonowa) as a Scottish woman, but offers no evidence for this supposition. The records of the Cracow assembly document only the fact that she was married to Scot, i.e. Robert (Wojciech) Hewison. Similarly, very little is known about the ancestry of Eva Forbes. Cf. Bieniarzówna and Małecki, *Dzieje Krakowa*, vol. II, pp. 204, 471; Wijaczka, *Handel zagraniczny*, pp. 98, 109, 216.

61 Kowalski, 'The Scots at the Cracow Customs', pp. 7, Table 1, no. 9.

62 Ibid., pp. 109, 138–40, 217.

63 'LM 15 Dec 1651', *KW*, f. 147.

64 'LComm', *KW*, ff. 43–89.

65 'Reiestr Dziatek Ochrzczonych których imiona w księgach kościelnych przedtym nie były wpisane Rejestrzyk od samych ich Rodziców zebrany y do tych ksiąg podany (1610–1657)', *KW*, ff. 14–16v; 'Reiestr Ochrzczonych w Zborze Wielkanockim y Lucianowskim (1631–1657)', *KW*, ff. 17–27.

66 Węgierski, *Kronika*, p. 110.

67 *PRSP*, p. 124.

68 'LM 20 October 1642', *KW*, f. 144.

69 'LM May 1648', *KW*, f. 146.

70 'LM 14 October 1637', *KW*, f. 98, 142.

71 The inscription in Polish reads '. . . przymiotowy cnot wizerunek żywy / zacności y przykładów konterfekt prawdziwy' – 'Epitaph of Suzanne Chambers née Sommer (1720)', sandstone, The Lapidarium, Evangelical-Reformed Church, Żychlin near Konin.

72 The inscription on the epitaph of Catherine Kin reads '. . . przez lat 16 znym potomstwo miała / ośmioro dostałego pięć ich ziemy dawszy / troie iest frasobliwych po niey pozostawszy . . .' (trans. during the 16 years of marriage, together they had eight children of whom five have passed away, and the three living ones are now in sorrow . . .). 'Epitaph of Catherine Paterson née Kin (1637)', sandstone, The Lapidarium, Evangelical-Reformed Church, Żychlin near Konin. (Please refer to Fig. 6.1.)

73 K. Górecka, *Pobożne matrony i cnotliwe panny: Epitafia jako źródło wiedzy o kobiecie w epoce nowożytnej* (Warszawa, 2006), pp. 123–6, 187–8, *passim*.

74 Among the so called *compatres* of twins George (Grigen) and Robert (Albert) Aidy (Ede), sons of John and Elisabeth (née unknown), baptised in St Peter and St Paul in 1648, there were only Scots, among them George Aidy (Grigen Ede), James Crighton (Jacob Kricht), Alexander Strachan (Strachon), Thomas Smart (Schmart), William Anderson, Robert Shearer (Albrecht Schirer), *Frau* Auchterlonie (Achterlon), and *Frau* Mill (Millis). 'LB 27 July 1648', APGd, sig. 356/3, f. 51.

75 The ethnicity of only several of such women could be confirmed, e.g. Anna née Hunter was a wife of Jan Dugiet, and Catherine née King, was married to Michał Kałaj: 'Reiestr Dziatek', *KW*, f. 15v; 'Reiestr Ochrzczonych', *KW*, f. 18v.

76 'Extract Variorum Casuum', *KW*, ff. 91, 92v.

77 Węgierski, *Kronika*, p. 71.

78 The Session decided that due to absences caused by Carmichael's mercantile activity, Robert Blackhall was to be appointed as his proxy. – Ibid., ff. 94v, 95v; 'Visitacje Zboru Wielkanockiego y Lucianowskiego', *KW*, ff. 160v, 161r, 161v, 164, 165v.

79 'Rejestr komunikantów 1657–1716', *KT*, f. 32v.

80 Ibid., f. 41.

81 'Raport zdany D. Jabłońskiemu (1704)', quoted in Łukaszewicz, *Dzieje kościołów*, pp. 425–6.

82 A. Biegańska, 'Andrew Davidson (1591–1660) and his descendants', *Scottish Slavonic Review* 10 (1998), p. 12; W. Kriegseisen 'Dzieje zboru ewangelicko-reformowanego w Sielcu k. Staszowa', part 1, in *Jednota* 1–2 (1989, XLVIII), pp. 22–6.

83 Kriegseisen, *Ewangelicy polscy i litewscy*, pp. 60, 205.

84 'Ztamtąd na koniec poszli na Sławkowską Ulice y wpadli tyłem do P. Thomasa Forbessa, którego śpiącego jeszcze zastawszy, skrzynie poodbijawszy, wiary wnich szukali, y wszystko znich wybrawszy, y wielkie szkody poczyniwszy, samego z Małżonką znieważywszy, odeszli.' (trans. Finally they went to Sławkowska Street and stumbled through the back door into the house of Thomas Forbes. While he was still asleep, they forced the coffers open and sought after heresies; and after taking all the spoils, causing much damage, and assaulting him and his wife, they left.) – 'Extract Variorum Casuum', *KW*, f. 94; cf. Węgierski, *Kronika*, p. 82.

85 'Extract Variorum Casuum', *KW*, f. 101; Węgierski, *Kronika,* p. 101.

86 One of the most prominent collaborators of Scottish origin was James Chalmer (Jakub Czamer), who on behalf of the occupants supervised plundering of Cracow's Catholic churches: Bieniarzówna and Małecki, *Dzieje Krakowa,* p. 376.

87 The pedlar stereotype has been challenged recently by Bogucka and Murdoch: M. Bogucka, 'Scots in Gdańsk (Danzig) in the Seventeenth Century', in *Ships, Guns and Bibles in the North Sea and Baltic States, c.1350–c.1700,* eds A.I. Macinnes, T. Riis and F. Pedersen (East Lothian, 2000), p. 41; S. Murdoch, 'Scotland, Europe and the English "Missing Link"', *History Compass* 5, issue 3 (2007), pp. 895–6.

7

'Men of noe credit'?

Scottish Highlanders in Poland–Lithuania, c. 1500–1800

David Worthington

Introduction

A letter dating from the early winter of 1772 suggests that the people of the Isle of Skye had come to consider Poland and the Polish people as the source of a potentially deadly threat. A Colin Mackenzie wrote in late November that year from the mainland town of Dingwall to George Gillanders, a factor for Kenneth Mackenzie, first Earl of Seaforth (1744–1781). Mackenzie had arrived there in haste from Stornoway in Lewis, reporting the spread of a fever. Following a summer of widespread crop failure in the Highlands and Islands, and coming in the year before Samuel Johnson and James Boswell's famous visit, his statement will come as no surprise to those with an interest in the eighteenth-century history of Scotland's north and north-west. What is more striking is that, later in his account, Mackenzie asserted that the Skye residents to whom he had spoken while making his return had claimed that the 'fever' in question was a variety of plague, and that it had arrived in Stornoway 'by a ship from Dantzick', that is, from the south-eastern Baltic port city of Danzig (Gdańsk).[1]

This dread of plague returning with a vengeance across the Baltic and North Seas to the far north-west of Scotland was, in a sense, warranted: British newspapers had reported some weeks before that Moscow, a couple of thousand miles to the east of Danzig, was in the throes of an outbreak. Yet, it might be asked why Mackenzie, or at least the people he spoke to on Skye, declared relatively healthy Danzig, instead, to have been the source.[2] The analysis provided in this chapter will suggest that his statement is best interpreted as a piece of counter-evidence in the study of what will be referred to as Scotland's 'first diaspora', especially as regards the merchants, soldiers, as well as religious and intellectual figures, who represented that dispersal in the southern Baltic region.[3] The argument will aim to correct previous assumptions as to the geographical origins of this body of emigrants, most widespread in that variety of accounts which have recorded the extensive movement of Scottish people to, most especially, Poland, from as early as the fourteenth century, but particularly during the sixteenth and seventeenth centuries.[4]

In finding a context for Mackenzie's claim in terms of the writing of the history of Scottish–Polish relations, it is necessary to address two problems.

The first of these has been a common failure in the historiography – and despite the social and religious tolerance associated at times, both then and since, with the post-1569 Commonwealth (*Rzeczpospolita*) of Poland–Lithuania – to acknowledge the sometimes unwelcome nature of that connection to contemporaries.[5] Few writers have sought to highlight that, in all areas of the public life of the Commonwealth, the experience of Scottish immigrants, male and female, was, like that of members of any other minority ethnic group, one characterised as much by xenophobia as by heartfelt welcome. Regarding those traders and merchants to be studied in the first part of the chapter, a leading Polish Renaissance poet's statement that 'Grocery and wares don't make a Scot a nobleman' is only one of numerous literary sources from the time which, as Arthur Williamson has explored, point to tensions in the relationship as waves of ambitious Scottish economic migrants arrived in the Commonwealth.[6] As soldiers too, the Scots in Poland may have been deemed to be heretical as often as they were considered hardy, while, as intellectual and religious figures, some of their hosts expressed openly their suspicions of uprooted Presbyterians, Episcopalians and especially, of course, anti-Trinitarians.[7] The second problem that the 'Dantzick' quote highlights is a factor considered even less frequently (except in one article by Steve Murdoch and in a recent book by James Hunter), namely, the need to examine a uniquely Highland aspect to the Scottish–Polish relationship and, one might add, to the Scottish connection with mainland Europe and Scandinavia more widely during the fourteenth to eighteenth century.[8] Highlanders have been mentioned in previous accounts of the Scots in Europe, of course. However, even to a seventeenth-century son of the eastern Highlands such as Sir Thomas Urquhart of Cromarty (1611–1660), assessment of a distinctively northern and western Scottish element amongst the emigrants seems to have been considered a moot point, and the assumption of nearly all historians who have written on the topic since has been that the overwhelming majority of the Scots in Poland hailed from east coast port towns situated somewhere between Inverness and Berwick.[9] To highlight some prominent instances, the German scholar, Thomas Alfred Fischer, argued in the years after 1900 that 'very few from the far west and of Celtic blood are to be found'.[10] Archibald Francis Steuart, writing in 1915, concurred, stating that Scottish merchants 'of pure Celtic origin' were 'comparatively rare' in the Commonwealth.[11] In 1969, Seliga and Koczy added that 'almost all Scottish immigrants arrived in Poland from the eastern part of Scotland . . . we come across the names of such Scottish towns as: Edinburgh, Aberdeen, Inverness, Dundee, Perth, St Andrews, Culross, Crail, Cupar Angus, Brechin, Montrose, Auchtermuchty, Berwick and others'.[12] Anna Biegańska reiterated, in 1986, that 'as far as can be ascertained, the Scots emigrating to Poland originated from over 140 localities situated chiefly in the east and north-east' of Scotland.[13] Most recently,

Waldemar Kowalski has asserted that, at least as regards birthbrieves (proofs of good birth sent on request from Scotland to the Polish authorities) they came mostly from 'harbours on the east coast and settlements lying close to the eastern coastline such as Brechin and Elgin', evidence which supported earlier observations that 'arrivals in Poland hailed mostly from eastern and north-eastern Scotland', with a preponderance from Aberdeen.[14] As regards point of departure, these scholars are all correct. However, with respect to place of origin, this is too simplistic an analysis, since it ignores the prevalence of rural–urban migration that, both then and ever since, has led Highlanders to the port towns of the Lowlands and from there, abroad.[15]

Trade

Considering the ongoing debate regarding the convulsive nature of commercial developments in the pre-nineteenth-century Highlands, a detailed assessment by historians of the experience of emigrants from the northern and western parts of Scotland in this sphere of late medieval and early modern European life is overdue. Certainly, if all parts of mainland Scotland from Inverness northwards and the whole of the Western Isles are considered 'Highland', a complexity of mercantile connections existed with Poland, a factor that challenges further the supposition that the region 'had relatively little contact with the outside world'.[16] One might commence with a letter from 1610 written by Thomas Chamberlain, the Stuart envoy in Elbing (Elblag) claiming that '. . . these Scotts [in Poland] for the most parte are heightlanders', adding that they were 'men of noe credit, a Company of peddling knaves'.[17] The writer, in dismissing any economic ingenuity on the part of the Highland emigrant male, was presumably employing a pejorative stereotype then in favour at Whitehall and perhaps also drawing on a cultural memory of instances such as that of 'Reichart of Wick, Kathnes', who, as early as 1471, had been tried alongside a wider group of Scots in Breslau (Wrocław) for 'vagabondage'.[18] Nonetheless, despite the conclusions drawn by Chamberlain along with those made more recently by Laurence Fontaine on the upland background of most pedlars in Europe, there is very little evidence of Highlanders operating as footloose trampers in Poland–Lithuania.[19] Deceptive or not, it is at the higher levels of civic life that both Polish and British sources indicate the presence of Highland merchants in the Commonwealth. Moreover, in such cases, interpretation of the relevant documents, many of the originals of which have been lost amid the destruction of twentieth-century warfare, suggests frequent and straightforward cooperation with emigrants from other parts of Scotland. Reliance on subsequently anglicised versions of previously Polish or German (and perhaps purely phonetic) renderings of Gaelic names may be problematic, an issue raised by a reference in Fischer's work to a source indicating that, in 1615, a 'Killianus Makkien' sold his garden and shed in Bromberg (Bydgoszcz) to a local English resident.[20] Yet, the subsequent loss or else dispersal of some of those documents used by Fischer and then by Steuart and his colleagues prior to the outbreak of World War I, does not prevent the modern-day historian confirming from the Main Archive of Old Records (*Archiwum Główne Akt Dawnych*) in Warsaw the information first given by the latter that a 'John Maknil' was, in 1577, a citizen of the town of 'Cowalow' [Kowalewo Pomorskie] in northern Poland, from where the outcome of a legal case presented him with property and a small sum that had reverted to the Crown on the death of a 'John Lenze . . . citizen of Rogozno of illegitimate birth', and with whom 'Maknil' had been in partnership.[21] From the same archive, the modern-day reader can also back up Steuart in his assertion that a 'Peter Makalienski' was employed at the royal Court in Warsaw in 1613 alongside several other merchants, including a resident in the town of Zamość called 'Jacobus Gorski/Gurski' (perhaps a reference to a distant Highland background too, *górski* meaning 'of/from the mountain' in Polish) alongside others named 'Fraser', 'Orem' and 'Jantson'.[22]

Moving to more fleeting visitors to Poland and returning to primary sources of Scottish provenance, the case of Donald Sligoe, an Inverness seaman, 'having gone a voyage to Danzick' warranted no special further remark or explanation in that town's seventeenth-century kirk session records. Hence, it is unsurprising that it remains difficult to assert just how many others involved in the trade of Inverness and its hinterland around that time made similar journeys. Evidently, some ventured to the southern Baltic ports on, for instance, Aberdeen- and, to a lesser extent, Dundee-registered ships, while others may have sailed from the Fife and Lothian ports. The sections of the Sound Toll Registers edited by Nina E. Bang and Knud Korst and published in 1930 are instructive here, at least from the eighteenth century, in elucidating a trade linking Campbeltown, Cromarty, Findhorn, Fort George, Kirkwall, Lerwick, Lochbroom, Lochinver, Stornoway, and even Strontian, with the Baltic. Louise Taylor recorded the activities of some traders who, as early as 1655, 'importit in ane boot from Caetnes [Caithness] 1900 sklaets [slates] gotten for them' into the far north, and again, on 1 July 1662, goods 'im portit by George Bruce, master of ane barke of Caetnes, with sklaits [slates] 3000', although the port of origin is in both cases unknown.[23] It is only in the early eighteenth century, however, that a satisfactory account for the Highland capital can be found. The letterbook of Bailie John Steuart (1676–?) comments frequently on trading connections linking Inverness with Danzig.[24] The Bailie's family came from Strathspey, although he served on the town's council from 1703 to 1716, shipping provisions from there to the western Highlands via the Pentland Firth. Nevertheless, Bailie Steuart was also instrumental in developing Inverness's trade with the southern Baltic.[25]

This involved the export not only of herrings, lamb skins and pork, but more occasionally fox, otter and wildcat furs, in return for barrel staves, timber, iron, glass, copper, soap, flax and rope, amongst other products.[26] Furthermore, the reader learns from the letterbook of several Highland merchants travelling to and from Danzig on this basis. In 1718, Steuart advised Alexander Greig, master of *The Alexander*, to sail there, while, in 1720, he laid out his 'Directions to Daniel Fraser on his Voyage to Dantzick'. One year later, the Bailie reported the possible arrival in the same port of his 'frind and broyr John McLeod', presumably a close relative of his second wife, Ann MacLeod of Drynoch on Skye: MacLeod was due to sail to Danzig in *The Margret*, a vessel that had already been doing the Inverness to Baltic route for several years. Further evidence comes from 1727, when the Bailie corresponded with a Mr Francis Grant, another merchant from the town, who was at that time in the southern Baltic port.[27]

Although this handful of Invernesians probably spent only a short time in Danzig and its hinterland, the question emerges as to the extent to which those Highland traders who settled there or more widely in Poland–Lithuania became immersed completely in their new surroundings or else developed a diasporic identity based on nationality. The evidence once again suggests similarities and overlaps with merchants from other parts of Scotland and thus points to the latter. Seliga and Koczy recorded a partial assimilation process with reference to the appearance of polonised interpretations of Scottish names in Polish sources, some of them perhaps pertaining to words transcribed or translated aurally from spoken Gaelic, and involving hence a confused rendering of Gaelic patronymics into the vernacular as single-word surnames. But, in those cases where the surnames given refer more clearly to people of Highland background, they provide us with tentative evidence relating to the lives of a minority of immigrants coming from the northern and western parts of the country. Some Highland émigrés were active members of urban communities in Polish towns, groups which would have been multinational and thus, of necessity, multilingual. In one year, 1677, in the city of Lublin, Francis Gern, Peter Gern and Alexander Paip were all guild members.[28] Without doubt, second- or even third-generation Highland traders are traceable in small numbers too on the list of contributors to the tax levied on British subjects living in the Commonwealth in 1650, a subsidy which the young Charles had called for while in exile following the regicide.[29]

More concrete evidence to back claims of a diasporic identification of Highlanders in Poland with their homeland (and analogous to that already evidenced amongst some Scottish lowlanders) comes in the involvement of some richer merchants from Easter Ross in providing subscriptions towards the restoration of Marischal College, Aberdeen's second university. Alexander

Paip was one of them. A son of Gilbert Paip of Muckle Rainy near Tain and Anne Munro of Petconnoquhy near Avoch on the Black Isle, Paip was a merchant and guild member in the city of Lublin from 1668, dealing in grain and wine.[30] In the 1680s, he settled in Danzig and, in 1706, along with his son, also Alexander and likewise a burgess in the southern Baltic port, joined with a Thomas Leslie in order to purchase the house that would subsequently serve as the city's 'Brittons Chapell'. Both Paips were buried in the St Peter and Paul Church there.[31] George Paip, a court servitor and wholesaler who lived on the main Market Square in Warsaw, and who also contributed to the restoration of Marischal College in 1700 by means of a payment of thirty guilders, was presumably a relative of theirs.[32]

'Of considerable wealth'? The Ross family network

An even more dramatic illustration of continued contacts with the home country than that to be found amongst the Paips is that visible in the biography of another son of Easter Ross, Alexander Ross, a merchant in Cracow, who married a Sophia French, with whom he had two sons, Alexander and David. In 1721, a sasine provided Ross with titles to the lands of Easter Kindeace near Nigg in Easter Ross, which he chose to rename Ankerville.[33] Although Marinell Ash asserted recently that sea flooding at high tides was such that he must have lived out 'a damp retirement' there, Ross made his presence felt.[34] By the time that Richard Pococke, Anglican Bishop of Meath, made his travels through the area in the mid-eighteenth century, the story of Alexander's life in Poland and his return had become colourful. Pococke related that:

> . . . we came to Ancherville, formerly the seat of one of the name of Ross, who from a very low beginning went into the service of Augustus of Poland . . . and being the only person who could bear more liquor than his Majesty, got to be a Commissary, came away with the plunder of churches &c. in the war about the Crown of Poland, purchased this estate of £100 a year, built and lived too greatly for it, was for determining all things by the Sabre; and died much reduced in his finances between twenty and thirty years agoe.[35]

As late as the mid-nineteenth century, Ross's presence lingered in the parish in spectral form.[36] The Cromarty-born polymath, Hugh Miller, recorded the following tale on passing Ankerville with a local informant, the subject of which is without doubt this same return emigrant:

> We passed onwards, and paused for a few seconds where the parish of Nigg borders on that of Fearn, beside an old hawthorn hedge and a few green

mounds. 'And here,' said my companion, 'is the scene of another ghost story, that made some noise in its day; but it is now more than a century old, and the details are but imperfectly preserved. You have read, in Johnson's *Life of Denham*, that Charles II, during his exile in France, succeeded in procuring a contribution of 10,000 pounds from the Scotch that at that time wandered as itinerant traders over Poland. The old hedge beside you, and the few green mounds beyond it, once formed the dwelling house and garden fence of one of these Polish traders, who had returned in old age to his native country, possessed, as all supposed, of considerable wealth. He was known to the country folk as the "Rich Polander". On his death, however, which took place suddenly, his strong-box was found to contain only a will, bequeathing to his various relations large sums that were vested, no one knew where. Some were of opinion that he had lent money to a considerable amount to one or two neighbouring proprietors; and some had heard him speak of a brother in Poland, with whom he had left the greater part of his capital, and who had been robbed and murdered by banditti, somewhere on the frontier territories, when on his return to Scotland. In the middle of these surmisings, however, the Polander himself returned, as if to settle the point. The field there to the right, in front of the ruins, was at that time laid out as a lawn; there was a gate in the eastern corner, and another in the west; and there ran between them a road that passed in front of the house. And almost every evening, the apparition of the Polander, for years after his decease, walked along that road. It came invariably from the east, lingered long in front of the building, and then, gliding towards the west, disappeared in passing through the gateway. But no one had courage enough to meet with it, or address it; and till this day the legacies of the Polander remain unpaid.'[37]

Although the Ross surname was by no means exclusive to the Scottish Highlands, an assessment of people of that family more generally can offer a revealing case study of migration from the western parts of what David Kirby and Merja-Liisa Hinkkanen suggest was a 'North Sea and Baltic cultural region'.[38] Whereas Highland Ross émigrés to England and the Netherlands during this period were most prominent as intellectual figures and as soldiers respectively, those who went to Poland seem to have been almost exclusively merchants. By the late seventeenth century, the trading activities of Scots named Ross are traceable in a remarkable range of positions in at least eleven Polish towns (as well as two in the grand duchy of Lithuania). Furthermore, although some of these locations, such as Danzig, Elbing, and Königsberg are on the Baltic coast, others – Kiejdany, Poznań, Warsaw, Lublin, Opatów, Raków, Chmielnik, Zamość, Tarnów and Cracow – lie deep inland.

In listing them briefly, Gdańsk, probably their first port of call on the southern Baltic, is the most appropriate place from which to start. As early as 1453, a Robert Ross was trading from there, while, from the late sixteenth to the mid-eighteenth century, a continuous Ross presence in the city is suggested both by the birthbrieves that some of them applied to the Scottish authorities for and from the records of St Elizabeth's Calvinist Church in the city. [39] Indeed, by the 1770s, one Charles Ross was involved in supporting the maintenance of a bursary that would allow Protestant scholars to cross from Poland to Scotland. [40] Danzig was frequently fought over by Catholic Poles and Protestant Swedes in early modern times, and scholars should be careful before assuming the allegiance of Scots who were there in times of warfare: in the 1620s, the life of one of the city's burgesses, James Ross, 'lieutenant and innkeeper', extended to spying for the former against the latter. [41]

Limited space here allows for other towns to be dealt with only briefly. As regards Rosses in Elbing (Elblag) a few miles to the east, the diary of General Patrick Gordon of Auchleuchries (1635–1699), a son of Aberdeenshire who served the Poles and Russians in the seventeenth century, is illuminating. In 1656, Gordon recorded having met a Scotsman called Wallace who told him that:

> . . . his comorad, Rosse, at the coming out of Elbing had bemoaned himself of a great paine in his head, which he said proceeded of excess of drink, and being then also drunk he could not hold up his head, and at last falling from his horse, he dyed. [42]

Further east along the Baltic coast in Königsberg (Kaliningrad), George Ross was a guild member in 1723, while going deeper into Lithuania, William Ross was an alderman in the town of Kėdainiai (Kiejdany) from where he assisted in the founding of a trading company for Protestants in 1731. Shifting back to the westernmost perimeters of what is now Poland, Albert and James Ross had been elders of the merchants' guild in Posen (Poznań), while, in the mid-seventeenth century, John or Jan Ross was trading from Chmielnik. [43] Wojciech Ross was a merchant in Warsaw at the same time as Jan Ross, while, around the same time, the aforementioned Patrick Gordon took a shine to the daughter of a landlord of one of the Polish guest houses he stayed in, who claimed to have been 'during the siege in Varso [Warsaw] by a Scotesman called John Rosse . . .', perhaps the same individual as the aforementioned Jan. [44] Christian Ross was a merchant and citizen in the same city in 1699. Furthermore, Warsaw was the centre of the Polish regal Court where Alexander and William Ross, two merchants who owned shops in the city's marketplace, were appointed special purveyors in 1697, in Alexander's case until 1703. [45] East of Warsaw, George Ross was an elder to the Scottish Presbyterian

Brotherhood in Lublin in 1701, and was listed again as such as late as 1726.[46] Two smaller towns slightly further to the west from there are Opatów, where an Alexander Ross was trading in 1650, and Raków, where the town council noted the activities of a John 'Russ' in 1655.[47] In Tarnów, three Ross merchants can be traced between 1600 and the 1620s, and, in Zamość, one.[48] Cracow was and remains a much larger city than any of those mentioned so far in inland Poland, excepting Warsaw. An individual named 'Rusek' was the Scottish factor there in 1603, while a William Ross was a postmaster in 1703, recorded as having been killed a few miles away in Myślenice in 1707. Finally, it may not just have been male Rosses who settled in southern Poland at this time: a George Gordon was married to an Ursula Russocka – a surname suggesting a Ross derivation – and their child baptised, also in Cracow, in 1736.[49]

The Army

Sometimes it was a combination of mercantile and military connections which led Highland men and women to live their lives out in the Commonwealth. The Baroque poet Wacław Potocki (1621–1696) imagined a Polish Army regarding which: 'It wouldn't be necessary for us to draft Germans and Englishmen / Pull peasants from flails nor Scots from their merchandise.'[50] However, it was probably as a soldier rather than as a ghostly apparition of a wealthy, if perhaps profligate, merchant that the figure of the Scottish Highlander was impressed most deeply on early modern citizens of the Commonwealth.[51] Most famously, there is a broadsheet showing some 'Irish' members of the Swedish Army at Stettin (Szceczin) in 1630, the men depicted being presumed often to be Highland veterans from the levies made for 'Mackay's Regiment' by Robert Monro (d. 1675). If so, they had probably been amongst the group who embarked in October 1626, 'from Cromartie in Scotland to Lugstad [Glückstadt] on the Elve [Elbe] by Sea' to serve in the Danish–Norwegian, and later Swedish, Armies.[52] Some Highlanders serving in the Polish military undoubtably came from this background, as shall be seen, the sometimes ambivalent view projected on them subsequently by the host society being perhaps encapsulated most obviously in the case of the Machlejds, a family which traces descent from a MacLeod in Swedish service who subsequently settled in Germany, and the Lutheran descendents of whom arrived in Poland only much later, as traders.[53] Another example of Highlanders finding themselves torn between the Swedish or Polish Army comes during the *potop* (deluge) into the Commonwealth in the 1650s, when Cranston's regiment, recruited for the Poles, served instead, following their predecessors in 'MacKay's Regiment', for the Swedes. Some of the veterans, nevertheless, took up residency in Poland. According to the diary of James

Fraser (1634–1709) minister of the parish of Wardlaw or Kirkhill near Beauly, William Fraser of Phopachy:

> . . . went abroad with Captain James Fraser, my Lord Lovat sonne, anno 1656, in the quality of an ensign in the Lord Cranston's regiment, for the service of Carolus Gustavus, King of Sweden; and after the peace he went up to Pole with other Scotsmen, and settled at Torn [Thorn, Toruń], where he married as a merchant.[54]

Homesickness seems to have got the better of William by 1670 when he 'was necessitat to take the occasion of a ship and come to Scotland to crave his own'. According to James Fraser, William:

> . . . continued here among his friends all the winter, and returned back in the spring, never to see his native country again. Two of his foster brothers ventured with him, Farqhar and Rory, very pretty boys.[55]

Church, university and cultural life

As intellectual and cultural migrants in Europe, Scots can be traced as university students, as clergy and, in a few cases, as prototype 'Grand Tourists' in the seventeenth and eighteenth centuries.[56] Thomas Urquhart claimed that they had been:

> held by all the inhabitants of *France,* to have been attended *(caeteris paribus)* with greater proficiency, then any other manner of breeding subordinate to the documents of those of another Country. Nor are the *French* the only men who have harboured this good opinion of the Scots, in behalf of their inward abilities; but many times the *Spaniards, Italians, Flemins, Dutch, Hungarians, Sweds,* and *Polonians,* have testified their being of the same mind, by the promotions whereunto, for their learning, they in all those Nations, at several times have attained.[57]

The place of Highlanders in the cultural and religious life of the 'Polonians' can thus be situated within the wider Scottish diasporic context already outlined. Alexander Campbell, listed as a 'Lithuanian', matriculated from the University of Königsberg in 1706, while Biegańska has recorded the activities of a Dominican in Poland named Thomas Makolroy.[58] One curious incident linking the Western Isles and Poland stems from Irish Franciscan activity in Scottish Gaeldom. In 1629, John Rakouski, a representative of the king of Poland at the Stuart Court, interceded to bring about the release of the Irish Franciscan priest, Cornelius Ward (d. 1641), then involved in the Franciscan mission to the Western Isles. The

English Government granted this on the basis that Ward leave for Poland with the Pole, although the Irishman seems to have travelled instead through Bohemia, then Rome, before arriving in the Commonwealth, and, once there, retreated quickly to Spain in order to make his return to the Three Kingdoms. However, no scholar from Scotland's north or west rose further and faster in scholarly circles in Poland than William Bruce, from Stanstill in Caithness, an individual covered in much more depth elsewhere in this volume by Anna Kalinowska.[59] In the course of his early career, William left the country of his birth for the University of Cahors. He moved on to Toulouse, Rome, and Würzburg, but seems to have arrived in the Commonwealth only in 1594 in which year he wrote in Latin and published his *Ad Principes popolumque Christianum de bello adversus ad Turcos gerendo* (Cracow, 1594) an encouragement to Christian kings and princes to join the Holy Roman Emperor in battle against the Ottoman Empire.[60] Fluent also in French and Italian, from 1596, Bruce lectured in Roman Law at the academy founded by the Polish chancellor Jan Zamoyski (1542–1605) in Zamość. Following an audience with the envoy to Poland of the Tatar khan, he published his *Epistola* (Görlitz, 1596) and then, in 1598, his description of Tatar customs *De Tartaris diarium Guilielmi Brussii Scoti* (Frankfurt on Oder, 1598), dedicated to Sir George Talbot of Grafton (1564?–1630), an Englishman resident at the Bavarian Court.[61] According to Sebastian Sobecki, these writings force us to question the authorship of the next text with which Bruce has often been associated, a detailed proto-anthropological publication from 1598, the *Relation of the State of Polonia and the United Provinces*. In Sobecki's opinion, the earlier attribution of this to George Carew, the Elizabethan diplomat who spent only two weeks in Poland in 1598, is more convincing, despite Bruce's familiarity with Zamoyski, and his much deeper knowledge of the various regions of the Commonwealth.[62] In any case, as early as 1597, the Caithnessian had left Zamość Academy and was in the employment of the Bishop of Olomouc in the Bohemian kingdom while, in 1600 or 1601, Zamoyski sent him to the Elizabethan Court, from where he made his way back to Scotland at least once. Following that, Bruce returned to Poland as Stuart ambassador, during which time he offered advice to Edward Bruce, first Lord Kinloss and Baron Bruce of Kinloss (1548/9–1611) and sent back portraits and amber jewellery to James VI and I and Anne of Denmark. Resident in Danzig from 1606, his last known action is an intervention in a case in Königsberg, where the Duke of Prussia was attempting to expel the Scottish immigrant population.[63]

Conclusion

To conclude, the situation whereby 'Dantzick' was seen as a potential source of plague and in which a return emigrant from Easter Ross, 'Ross the Polander', was recalled, correctly or not, as a boastful drunkard or as a ghostly presence, might lead easily to a misleading impression being given of the historical connection of the Highlands of Scotland with Poland–Lithuania. This aspect of the Scottish–Polish tie has most definitely not been 'over-celebrated' in Scottish or Polish historiography, but, on the contrary, under-represented to the point of hardly being mentioned. The reasons behind this require more research.[64] Although a notion of 'diasporic memory' has developed recently amongst scholars, more rarely considered is the possibility that historical diasporas might have been transformed completely or even ceased to exist over time.[65] By the late eighteenth century, figures such as William Bruce – who, during his lifetime, must have attracted considerable attention from his hosts – had slipped from collective memory in Scotland, and, curiously, the Highland link to Poland, even more than the Lowland one, was viewed, if at all, it would seem, in an unfavourable light. But, this does not reflect the situation as it would have appeared a century earlier, when, in 1669–70, at Bruce's old academy in Zamość an 'Andreas Simonis Machayski' was following in his footsteps, and where emigrants from the far north and west could have been found participating, by no means always as 'men of noe credit', in every aspect of life in the Commonwealth.

It must be hoped that the attempt to highlight the existence of a Highland element amongst the Scots in Poland here has helped expose also the complexity of the problem of interpreting place of origin when it comes to studying emigration from Scotland's north and west, especially within the British Isles and Europe, and that it will lead to a questioning of what we mean by the 'integration' or otherwise of this particular body of members of the diaspora. Much of the writing of academics on the Scots in Poland that existed prior to the 1980s was written in a manner that, either implicitly or explicitly, promoted the idea of an especially close relationship between the two countries, and one involving only Lowland males. Yet, a significant minority of Highlanders in the 'first diaspora' settled too in Poland–Lithuania, and sometimes in places that lie today within the borders of Germany, Ukraine, Lithuania, or Belarus. Expanding our horizons to consider a dispersal involving members of the adult population in Scotland's north and west, and embracing the entirety of Christendom prior to the Enlightenment imagining of both a peripheralised eastern Europe and a marginalised Scottish Highlands – lies as one of the many important tasks remaining to be addressed by future scholarship on emigration from Scotland during the late medieval and early modern periods.[66]

Notes

1 Mackenzie assured Gillanders that claims of the arrival of plague from Danzig contradicted an article the day previously in the *London Gazette,* but

recommended that Gillanders and 'Doctor Macaskill' send a letter to the *Caledonian Mercury* to dispel the rumour. See 23 November 1772, Dingwall, Colin Mackenzie to George Gillanders, Papers of the Gillanders Family of Highfield, National Archives of Scotland (hereafter NAS), GD427/204.

2 A ship from Danzig had been feared as the source of a 'strange sickness' by the residents of Aberdeen in 1500 and its crew isolated on pain of death on coming ashore. See E. Patricia Dennison, David Ditchburn and Michael Lynch, eds, *Aberdeen before 1800: A New History* (East Linton, 2002), p. 74. In 1698, a disastrous Polish harvest had taken place simultaneous to the famine in Scotland, and, presumably, cut off emergency grain supplies from there. Moreover, the kirk session records of Inverness indicate that, in 1708, the Privy Council had ordered them to pray 'anent the plague and pestilence raging noe in Danzich and Pole'. See A. Mitchell, ed., *Inverness Kirk Session Records, 1661–1680* (Inverness, 1902); J. P. Byrne, *Daily Life during the Black Death* (Abingdon, 2006), pp. 293–4. For accounts of 'English sweat' in Danzig in 1528, see John D. Fudge, 'Corollaries of Commerce between England and Gdańsk (Danzig) in the Fifteenth and Sixteenth Centuries: Romance, Heresy, Employment and Epidemic' in *Britain and Poland–Lithuania: Contact and Comparison from the Middle Ages to 1795*, ed. Richard W. Unger (Leiden, 2008), pp. 226–7. Indeed, documentary sources allow the casual reader to find evidence of expatriate Scots in the Polish towns of Cracow and Żmigród having taken charge of caring for victims of the plague there in the seventeenth century. John Scot, a barber, became a leader of a group fighting the epidemic of 1677–9 in Cracow, as a reward for which the town authorities granted him a pension and honorary citizenship. See Anna Biegańska, 'The Learned Scots in Poland (From the Mid-Sixteenth to the close of the Eighteenth Century)' in *Canadian Slavonic Review*, 43(1), (2001). In Żmigród, Mr George Ross collected money for the plague-stricken. See A. Francis Steuart, ed., *Papers Relating to the Scots in Poland 1576–1793* (Edinburgh, 1915) p. 171.

3 It is necessary to give a definition of what is meant here by 'diaspora'. For this, the argument of Robin Cohen proves useful. Cohen's list of nine 'Common features of a diaspora' reflects a focus on settlement problems within multiple host societies and thus offers a comparatively narrow interpretation. Robin Cohen, *Global Diasporas* (London, 1997), p. ix.

4 A full bibliography of sources for this theme would be of great use to historians. For the most effective, concise bibliographic summaries, see Anna Biegańska, 'A Note on the Scots in Poland, 1550–1800', in *Scotland and Europe, 1200–1850*, ed. T. C. Smout (Edinburgh, 1986) pp. 157–66; Waldemar Kowalski, 'The Placement of Urbanised Scots in the Polish Crown during the Sixteenth and Seventeenth Centuries', in *Scottish Communities Abroad in the Early Modern Period*, eds Alexia Grosjean and Steve Murdoch (Leiden, 2005), pp. 53–104.

5 Steve Murdoch's assertion in a recent publication that the Scottish–Polish connection has, where studied, been 'over-celebrated' has some substance. See Steve Murdoch, *Network North. Scottish Kin, Commercial and Covert Associations in Northern Europe, 1603–1746* (Leiden, 2006) p. 254. Murdoch has since developed this argument in another article. See Murdoch, 'Scotland, Europe and the

English "Missing Link"', *History Compass,* 5/3 (2007), pp. 890–913. One very early example of a Scot lauding such a tradition is Sir Thomas Urquhart of Cromarty (1611–1660) who applauded the 'fidelity, valor and gallantry' of those Scots who had gone to Poland and to other parts of the Continent to fight in the Thirty Years' War (1618–48). See *The Works of Sir Thomas Urquhart of Cromarty, Knight,* several editors (Maitland Club, Edinburgh: 1834), pp. 213–14; Stanislaw Seliga and Leon Koczy, *Scotland and Poland: A Chapter of Forgotten History* (Dundee, 1969).

6 Arthur H. Williamson, 'The Nation Epidemical: Scoto-Britannus to Scoto-Polonus', in *Britain and Poland–Lithuania,* ed. R. Unger, pp. 287–304.

7 Conversely, the trickle of Polish migrants to Scotland prior to the late nineteenth century might also have claimed xenophobia. One central European scholar, Pawel Krawar, a Silesian, was burnt to death in St Andrews for heresy in 1411. See David Worthington, *Scots in Habsburg Service, 1618–1648* (Leiden, 2003), p. 18. Polish soldiers were a much rarer sight in Scotland, even in the era of nineteenth-century romanticism surrounding the Sobieski Stuart brothers. As merchants moreover, the presence of some Poles in the English Jamestown colony of Sir John Smith after 1607 is unusual, there being, it seems, little to attract them to Scotland or England.

8 Steve Murdoch, 'More than just "Mackay's" and Mercenaries: Gaelic Influences in Scandinavia, 1580–1707', *Transactions of the Gaelic Society of Inverness,* 60 (1997) pp. 161–85; James Hunter, *Scottish Exodus: Travels in Search of a Worldwide Clan* (Edinburgh, 2007). Although this paper cannot claim to have exhausted the archival material available on this theme, the leading Danish scholar Thomas Riis's initial identification on the basis of name alone a 'Peter Posepiber' ('Peter the Bagpiper') as a Gael domiciled in mid-1630s' Denmark, emphasises the kind of pitfalls that exist.

9 Thomas Urquhart, *Ekskybalauron: or, The discovery of a most exquisite jewel, more precious then diamonds inchased in gold, the like whereof was never seen in any age; found in the kennel of Worcester-streets, the day after the fight, and six before the autumnal aequinox, anno 1651. Serving in this place, to frontal a vindication of the honour of Scotland, from that infamy, whereinto the rigid Presbyterian party of that nation, out of their coveteousness and ambition, most dissembledly hath involved it* (London, 1652), pp. 171–5.

10 T. A. Fischer, *The Scots in Eastern and Western Prussia* (Edinburgh, 1903), p. 151.

11 Steuart, ed., *Papers,* p. xxiii. Beatrice Baskerville completed parts of the introduction to that work.

12 Seliga and Koczy, *Scotland and Poland,* p. 9.

13 Biegańska, 'A Note on the Scots in Poland'.

14 Kowalski pointed to a possible exception to the rule in Cracow, in the case of birthbrieves relating to Scots, one apparently from Birsay (Orkney) and another from Dumfries. See Waldemar Kowalski, 'Kraków citizenship and the Local Scots, 1509–1655' in Unger ed., *Britain and Poland–Lithuania,* pp. 269–72.

15 T. M. Devine, 'Temporary migration and the Scottish Highlands in the nineteenth century', *Economic History Review,* 33 (1979), pp. 344–59.

16 T. C. Smout, *Scottish Trade on the Eve of Union* (Edinburgh, 1963) p. 118. Smout includes Inverness and also Tain, Dornoch, Dingwall and Fortrose as 'North-East' ports.

17 29 November 1610, Elbing (Elbląg), Thomas Chamberlain to Robert Cecil, cited in Robert I. Frost, 'Scottish Soldiers, Poland–Lithuania and the Thirty Years' War', in *Scotland and the Thirty Years' War*, ed. Steve Murdoch (Leiden, 2001), p. 194. For Salisbury's distraught state of mind at this time see, Pauline Croft, 'Cecil, Robert, first earl of Salisbury (1563–1612)', *Oxford Dictionary of National Biography* (Oxford, 2004), online edition, Oct 2008 [http://www.oxforddnb.com/view/article/4980, accessed 27 Jan 2009].

18 The anglicisation from German is Fischer's. See T. A. Fischer, *The Scots in Germany*, pp. 31, 241–2.

19 Laurence Fontaine, *History of Pedlars in Europe* (Oxford, 1996).

20 Fischer, *The Scots in Germany*, p. 109.

21 This document lies today in the post-war Main Archive of Old Records in Warsaw, Archiwum Główne Akt Dawnych (hereafter AGAD), Metryka Koronna (hereafter MK), Księgi Wpisów, 115, f. 293. The original refers to 'pro Honesto Joanne Maknil Scoto . . . Ioannis Lenze oppidam Rogosnen donatur'. See also Steuart ed., *Papers*, p. 2.

22 AGAD, Metryka Koronna, Księgi Wpisów, 155, f. 4. See also Steuart ed., *Papers*, p. 8. If rendered phonetically, 'Makalienski' would be closer to a Polish interpretation of 'Peter of MacGill-Eain' as rendered in Gaelic than the anglicised version, 'Maclean'. It seems to have been very rare for Scots to have been awarded the '-ski' or '-owski' suffix to their surname, a form indicating often a geographical location and noble status.

23 For Aberdeen, see Louise B. Taylor, ed., *Aberdeen Shore Work Accounts 1596–1670* (Aberdeen, 1972). This work is confusing and does not paint a full picture of Aberdeen's connections with Danzig, since she takes references to 'Dansken' to mean Denmark. See also Louise B. Taylor, ed., *Aberdeen Council Letter Books 1552–1681*, 6 vols, (Aberdeen, 1942–1961); *Register of Burgesses of the Burgh of Aberdeen*, 3 vols, (Aberdeen, 1890–1908); A. H. Millar, ed., *The compt buik of David Wedderburne, merchant of Dundee, 1587–1630* (Edinburgh, 1898); Nina E. Bang and Knud Korst, eds, *Tabeller over Skibsfart og Varetransport gennem Øresund 1661–1783 og gennem Storebælt 1701–1748*, 4 vols, (Copenhagen, 1930), vol. 1. See also, Aberdeen Council Archives, Registers of Deeds, 1st Series and Propinquity Books, vol. 1, 1637–1732, ff. 170, 179, vol. 2, 1733–1765, f. 44.

24 W. Mackay, ed., *The Letterbook of Bailie John Steuart (1715–1752)* (Edinburgh, 1915) For Inverness's disrupted and very sporadic earlier trade with the Baltic ports, see James Miller, *Inverness* (Edinburgh, 2004), chs 5, 6. See also NAS, Exchequer Records: Customs Books (First Series, 1620–1), E71/26/1; (Second Series, 1668–1696), which shows customs accounts for Inverness (a 'customs precinct'), Ross and Caithness, linking them sporadically from 1620 with the English, Dutch, French and Norwegian trade, but not directly with the Baltic. Further details of Inverness's seventeenth-century trade with these same locations is contained in E72/11/1–19. More on the town's burgh life at the time can be

found in the Highland Council Archives (HCA): Burgh Court Book, 1602–1621, B1/1/1/3; Burgh Council Minutes, 1619–1655, B1/1/1/3A, much of it printed in William Mackay and H. C. Boyd, eds, *Records of Inverness*, 2 vols, (Aberdeen, 1911).

25 His account also mentions merchants such as Robert Mackay in Rotterdam, Hugh Ross in Gothenburg, Alexander Ross in Copenhagen, and Daniel Mackay in London. See Mackay, ed., *The Letterbook*.

26 Mackay, ed., *The Letterbook*, p.21; Ewan G. MacDonald, 'A History of Commercial Relations between Scotland and Poland from 1550 to 1750', University of Strathclyde MLitt Thesis (1970) pp. 16–17, 65, 74–5, 79. In organising this, Steuart drew on his contacts with two Scottish factors, both Lowlanders, in Danzig 12 June 1715, Danzig, (Andrew?) Marjoribanks and ? Coutts to Alexander Mackintosh, NAS, GD23/6/30; Smout, *Scottish Trade*, p. 98.

27 8 April 1727, Inverness, Steuart to Mr Francis Grant, in Mackay, ed., *The Letterbook*, p. 275.

28 For more evidence, see Dmitry Fedosov, ed., *Diary of Patrick Gordon of Auchleuchries, Volume 1: 1635–1659* (Aberdeen, 2009).

29 From the city of Poznań, one of the richer merchants, Dawid Makabey, contributed 5,000 florins, while a Jakub Makaroi paid 20 florins. Jan Ross contributed from Chmielnik, Woyciech Ross from Warsaw, Iakub Fresser from Krosno, Tomas Argiel from Lublin, Wilhelm Makki from Mława, and Hektor Magga from Gniew. Elsewhere, the names of Christine Allanach, Albert and George Bruce, James Macilroy and Donalt MacLachlan besides several other individuals named Ross, Robertson or Sinckler, are similarly suggestive of far northern or western Scottish provenance. See Andrew P. Pernal and Rosanne P. Gasse, 'The 1651 Polish Subsidy to the Exiled Charles II', *Slavonic Papers*, 32 (1999), pp. 21, 29.

30 'Petconnoquhy', 'Pittanochtie' or 'Pittonarthie' became later Rosehaugh. See W. P. Watson, *Place Names of Ross and Cromarty* (London, 1904), p. 131.

31 Anna Biegańska, 'Subscribers from Poland to the Restoration of Marischal College in the late Seventeenth Century', in *The Universities of Aberdeen and Europe*, ed. Paul Dukes (Aberdeen, 1995), p. 161.

32 Biegańska, 'Subscribers from Poland', p. 162.

33 Francis Nevile Reid, *The Earls of Ross and their Descendants* (Edinburgh, 1894), p. 22. The etymology of Ankerville is explained in Watson, *Place Names*, p. 53.

34 Marinell Ash, *This Noble Harbour: A History of the Cromarty Firth* (Bristol, 1991), pp. 143–5.

35 Cited in Nevile Reid, *The Earls of Ross*, p. 22.

36 Hugh Miller, *Scenes and Legends from the North of Scotland* (Edinburgh, 1869), pp. 361–2.

37 Ibid.

38 David Kirby and Merja-Liisa Hinkkanen, *The Baltic and the North Seas* (London, 2000).

39 Fisher, *The Scots in Germany*, p. 12.

40 Steuart, ed., *Papers*, p. 336.

41 Steve Murdoch, *Network North. Scottish Kin, Commercial and Covert Associations in Northern Europe, 1603–1746* (Leiden, 2005), pp. 364–6.

42 Nevile Reid, *The Earls of Ross*, pp. 97–103; Alexander M. Ross, *History of the Clan Ross with Genealogies of the Various Families* (Dingwall, 1932).

43 Kowalski, 'The Placement of Urbanised Scots', p. 89.

44 Pernal and Gasse, 'The 1651 Polish Subsidy', pp. 19, 21, 29.

45 Steuart, ed,. *Papers*, pp. 26–7, 336.

46 Ibid., pp. 173, 208.

47 Kowalski, 'The Placement of Urbanised Scots', pp. 92, 95.

48 Ibid., p. 100.

49 Steuart, ed., *Papers*, pp. 30, 105.

50 Kowalski, 'The Placement of Urbanised Scots', p. 84.

51 Murdoch, 'More than just "Mackay's"'; Aonghas MacCoinnich, '"His spirit was given only to warre": Conflict and Identity in the Scottish Gàidhealtachd, c. 1580–1630', in *Fighting for Identity: Scottish Military Experience, c. 1550–1900*, eds Steve Murdoch and Andrew Mackillop (Leiden, 2002): pp. 133–63.

52 William S. Brockington Jr., ed., *Monro, His Expedition with the Worthy Scots Regiment called Mac-Keys* (London, 1999), p. 117.

53 Hunter, *Scottish Exodus*, pp. 54–62; Krystyna Machlejd, *Saga Ulrichowsko-Machlejdowska* (Warsaw, 2006). Besides the Machlejds, Seliga and Koczy reported the awarding of titles of nobility to a Mackay and a Macfarlant in early modern times. See Seliga and Koczy, *Scotland and Poland*, p.13.

54 William Mackay, ed., *Chronicles of the Frasers: the Wardlaw manuscript entitled 'Polichronicon seu policratica temporum' or 'The true genealogy of the Frasers', 916–1674* (Edinburgh, 1905) p. 424

55 Ibid.

56 The 'Grand Tourists' included James Fraser and Alexander Gordon of Navidale. See J. M. Bulloch, *The Gay Adventures of Sir Alexander Gordon, Knight of Navidale* (Dingwall, 1925).

57 Urquhart, *Ekskybalauron*, p. 188.

58 Anna Biegańska, 'In Search of Tolerance: Scottish Catholics and Presbyterians in Poland', *Scottish Slavonic Review*, 17 (1992), p. 49. See also Cathaldus Giblin, O.F.M. *Irish Franciscan Mission to Scotland, 1619–1646* (Dublin, 1964): pp. 174, 184–5.

59 Biegańska, 'Subscribers from Poland', p. 146.

60 Stanisław Kot, 'William Brus', *Polski słownik biograficzny* (Cracow, 1935). A 'Gulienus Brussius' also enrolled at the University of Cracow. See Kowalski, 'The Placement of Urbanised Scots', p. 95.

61 Antoni Krawczyk, 'The British in Poland in the Seventeenth Century', *The Seventeenth Century*, XVII, 2 (2002), p. 263.

62 Sebastian Sobecki, 'The Authorship of *A Relation of the State of Polonia, 1598*', *The Seventeenth Century*, 18 (2) (2003), pp. 172–9. The author noted the 'diversity of sects even Turcisme and Islam' in the Commonwealth and drew the conclusion that 'warre for religion is avoided' in the Commonwealth. This is covered in Anna Kalinowska's chapter in this volume and also in Biegańska, 'In Search of

Tolerance', p. 50; J. K. Fedorowicz, *England's Baltic trade in the early seventeenth century: A Study in Anglo-Polish commercial diplomacy* (Cambridge, 1980), pp. 17–18. See also 26 June 1606, Elbing, Bruce to Kinloss, Archiwum Państwowe w Gdańsku, MS.300 R/Bb 32, ff. 25–7.

63 Kot, 'William Brus'; G. M. Bell, *A Handlist of British Diplomatic Representatives 1509–1688* (London, 1990), p. 214. See also H. Gmiterek, ed., *Album Studentów Akademii Zamojskiej 1595–1781* (Warsaw, 1994), p. 254.

64 Murdoch, *Network North,* p. 254.

65 Andreas Huyssen, 'Diaspora and Nations: Migration into Other Parts', *New German Critique,* 88 (2003), pp. 147–64. In the Scottish case, an important stage in bringing about this 'rediasporisation', to borrow an unwieldy term from Jonathan Boyarin, involved a process of forgetting. See James Clifford, 'Diasporas', *Cultural Anthropology,* 9 (3), (1994), p. 305.

66 Larry Wolff, *Inventing Eastern Europe: The Map of Civilization on the Mind of the Enlightenment* (USA, 1994).

8

'The Penury of these Malignant Regions'
Comparing the Rural Economies of the Scottish Highlands
and the Polish–Lithuanian Commonwealth in the Early
Modern Period

Robert I. Frost

Enlightened contempt

In his elegant essay 'Of Refinement in the Arts', David Hume observed that:

> In rude unpolished nations where the arts are neglected, all labour is
> bestowed on the cultivation of the ground; and the whole society is divided
> into two classes, proprietors of land and their vassals or tenants. The latter
> are necessarily dependent, and fitted for slavery and subjection; especially
> where they possess no riches, and are not valued for their knowledge in
> agriculture; . . . The former naturally erect themselves into petty tyrants;
> and must either submit to an absolute master for the sake of peace and
> order, or if they will preserve their independency, like the ancient barons
> they must fall into feuds and contests among themselves, and throw the
> whole society into such confusion as is perhaps worse than the most
> despotic government.[1]

It is hard to escape the conclusion that Hume had the Polish–Lithuanian
Commonwealth in mind when he wrote this passage. It came almost immediately after he had mentioned it in disparaging terms:

> Of all EUROPEAN kingdoms, POLAND seems the most defective in the
> arts of war as well as peace, mechanical as well as liberal; yet it is there that
> venality and corruption do most prevail. The nobles seem to have preserved
> their crown elective for no other purpose, than regularly to sell it to the
> highest bidder. This is almost the only species of commerce, with which
> that people are acquainted.[2]

Such damning verdicts on the Polish social and political system were common-
place after 1750, when the Commonwealth's apparent descent into political
anarchy or 'confusion' had made it the laughing-stock of Enlightened Europe.
A political system in which citizenship was restricted to the nobility (*szlachta*)
was not to the taste of most Enlightened thinkers apart from Rousseau, who

rather liked the fierce resistance to central authority which was its hallmark. Hume certainly did not approve: in another essay, he drew a distinction between the Venetian system of government by what he termed patrician oligarchy – which he commended – and the Polish system of government by 'feudal nobility' – which he condemned – as two incarnations of aristocratic government:

> In the VENETIAN government the whole body of nobility possesses the whole power, and no nobleman has any authority which he receives not from the whole. In the POLISH government every nobleman, by means of his fiefs, has a distinct hereditary authority over his vassals, and the whole body has no authority but what it receives from the concurrence of its parts.

The Venetian model was, according to Hume, much to be preferred:

> A nobility, who possess their power in common, will preserve peace and order, both among themselves, and their subjects; and no member can have authority enough to controul the laws for a moment. The nobles will preserve their authority over the people, but without any grievous tyranny, or any breach of private property; because such a tyrannical government promotes not the interests of the whole body, however it may that of some individuals. There will be a distinction of rank between the nobility and people, but this will be the only distinction in the state. The whole nobility will form one body, and the whole people another, without any of those private feuds and animosities, which spread ruin and desolation every where. It is easy to see the disadvantages of a POLISH nobility in every one of these particulars.[3]

Hume found the *szlachta* to be a peculiarly oppressive class:

> Ten thousand, even though they were not annually elected, are a basis large enough for any free government. It is true, the nobles in POLAND are more than 10,000, and yet these oppress the people. But as power always continues there in the same persons and families, this makes them, in a manner, a different nation from the people. Besides the nobles are there united under a few heads of families.[4]

Hume was not the only Scot whose attention was caught by the political decline of Poland–Lithuania. If learned Scots had, on the whole, shown relatively little interest in the Commonwealth in the seventeenth and early eighteenth centuries, as I discuss in another essay in this volume (see Chapter 3), by the late eighteenth century its apparent political collapse provoked reflection. Whereas in the mid-seventeenth century, Poles had tended to look with disdain on Scotland as a poor country mired in heresy and civil war, by the second half of the eighteenth century it was the turn of learned Scots to draw moral lessons. The renewed interest in Poland–Lithuania in late eighteenth-century Scotland, however, in part stemmed from a domestic agenda: as Colin Kidd has pointed out, Hume's attack on this supposedly degenerate aristocratic system was in fact a thinly veiled assault on his native Scotland, which had come to be linked to Poland in Enlightened discourse as two examples of states which the grip of feudalism had condemned to poverty and backwardness.[5] Kidd suggests that for Hume, as for other luminaries of the Scottish Enlightenment, Scottish exceptionalism was not, as Buchanan had argued in the sixteenth century, one of 'high antiquity and ancient constitutionalism', but a less positive phenomenon, deriving from the high degree of feudalisation in Scottish society and the 'remarkable tenacity of feudal institutions', above all in the Highlands.[6] Hume did not explicitly link Scotland and Poland – Kidd suggests he did not have to – but William Robertson did, in a passage in which he identified Scotland's lack of great cities as a major factor contributing to the grip of the nobility on power: 'Laws and subordination take rise in cities; and where there are few cities, as in Poland, or none as in Tartary, there are few or no traces of any sort of police.'[7]

It is not surprising that the comparison between Poland and Scotland, and in particular the Highlands of Scotland, should leap so readily to Enlightened minds. For despite the Enlightenment's conceptual reconfiguration of Europe into an 'advanced' west and a 'backward' east,[8] the poverty of the Highlands matched anything found east of the Elbe. Certainly, the accounts of eighteenth-century travellers in both regions are remarkably similar, as is the condescending tone they adopt. William Coxe, travelling through Poland in 1778, remarked that: 'the roads were bad, the villages few and wretched beyond description; the hovels all built of wood seemed full of filth and misery, and every thing wore the appearance of extreme poverty'.[9] Between Cracow and Warsaw he found that: 'The natives were poorer, humbler, and more miserable than any people we had yet observed in the course of our travels: wherever we stopped, they flocked around us in crouds; and, asking for charity, used the most abject gestures.'[10] The Abbé Ségur, in Poland in 1784, wrote of the 'poor population . . . dirty villages; cottages little different from savage huts; everything makes one think one has been moved back ten centuries, and that one finds oneself amid hordes of Huns, Scythians, Veneti, Slavs, and Sarmatians'.[11] Travellers regularly complained of the dirt, poverty, indolence and savagery of the local peasants.

The terms used could have been lifted from contemporary descriptions of the Highlands. In 1769, Thomas Pennant noted that the 'houses of the peasants in *Lochaber* are the most wretched that can be imagined'.[12] Just as in Poland–Lithuania, travellers commented on the squalid living conditions of the peasantry, their primitive agricultural techniques, the roughness of their clothes, the nakedness of the children and the fact that most people went barefoot. John Knox found the Highlands full of 'scenes of human misery in all its shapes; unalleviated by the cheering rays of hope or any of the comforts, which the lower ranks of mankind, inhabiting richer soils, enjoy in a certain degree'. He reflected glumly on the fact that:

> A tract of land, that composes a fifth part of Great Britain, appeared, with some few exceptions, to be in a state of nature; a great body of people . . . dragging out a wretched existence, perishing through want, or forced by wild despair to abandon their country, their kindred, and friends, and to embark, moneyless and unknown, the indented slaves to unremitting toil and drudgery, in boundless deserts, at the distance of 3,000 miles.[13]

Commentators on both the Highlands and Poland–Lithuania shook their heads in despair over the fact that agricultural implements and carts were constructed of wood, with hardly any iron used.[14]

Such parallels could be multiplied many times over, but it was not just that the Highlands and Poland–Lithuania provided travellers with visions of a rural poverty whose manifestations were strikingly similar: 'the penury of these malignant regions', as Dr Johnson termed it with regard to the Highlands.[15] Enlightened attempts to explain the economic woes of both countries invariably alighted on the same cause: poverty and underdevelopment were due to the abject dependence of the rural populations upon their masters in a condition which observers did not hesitate to call slavery. As Coxe remarked:

> The peasants in Poland, as in all feudal governments, are serfs or slaves; and the value of an estate is not estimated so much from its extent, as from the number of its peasants, who are transferred from one master to another like so many head of cattle.

On the road from Warsaw to Białystok he observed that:

> The peasants are perfect slaves, and their habitations and appearance corresponded with their miserable situation: I could scarcely have figured to myself such objects of poverty and misery.[16]

A French officer who had served in the Polish Army and was reasonably well-disposed towards the Poles, wrote that:

The Poles are perhaps more backward in respect of their knowledge than the Caribbeans. I mean the common people. These poor unfortunates have no idea of either property or liberty. Crushed under the weight of the most abject misery, they are little more than machines whom their lords use five days in the week to work their lands; the labour of the sixth day must sustain them throughout the week.[17]

Like Hume, Adam Smith had not visited Poland–Lithuania himself, but he also fulminated at its feudal backwardness, claiming in the first volume of the *Wealth of Nations* that: 'Poland, where the feudal system still continues to take place, is at this day as beggarly a country as it was before the discovery of America.'[18] In the chapter entitled 'Of the Discouragement of Agriculture in the antient State of Europe after the Fall of the Roman Empire', he argued that the spread of primogeniture and systems of entail, unknown to the Romans, had held back the development of European agriculture:

In those disorderly times, every great landlord was a sort of petty prince. His tenants were his subjects. He was their judge, and in some respects their legislator in peace, and their leader in war . . . The security of a landed estate, therefore, the protection which its owner could afford to those who dwelt on it, depended upon its greatness. To divide it was to ruin it, and to expose every part of it to be oppressed and swallowed up by the incursions of its neighbours. The law of primogeniture, therefore, came to take place, . . . in the succession of landed estates.[19]

He argued that these great landed proprietors were unlikely to improve the land; still less those under them, who were tenants-at-will, or effectively slaves tied to the land and subject to their lord's jurisdiction. While he recognised that not all systems with large-scale landed proprietors were necessarily based on serfdom, or slavery as Smith termed it, in Poland, along with Russia, Bohemia, Moravia and parts of Germany, the pernicious effects of serfdom on agricultural improvement were most apparent. He concluded that:

The experience of all ages and nations, I believe, demonstrates that the work done by slaves, though it appears to cost only their maintenance, is in the end the dearest of any. A person who can acquire no property, can have no other interest, but to eat as much, and to labour as little as possible. Whatever work he does beyond what is sufficient to purchase his own maintenance, can be squeezed out of him by violence only, and not by any interest of his own.[20]

Such sentiments were echoed by contemporary observers of the Highlands, who saw the clan system as the main reason for Highland backwardness. In 1740, Sir Alexander Murray attacked:

> the dangerous and more than kingly heretable Powers, Courts and Jurisdictions in *Scotland*, whose Power and Interest are directly opposite and destructive to those of the Common Good, and do solely consist in the Divisions, Disunion and Troubles of the whole State, and Slavery, Ignorance, Idleness, Poverty, Thefts and Miseries of the People.[21]

A report on the condition of the Highlands in 1750 observed of the Sinclairs in Caithness that 'the Common People are Slaves, in proportion to the Distance of their Country from the Center of Justice' and added that in the county there were over 1,500 men, 'but by Reason of the prodigious Slavery and Poverty of the Commons, more than half of them are but pitifull half-starved Creatures, of a Low Dwarfish Stature, whom a Stranger would hardly believe to be Inhabitants of Great Britain'.[22] In this discourse, as Kidd has pointed out, the anti-noble sentiments of Jacobite writers such as Patrick Abercromby and William Mackintosh of Borlum, who attributed Scotland's 'barbarous Gothish manner of husbandry' largely to the 'thraldom of the commons', were purloined by anti-Jacobite whiggish improvers, who argued that the pernicious effects of the clan system were not confined to the ability of clan chiefs to raise their followers in armed rebellion against the Crown.[23]

Hindsight

Jan Rutkowski (1886–1949), the great interwar historian of the early modern Polish and French rural economies, warned historians of the dangers of placing too much weight on the subjective opinions found in literary sources, or the works of publicists and legal writers, who usually had a political agenda.[24] Rutkowski, who knew Marc Bloch and was strongly influenced by the *Annalistes*, worked for many years in the National Bureau of Statistics, and argued that historians should eschew such unreliable sources in favour of more objective records of the agricultural economy. He was a powerful advocate of the comparative method, which, he argued, was the necessary surrogate for experiment in the historical sciences.[25] In the rest of this essay I would like to explore the implicit parallels drawn by enlightened philosophers between the rural economies of the Polish–Lithuanian Commonwealth and the Highlands of Scotland, and ask whether the apparently similar reactions of travellers to the rural poverty of the two countries really do bear out the Enlightened diagnosis of those ills. Before doing so, however, it is first necessary to consider the rather different contexts in which historians in Poland and Scotland have examined their rural economies.

For Rutkowski's warning is highly relevant: the shadow cast by the negative verdicts of the Enlightenment on both the Highlands and the Polish–Lithuanian Commonwealth is a long one. There are good reasons why this should be so. Quite apart from the problem of rural poverty which so animated eighteenth-century commentators, the Highlands and Poland–Lithuania both saw dramatic and rapid political change in the eighteenth century, the outcome of which established a framework for historical analysis down to the present day. In the case of the Highlands, the 1707 Anglo–Scottish Union and the dismantling of the clan system, both juridically and socially, in the aftermath of the 1745 Jacobite rebellion initiated a series of developments that altered the face of the Highlands forever; in Poland–Lithuania, the partitions of 1772, 1793 and 1795 destroyed the old Commonwealth and removed it from the map of Europe. Thus historians of the Highlands and of Poland–Lithuania have, in their different ways, had to grapple with the problem of hindsight, and accounts of civilisations overly coloured by knowledge of the difficult circumstances in which they ended. Yet whereas in Poland the Enlightenment's negative view of the pre-partition rural economy has only recently been challenged, in Scotland, Enlightened views of the Highlands were rudely and comprehensively rejected during the nineteenth century in popular accounts and, to a somewhat lesser extent, in more academic works.

Thus Polish historians have traditionally accepted the Enlightenment critique of the 'feudal system', and have placed serfdom, or the 'second serfdom' as Engels misleadingly but influentially christened it, at the centre of analyses of the problem of the Commonwealth's social and political back-wardness, presenting it as one of the major barriers to modernisation.[26] If, as Rutkowski points out, even historians such as Michał Bobrzyński (1849–1935), who blamed the partitions on internal, not external, factors, did not place particular emphasis on the role of serfdom in the collapse of the Commonwealth, they were certainly highly critical of its negative effects. It was more German and Russian historians, keen to justify the partitions by demonstrating that Poland–Lithuania had decayed to the extent that it no longer deserved to keep its statehood, who condemned the pernicious effects of the serf economy and linked it to the Commonwealth's collapse, passing over in silence the awkward fact that in both Germany and Russia serf econo-mies existed which in some aspects were considerably more onerous than that of Poland–Lithuania.[27] In the Russian partition in particular the view of the Polish–Lithuanian serf-economy as peculiarly oppressive was encouraged, as it helped set the Lithuanian, Belorussian and Ukrainian peasantries against their noble masters, the vast majority of whom were Polish-speaking by the late eighteenth century, even if most did not yet regard themselves as Poles. It was a successful strategy: to this day across wide stretches of eastern Europe the term *polskie pany* (Polish lords) symbolises arrogant, aristocratic oppression.

Rutkowski himself believed that the state of the Polish rural economy was an important contributing factor to the partitions, criticising in particular the defective 'public morality' of the *szlachta* for the skewing of the rural economy in their own interests.[28] His work was thus well regarded in the Polish People's Republic, which ensured that negative interpretations were institutionalised between 1945 and 1990. In broad outline, the legal enserfment of the peasantry from the mid-fifteenth to the early sixteenth century and the shift from a rural economy based on rents in cash and in kind to one founded on labour-service was presented as a retrograde step, in which the legal and economic advantage shifted decisively towards the *szlachta*, who enjoyed a monopoly of political power after 1572, and of judicial power over their peasants from 1518. The negative effects of the ending of the economic boom of the long sixteenth century after 1620, which hit an economy heavily based on the export of grain and other agricultural products, were exacerbated by political decay and an almost unbroken cycle of devastating wars between 1648 and 1721. Nobles sought to maintain their incomes by degrading the tenancies of their peasants and ratcheting up the burden of serfdom; thus by the mid-eighteenth century, the Polish–Lithuanian peasantry was reduced to the wretched state in which Coxe and other western travellers found it.

The situation with regard to the history of the Highlands is rather different. For while the Polish peasant is still very much with us, his Highland counterpart is long gone, and the circumstances of his departure were harsh. In consequence, almost immediately the scouring of the Highlands after the collapse of the 1745 Jacobite rebellion was over, the romanticisation of early modern Highland society began, to be sealed by that stern post-Enlightenment populist, Sir Walter Scott. The Enlightenment view of the clan system as the shameful remnant of an unlamented feudal past was replaced by a new image of the Highlander, the basis of what Tom Devine terms modern 'highlandism', in which the culture even of Lowland Scots, whose eighteenth-century predecessors regarded the Highlanders as little more than bare-arsed and distinctly plebeian bandits, is to this day defined by the sentimental and wistful tartan flummery which now constitutes the image of Scotland across the known world.[29] Even if Scott's romantic tory heart never quite dominated his flinty whiggish head, by the end of the nineteenth century – with gracious encouragement from that most romantic of Highland landowners, Queen Victoria – the transformation of the image of the Highlands was all but complete.[30]

This process, with its idealisation of the pre-Culloden clan system, marked a dramatic shift, an important aspect of which was the attachment to communal values which the clan was seen to embody. In the 1770s, Dr Johnson had been cautiously optimistic about the future of the Highlands, suggesting in a famous passage that the power of clan chiefs and the forces of commercialisation would eventually lift them out of the primitive state which he so deplored:

> There was perhaps never any change of national manners so quick, so great, and so general, as that which has operated in the *Highlands*, by the last conquest and the subsequent laws. We came thither too late to see what we expected, a people of peculiar appearance, and a system of antiquated life. The clans retain little now of their original character; their ferocity of temper is softened, their military ardour is depressed, their contempt of government subdued, and their reverence for their chief abated. Of what they had before the late conquest of their country, there remain only their language and their poverty . . . That their poverty is gradually abated, cannot be mentioned amoung the unpleasing consequences of subjection. They are now acquainted with money, and the possibility of gain will by degrees make them industrious.[31]

A century later, Andrew Lang's censorious introduction to his 1898 edition of the 1750 report on the condition of the Highlands quoted above reveals that much had changed. Although Lang was in favour of 'improvement', he had a very different view of early modern Highland society to Dr Johnson. He complained that the report was 'the work of a person violently Whiggish and Protestant, and must, therefore, like most contemporary accounts of the Highlanders by Englishmen or Lowlanders, be read with every allowance for prejudice'.[32] He suggested that:

> to observers entirely out of sympathy with clan loyalty and Celtic romance, the poorer classes in the Highlands seemed to be in a desperate posture of slavery, poverty, and ignorance . . . these spectators (Whigs, of course) saw none of that golden age, none of these good old times which tradition beholds in the distance behind Culloden. These English and Lowland spies on the land bring back from several districts a tale of actual starvation, of hungry clansmen and hard-fisted chiefs.

before concluding by once more blaming the English, a refrain which has become common in popular accounts of Highland history:

> The Highland question is greatly the result of English negligence. Had Cromwell's policy been steadily carried through, had roads been made into the remote districts, the clan system would not have lingered till it was

destroyed so late at a single blow. The clans would have accommodated themselves gradually to new conditions, like the Clans of the Border, whereas they suffered a social revolution imposed from above.[33]

One might wonder in the light of Ireland's experience just how being pacified by Cromwell differed from being pacified by Cumberland, but Lang was perhaps right to criticise the report's author, who invariably found that members of clans who supported the government were more manly than their benighted Jacobite counterparts: talking of the McKays of Strathnaver, whose 'Affection . . . to our Happy Constitution is well known', he continued: 'nor are the Common People here such Slaves or Dwarfs as are their Neighbours of Caithness [the Sinclairs], but are a Tall, Strong, Well-Bodied People'. [34] Apparently it was Jacobitism, not porridge, which stunted the growth.

Lang's idealisation of clan society and his presentation of life in the pre-Culloden Highlands as a golden age represents a fundamental rejection of the perspective of the Enlightened reformers. It is his approach, rather than that of Hume, Smith or Johnson, which dominates the popular view of Scottish history to this day. The aching poignancy of the Highland Clearances – in part, as Johnson pointed out, a result of the subjection of the clan to its chief – and the pathos of glens studded with the crumbled ruins that once housed a vanished population casts a powerful spell. Thus, whereas in Poland the popular view tends to uphold the Enlightenment analysis, condemning the *szlachta* for entrenching a backward, feudal economy and emphasising the terrible lot of the peasantry, in Scotland, it is the abandonment of the clan chiefs of the principles of clan society in favour of economic modernisation after the disasters of the Jacobite rebellions which is excoriated. Modernisation and the commercial forces praised by Johnson, not backwardness and poverty, are therefore seen as the main tragedy of the Highland past, a view which John Prebble's classic popular account of the Highland Clearances, published in 1963 and still in print, did much to form.[35]

This process has had a considerable impact upon the writing of the history of the rural economy of the early modern Highlands, and means that scholars working on it operate in a very different context to their colleagues in Poland, where to this day what has recently been termed the 'black legend of the Polish village' still exercises a powerful grip on the popular mind.[36] A new generation of historians in post-Communist Poland is beginning to reassess the issues, freed from the shackles of Marxist – or, more properly, Soviet – paradigms, but they do so against a background of a relentlessly negative stereotype, despite the fact that the works of economic historians in the People's Republic of Poland, apart from a brief Stalinist interlude from 1948 to 1956, were far less dogmatic and far more subtle than anything produced in the other states of the Soviet bloc. With a strong tradition of *Annaliste* historiography dating from the early 1930s, when Rutkowski and Franciszek Bujak founded the *Roczniki Dziejów Społecznych i Gospodarczych* along *Annaliste* lines, historians such as Marian Małowist, Witold Kula, Jerzy Topolski and Antoni Mączak gained deserved reputations outside Poland for their contributions to the debate on the transition from feudalism to capitalism which dominated early modern economic history outwith as well as within the Soviet bloc into the 1980s. Polish scholars had a significant impact on western debates, not least through Kula's brilliant *Economic Theory of the Feudal System*, which argued that the manorial system led the Commonwealth up an economic blind alley, and which, furnished with an admiring preface by Fernand Braudel, was widely translated.[37] Kula subtly used the concept of centre-periphery to challenge the extent to which endogamous forces leading to capitalism existed within the Polish feudal economy, something his detailed archival study of industrial enterprises in the eighteenth-century Commonwealth had led him to question.[38]

Scotching the myths

In both Poland and Scotland, academic historians, over the last thirty years or so, have at last begun to challenge the rather different popular stereotypes of their respective rural economies. Much of this work has been based on a rigorous use of estate records of which Rutkowski would undoubtedly have approved. What has this work revealed with regard to the claims of Enlightened observers? At the heart of the Enlightened critique of the rural economies of the Highlands and Poland–Lithuania was its attack on the dependence of the peasantry on their 'feudal' masters. Even a cursory glance at the two cases, however, suggests that there were fundamental differences between them which do much to explain the contrasting historiographical traditions. The most obvious is that Poland–Lithuania lacked the social phenomenon of clanship which meant, as Allan Macinnes argues, that the relationship between the chief and other clan members was not simply economic, but a political, social and cultural entity that was a mixture of 'feudalism, kinship and local association'.[39] For all that Marxist historians used the term 'feudal' with regard to Poland–Lithuania, whatever else the imposition of serfdom brought, the Commonwealth saw nothing comparable to the feudal systems of power in the medieval west, with their codes of feudal law, vertical ties of lord and vassal, and the feudal systems of land tenure, the vestiges of which survived in Scotland until abolished by Tony Blair's Government. While certain wealthy Lithuanian and Ukrainian magnates had the ability to mobilise substantial numbers of men for short periods of time in the so-called 'private armies' which so impressed Enlightened observers, these, however, were based on military tenancies and clientage networks which certainly did not constitute any social system remotely like clanship.[40]

The clan system undoubtedly did much to mitigate the harsher aspects of landlord-tenant relationships, not least through rent rebates and the distribution of grain from the chiefs' well-stocked girnals to relieve destitution and famine in the frequent crises which were unavoidable in a subsistence economy carried on in difficult terrain and a harsh northern climate.[41] Indeed, the increasing burden of famine relief in the early nineteenth century as the population was growing proved a powerful incentive for landlords to clear their lands and persuade their tenants to emigrate or resettle along the coast to engage in a mixed economy of farming, fishing and industrial labour. Arable cultivation, given the climatic and soil conditions of the Highlands, was necessarily a precarious and marginal activity, with traditional strains of oats and barely rendering yield ratios of 1:3–4, and agriculture had a low capacity for generating capital.[42] Long before Culloden, it was clear that the rural economy was in trouble:

> The problems of [the Highlands] were deeper and more structural in nature, and cannot be put down to the relentless assertion of new political forces or land uses . . . the Highlands and Islands had too many people dependent on too little arable land. This was a predicament it faced before its Jacobite aspirations had been dashed at Culloden and certainly before sheep began to displace men.[43]

Although Dodgshon estimates that around 1650 on average there were some 3–4 acres (1.2–1.6 hectares) of arable land per family in the Highlands, there was a steady downward trend as population grew: by the late eighteenth century, the average plot may have been as little as 2.5 acres (1 hectare). It is hardly surprising that eighteenth-century travellers found a picture of misery, and clicked their tongues at the poor diet of the Highlanders.[44]

Of course, the agricultural economy in the Highlands was more pastoral than arable, and the raising of cattle for the southern market played an increasingly important role, but such figures give pause for thought to a historian of Poland–Lithuania. The 'black legend of the Polish village' depended on the premise that the establishment of large-scale demesne farming after the sixteenth century created a situation in which the peasant laboured on the lord's manor for up to five or even six days per week, while his personal plot was farmed largely for subsistence: as Kula argues, not only was 'feudalism . . . a system based on large landed property', but it was 'characterized by the prevalence of small productive units and by a non-commercialized natural economy'.[45] To what extent is this true? Kula himself accepted that his ideal type of a small peasant plot, operating according to a completely natural economy, obliged to provide the lord only with labour-service and capable at most of simple reproduction, in practice hardly ever existed; nevertheless he insists that '[a]n economic system based on the demesne and serfdom entails an agrarian regime in which the peasant plot is, in principle, generally a subsistence unit and no more', arguing that in a pre-capitalist economy the market was subject to different laws.[46]

Yet, as Kula admits, peasants needed access to the market to raise money to pay their taxes and debts; the evidence suggests that Polish–Lithuanian peasants were far from isolated from market forces, even if, as Kula insists, those market forces were functioning in what he terms 'a non-market milieu'. Polish–Lithuanian peasants did operate to a considerable extent within a market milieu, even if an imperfect one, and were far more engaged with the market than their Highland counterparts scratching a bare subsistence living from their tiny plots, even allowing for the emphasis by Macinnes and others on the growing commercialisation of Highland agriculture long before Culloden.[47] Certainly, the majority of Polish peasants farmed plots that were much larger than those of their Highland counterparts. By the sixteenth century, a substantial group of wealthier peasants (kmiecie) had emerged, with many farming personal holdings of one hide (łan), approximately 16–17 hectares (40–42.5 acres), and a larger group with holdings of half a hide: of 625 landholding peasants in 38 royal villages around Poznań in 1564–5, 34 per cent held one hide, with 60 per cent holding half a hide.[48] In addition to the landholding peasantry with these relatively large farms, there was a large class of poorer inhabitants in every village: zagrodnicy, who farmed smaller plots, cottars (chałupnicy), who lived in their own hut (chałupa) but had at best a garden rather than arable land, and komornicy, rural labourers who did not have a dwelling of their own. These all hired out their services to lords or, indeed, other peasants, often being engaged to provide labour-rent on behalf of wealthier peasants. Even in the eighteenth century, when war, recession and the subdivision of peasant plots had considerably reduced the size of holdings, the majority of peasant farms were in the hands of small and middling kmiecie and zagrodnicy farming plots of up to 8 hectares (20 acres): these two categories constituted 57 per cent of the 17,375 farms from all areas of Poland studied by Rutkowski, with only 15.1 per cent of holdings in the hands of those who did not farm their own plots (chałupnicy and komornicy). There was still a class of wealthier kmiecie farming plots of over 8 hectares, though it now held only 3.8 per cent of peasant farms.[49]

Thus, even in the eighteenth century, undoubtedly a difficult time for the Polish rural economy, a substantial proportion of the peasantry still held far larger farms than were necessary for simple subsistence. The contrast with the Highlands is stark: as Dodgshon has shown, the actual structure of Highland townships was often based on a substantial proportion of sub-tenants holding tiny plots of land, while the majority of the land was held by the tacksmen or a group of head-tenants: thus of fourteen tenants in the township of Caillig on Tiree in 1652, four held more than three-quarters of the arable land, with the rest barely holding enough to sow one or two bolls of grain.[50] Moreover, Polish–Lithuanian peasants in practice enjoyed rather more security of tenure than their Highland counterparts. While in theory the lord could deprive tenants of their holdings at will, and occasionally did, much of the rural economy was based on a range of hereditary, long- and short-term leases, with the longer leases often being defined over periods of several decades or even generations.[51] In contrast:

> the Highland élite was the most absolute of all. They had enormous capacity to displace population and radically alter settlement structure. The peasantry possessed land but did not own it; there were therefore few of the obstacles which restrained seigneurial power in many European societies. The vast majority of the small tenantry had no leases and held land on an annual basis. Below this rent-paying group and forming as much as one third to one half of the population of some estates in the nineteenth century, was an undermass of semi-landless subtenants who paid no rent directly to the proprietor. Most inhabitants on a typical Highland property were therefore liable to eviction at the landlord's will.[52]

As Dodghson points out, Dr Johnson particularly condemned the inhumanity of this insecurity of tenure, which is what made the Clearances possible.[53] Neverthless, historians of Scotland, despite stressing the power of clan chiefs and questioning the myth of the clan as a real kinship group, have emphasised that the spirit of clanship played an important role in mitigating the harsh letter of the feudal law. Whereas the legal powers of Polish–Lithuanian nobles over their serfs are routinely seen in a negative light and are taken to indicate the abject position of the peasantry, Scottish historians have taken a much more positive view of the baronial courts:

> while landowners were strongly aware of their position as the heads of local communities and part of more or less extensive kinship and clientage networks, they were not very conscious of being part of a group with common economic and political interests. Scottish society, from noble to cottar, was bound by vertical linkages based on reciprocal obligations of paternalism and deference. There was a good deal of consensus in rural society between landlord and tenant. This was shown in the operation of baron courts and in the birlay courts that sometimes existed under them.[54]

The relationship between Highland chiefs and their tenants before the abolition of the Heritable Jurisdictions in 1747 is generally presented in a positive light, as the central pivot of an occasionally harsh, but largely benevolent, paternalistic regime in which:

> the judicial privileges of the baron court, though valuable to the laird, had a real function in rural society by providing the tenants with quick and probably fairly impartial justice in their disputes with one another.[55]

Polish historians have also in recent years begun to attack the all but universal assumption that the loss of the right of appeal for peasants to the royal courts in 1518 necessarily brought about a sharp and sustained worsening of their position. This process began with a pioneering article in 1978, in which Andrzej Wyczański asked the radical question of how bad life actually was for peasants in sixteenth-century Poland. He questioned the extent to which the 1518 act made a real difference, and pointed out that even after that date cases did find their way to the royal courts.[56] In any case, the legislation only affected peasants on the nobility's private estates: peasants on royal estates – a fifth of the Commonwealth's cultivated land, much of it granted on lifelong leases to wealthier noblemen – could and did complain to the Referendary Court, which did not always take the part of the noble leaseholder.[57] Much work remains to be done on the operation of the equivalent of Scottish baronial courts, but the few records that have been published suggest that the standard bleak picture of the operation of noble justice may need some adjusting: as in Scotland, these courts enabled disputes between villagers to be settled relatively swiftly and effectively.[58] Some contemporary accounts bear out this impression. Bernard Connor, as an Irishman someone who knew something about impoverished peasantries, observed at the end of the seventeenth century:

> I cannot but admire at the honest and good Temper of the *Polish* Gentry; for tho' their Liberty is extraordinary; tho' they have Power of Life and Death over their Subjects; tho' they are in a manner above their own Laws, and tho' Justice is administer'd in *Poland* more slightly that in any other Country, yet Dr *Connor* says, that all the while that he was in that Kingdom, he neither saw, nor heard of any Murther or Slaughter, or of any Barbarity or Cruelty committed by the Gentry on their Subjects.[59]

Connor's views, based on considerable knowledge derived from a long stay in Poland at the court of John III Sobieski (1674–96), deserve to be given rather more weight than the rapidly formed impressions of travellers such as Coxe, who, as Larry Wolff points out, were conditioned to find a backward and impoverished country. If one looks at travellers' reports before 1700, the picture they paint of Polish agriculture is very different. They certainly noted the peasantry's lack of freedom, but they also praised the fertility of the coun-tryside, and were often complimentary. Connor observed that: 'Notwithstanding the Peasants in *Poland* being born Slaves, and having no manner o[r] Notion of Liberty, [they] live very well satisfy'd and contented.'[60] After an account of the rough usage of peasants while harvesting their lord's grain, he added:

> I should think now, these poor Wretches the most miserable Creatures breathing; but they on the contrary, never having known any better Condition; and having seen their Fathers Slaves before them, are well satis-fied and contented with their Servitude. But however, they have this Happiness, that they seldom want for Victuals and Drink; for their Wives chiefest Employment is to provide them with that.[61]

Ulrich Werdum, travelling in Poland in the 1670s, reported that there was a copious supply of the necessities of life, which were extremely cheap; he concluded that Poland was a blessed country, with productive agriculture, healthy air and rivers full of fish. He was not slow to comment when he passed through poor villages, but he also noted when they were well built or fertile. Near Jarosław in Ruthenia, he travelled through 'the most fertile land which one could ever find under the Sun, which stands among the most fruitful hills and valleys'.[62]

These testimonies are very different from the bleak pictures painted by Coxe and Ségur, and they suggest that Rutkowski was right to warn against depictions of the rural economy which adopt terms such as 'oppression', 'servitude' and 'complete lack of freedom' from literary sources.[63] They suggest that Wyczański's question is a very pertinent one; in his article, he analyses the material well-being of the Polish peasantry in the late sixteenth century. Challenging the importance accorded to the international demand for grain in traditional theories of the development of the manorial economy, he suggests that no more than 2.5 per cent of Poland's grain was exported in the sixteenth century,[64] thereby fundamentally challenging Kula's assertion that the 'feudal system' was defined by minimal peasant contact with the market, and argues that the peasant economy was heavily engaged in markets. This fact is clear not least from the size of cash payments made in villages for the transfer of property and other similar transactions: Connor mentions the case of a peasant who purchased the liberty of his son for 400 crowns so that he could go to university, and as Inglot points out, land transactions were extremely common between peasants. Peasants rented and even bought land from lords in addition to their basic holding, clearly for market production.[65] Wyczański calculated that in the late sixteenth century the sale of rye and oats from a one-hide peasant holding would realise 33–38 złoties per annum, (roughly £3–4 sterling) which does not include earnings from the sale of animal products (wool, cheese, butter, milk) or of flax, linen, fruit and vegetables, all of which played important parts in peasant economies, and brought earnings up to 53–61 złoties (c. £5–6 sterling). Real earnings had risen up to fourfold since 1500.[66] The large latifundia of the magnates were undoubtedly better suited to the complex commercial operation of grain export, which was the reason for their formation, but many of the largest were concentrated in the east and south-east; and in the heartland Polish provinces of Wielkopolska, Małopolska and, especially Mazovia, estates tended to be smaller. Peasant production was much more oriented to the internal market, and it is worth remembering that peasant plots, not demesne estates, constituted by far the majority of cultivated land: the Josephine cadaster undertaken in the Austrian partition after 1772 revealed that they constituted no less than 75 per cent of acreage.[67] Moreover, it is clear that yield ratios were considerably higher on the peasants' own plots than on the lord's demesne, worked by labour-service: one estimate for sixteenth-century Mazovia suggested ratios as high as 1:8.75 for rye, 1:10.5 for wheat, 1:12 for barley and 1:8.1 for oats. If these estimates have been questioned, it is clear that, for peasant holdings, they were far in advance of those widely quoted in the general literature to indicate the lack of productivity of the serf economy, which were based on demesne figures.[68] They were certainly considerably greater than yield ratios in the Highlands, and even the most cautious figures suggest that there was a substantial surplus of produce to market.

Research following the fall of Communism, which no longer has even to pay lip-service to the old picture of a savagely oppressive system, is now confirming many of Wyczański's findings. The assumption that the manorial economy and the so-called 'second serfdom' arose because of extra-economic coercion by the *szlachta* is coming under increasing attack. While the growing political power of the nobility was central to the construction of the legal framework for serfdom, the substitution of labour-rent for rents in cash and in kind in the fifteenth century was much more of a pragmatic bilateral response to worsening economic conditions than the result of laws passed by the Sejm. In the face of a growing shortage of specie, peasants were often only too happy to commute rents in cash or kind into the initially far from onerous labour-rents of one or two days per week, which enabled them to concentrate on marketing the surplus produced on their own plots, and meant that they, not the lord, were able to profit from their own produce, as rents in kind were substantially reduced to allow for the introduction of labour-rents. [69]

Thus, over the early modern period, as Rutkowski had hinted, the Polish–Lithuanian economy was far more flexible and responsive to market forces than has often been recognised. By no means all of the Commonwealth saw the triumph of the great demesne estates which formed the basis for Kula's theoretical model. Much of Royal Prussia, which contained great trading ports that made export easy, retained cash rents throughout the period. The mountainous Carpathian region, where pastoral farming was widespread, sustained an economy much more comparable to the Highlands, in which demesne farming failed to penetrate and rents, largly in kind, dominated.[70] The extent of labour-service undoubtedly increased, but the popular misconception which sees peasants working the whole week on the lord's demesne is fundamentally misguided: labour was provided out of the peasant household, and the head of the family might himself work relatively infrequently on the lord's land. Moreover, as economic conditions changed, the balance between rents paid in cash, kind, or labour-service fluctuated; there was undoubtedly a strong move towards large-scale demesne farming in the sixteenth century to meet the demand for grain from western Europe, but, by the eighteenth century, the trend was actually in the other direction.

There is one final contrast which might be drawn. Historians of the Highlands have stressed that it was the growing role of the state which, long before 1745, chipped away at the power of clan chiefs and fostered the forces of commercialisation.[71] In Poland–Lithuania, however, the undoubted weakening of royal power from the mid-fifteenth century meant that if the state was not able to protect peasant interests very effectively, there were advantages to be derived from its lack of interference. Unlike in Russia, where the state actively pursued and returned to their masters serfs who absconded, there was little that Polish–Lithuanian lords could do to recover those of their peasants who decided to seek their fortunes elsewhere; another indication, as Rutkowski argues, that historians should be wary of reading actual conditions on the ground on the basis of legislation, of which there was a great deal which sought to curtail peasant freedom of movement. In practice, the phenomenon was widespread, and serfs fleeing their masters did not necessarily have to take great precautions to hide their departure: it is clear that the two peasant families who absconded from one estate in the palatinate of Troki in Lithuania in 1585, taking with them two horses, three oxen, four bullocks, twelve mature sheep, eighteen young sheep, three goats, six mature pigs, twelve young pigs, twenty piglets, six mature geese, twenty-four goslings, twenty chickens, four barrels of rye, six of barley, twelve of milled rye, plus seedcorn, cloth and other items, must have prepared their move well; they would not have been hard to track down *en route* to their new holding on another estate.[72] The removal of such a substantial inventory of stock from one landlord to another is a reminder that while, in contrast to the Highlands, there was a great deal of fertile land in Poland–Lithuania, there was a relative shortage of labour to work it. Peasants, especially of the wealthier sort, were in short supply, and landlords could not treat them too badly.

There was another advantage of the weakness of the state: the nobility's control of taxation meant that the burden of the state on peasant incomes was far lower than elsewhere in Europe. Recent work on comparative peasant incomes suggests that the Polish–Lithuanian system was rather less burdensome than hitherto supposed. Piotr Guzowski has calculated that for the sixteenth century, when many European states saw a marked increase in taxation, Polish peasants did rather well. If a Polish peasant with a 16.8-hectare holding paid 12 per cent of his grain production in rent and taxes in the fifteenth century (9 per cent for an 8.4-hectare holding), this compares with 10 per cent for a 7.28-hectare holding in England, 20 per cent for holdings of 6 and 9 hectares in Languedoc and Normandy respectively, and 25 per cent for a 6-hectare holding in the Paris region. By the sixteenth century, the difference had become even starker: if a Polish peasant was now paying 20 per cent of his grain production in rent and taxes on a 16.8-hectare holding, and only 10 per cent on an 8.4-hectare holding, this on average compared well with his English equivalent, who was paying 15 per cent (7.8 hectares), but was considerably better than was the case in Languedoc (25 per cent, 6 hectares); Brandenburg (23.5 per cent, 16 hectares); Castile (33 per cent); the Paris area (40 per cent, 6 hectares) or Muscovy (40 per cent, 16.5 hectares).[73] Leaving on one side the issue of taxation, these figures suggest that the seigneurial regime in Poland–Lithuania was less demanding than in the Highlands, where, if Dodgshon's estimates are correct, tenants paid as much as 40–55 per cent of their (small) barley crop and 7.5–10 per cent of their oat crop in rent in 1541. The proportion of the barley crop surrendered in the seventeenth century fell to 20–25 per cent, but the fact that the proportion of the oat crop, which was far more important to the family's subsistence, had risen to 13.5–18 per cent may have been more burdensome.[74] Given that there was little or no surplus to market, these figures suggest that Highland peasants were much worse off than their Polish–Lithuanian counterparts.

Black and white legends

Thus it seems that despite the 'black legend of the Polish village' and the sentimental nostalgia which surrounds the pre-Culloden clan system, the demands of the *polskie pany* may have been rather less onerous to their serfs than those of the Highland chiefs on their supposed kin in the great family of the clan. Any such conclusion, however, would need substantially more research before it could be confirmed. Whatever this excursion to Rutkowski's laboratory of comparative history has revealed, perhaps only one firm conclusion can as yet be reached: for all the apparently similar manifestations of poverty that eighteenth-century travellers discerned in the Highlands of Scotland and Poland–Lithuania, the great paladins of the Enlightenment were mistaken. The underlying causes of the 'penury of those malignant regions' were very different, as were the manifestations of 'feudal' power which Enlightened philosophers saw as responsible for it. The Highlands may yet have been a rude, unpolished nation in Hume's day, even allowing for the well-established taste of some Highland chiefs for claret and Belgian lace, but that is scarcely a charge that can be sustained against the great magnates of Poland–Lithuania, who, by the eighteenth century, were among the wealthiest landowners in Europe.[75] Smith, too, got it wrong: primogeniture and entails were concepts that were alien to the Polish nobility. Only seven entails were ever allowed by the Polish Sejm, six of them at the end of the sixteenth century, and three of those were for different branches of the Lithuanian Radziwiłł family.[76] It was partible inheritance and the consequent subdivision of holdings – also a problem for the Highland tenant – which made it difficult for many Polish noble families to sustain agricultural improvement, and it was in fact on the great estates of the powerful magnate families that the latest agricultural fashions were most likely to be followed. It is, perhaps, time, however, to reappraise the black and white legends, and to escape the long intellectual shadow cast by the Enlightenment, to look anew at the rural economies of Poland–Lithuania and the Highlands from below, not above, with peasants as economic actors, rather than passive victims of oppression or romanticised figures in a mythical, timeless world.

Notes

1 David Hume, 'Of Refinement in the Arts' in *Political Essays*, ed. Knud Haakonssen (Cambridge, 1994), pp. 111–12.

2 Ibid., p. 111.

3 Hume, 'That Politics may be reduced to a Science', in Hume, *Political Essays*, pp. 5–6.

4 Hume, 'The Idea of a Perfect Commonwealth', ibid., p. 228.

5 Colin Kidd, *Subverting Scotland's Past. Scottish Whig Historians and the Creation of an Anglo–British Identity 1689–1830* (Cambridge, 1993), pp. 178–80.

6 Ibid. p. 181.

7 William Robertson, *The History of Scotland during the Reign of Queen Mary and King James VI till his Accession to the Crown of England* (Fifth edition, London, 1769), p. 26. Robertson tempered the severity of his judgement a little in later editions, altering the last sentence to 'a well-arranged police'.

8 See Larry Wolff, *Inventing Eastern Europe: The Map of Civilization on the Mind of the Enlightenment* (Stanford, 1994).

9 William Coxe, *Travels into Poland, Russia, Sweden and Denmark* 3 vols (London, 1784), III, p. 169.

10 Ibid., p. 202.

11 Quoted by Wolff, *Inventing Eastern Europe*, p. 19.

12 Thomas Pennant, *A Tour in Scotland 1769* (Chester, 1771), p. 11.

13 John Knox, *A View of the British Empire, more especially Scotland; with some Proposals for the Improvement of that Country, the Extension of its Fisheries, and the Relief of the People* (London, 1784), p. i.

14 *Letters from a Gentleman in the North of Scotland to His Friend in London* 2 vols (London, 1754) II p. 135; cf. Coxe, *Travels* III, p. 279.

15 Samuel Johnson, *A Journey to the Western Islands of Scotland* in *The Works of Samuel Johnson, LL.D. A New Edition in Twelve Volumes with an Essay on his Life and Genius by Arthur Murphy Esq.* VIII (London, 1796), p. 310.

16 Coxe, *Travels* III, pp. 155, 249.

17 *Voyage en Allemagne et en Pologne, commencé en 1776. par M. de L.S.M.A.S.D.P.* (Amsterdam and Paris, 1784), pp. 147–8.

18 Adam Smith, *An Inquiry into the Nature and Causes of the Wealth of Nations* I.xi.n, eds R.H. Campbell and A.S. Skinner, 2 vols (Oxford, 1976) I, p. 256.

19 Ibid., I, pp. 382–3.

20 Ibid., I, pp. 387–8.

21 Sir Alexander Murray, *The True Interest of Great Britain, Ireland and our Plantations* . . . (London, 1740), p. v.

22 Andrew Lang, ed., *The Highlands of Scotland in 1750* (Edinburgh, 1898), pp. 6, 7.

23 Kidd, *Subverting Scotland's Past*, pp. 168–70.

24 Jan Rutkowski, 'Poddaństwo włościan w XVIII wieku w Polsce i niektórych innych krajach Europy', in *Wieś Europejska późnego feudalizmu (XVI-XVIII w.)*, Jan Rutkowski, ed. Jerzy Topolski (Warsaw, 1986), pp. 31–2.

25 Ibid., p. 35. For Rutkowski, see Jerzy Topolski, 'Jan Rutkowski', *Polski Słownik Biograficzny* XXXIII, pp. 227–30.

26 For brief introductions to the problem in English, see William Hagen, 'Village life in East-Elbian Germany and Poland, 1400–1800: subjection, self-defence, survival', in *The Peasantries of Europe, 1400–1800*, ed. Tom Scott (Harlow, 1998), pp. 145–89, and 'Subject farmers in Brandenburg-Prussia and Poland: village life and fortunes under manorialism in early-modern Central Europe', in *Serfdom & Slavery. Studies in Legal Bondage*, ed. Michael Bush (Harlow, 1996), pp. 296–310.

27 Rutkowski, 'Poddaństwo włościan', pp. 27–9.

28 Jan Rutkowski, 'Gospodarcze podłoże rozbiorów Polski', in Rutkowski, *Wieś europejska*, pp. 375–86.

29 See T. M. Devine, *The Scottish Nation 1700–2000* (London, 1999), pp. 231–45.

30 For a discussion of Scott's ambivalence towards the romanticisation of the Highlands which argues that he should not be seen as the uncritical constructor of Highlandism, see Alison Lumsden, '"Beyond the dusky barrier". Perceptions of the Highlands in the Waverley novels', in *Mìorun Mòr na Gall, 'The Great Ill Will of the Lowlander'? Lowland Perceptions of the Highlands, Medieval and Modern*, eds Dauvit Broun and Martin MacGregor (Glasgow, 2009), pp. 158–86. See also Peter Womack, *Improvement and Romance. Constructing the Myth of the Highlands* (Basingstoke, 1989).

31 Johnson, *A Journey to the Western Islands*, p. 277.

32 Andrew Lang, 'Introduction', in *The Highlands of Scotland in 1750*, Lang, ed., p. viii.

33 Ibid., pp. xi, lxiii.

34 Lang, ed., *The Highlands of Scotland in 1750*, pp. 9, 11. The Sinclairs, a non-juring clan of Jacobite sympathy, in fact remained consistently neutral in all the risings: Allan Macinnes, *Clanship, Commerce and the House of Stuart, 1603–1788* (East Linton, 1996), pp. 190, 248.

35 John Prebble, *The Highland Clearances* (London, 1963).

36 Magdalena Śluszarska, 'Przedmowa', in *Dwór, plebana, rodzina chłopska. Szkice z dziejów wsi polskiej XVII i XVIII wieku*, ed. Magdalena Śluszarska (Warsaw, 1998), p. 6.

37 Witold Kula, *Teoria ekonomiczna ustroju feudalnego* (Warsaw, 1962). The English version, *An Economic Theory of the Feudal System. Towards a model of the Polish economic system 1500–1800* (London, 1976) was, unfortunately, translated from the Italian edition, not the original Polish.

38 J. Kochanowicz, 'Czy w Polsce nowożytnej był feudalizm?' *Roczniki Dziejów Społecznych i Gospodarczych* 58 (1998), p. 199.

39 Macinnes, *Clanship*, p. 1.

40 See Maciej Siekierski, 'Landed wealth in the Grand Duchy of Lithuania: the economic affairs of Prince Nicholas Christopher Radziwiłł (1549–1616)', *Acta Baltico-Slavica* XX (1989) pp. 239–308; XXI (1992), pp. 195–300; Urszula Augustyniak, *W służbie hetmana i Rzeczypospolitej. Klientela wojskowa Krzysztofa Radziwiłła (1585–1640)* (Warsaw, 2004).

41 Robert Dodgshon, *From Chiefs to Landlords. Social and Economic Change in the Western Highlands and Islands, c. 1493–1820* (Edinburgh, 1998), pp. 95–7, 238; T. M. Devine, 'The Highland Clearances', in *Exploring the Scottish Past. Themes in the History of Scottish Society*, T. M. Devine (East Linton, 1995), p. 133.

42 Macinnes, *Clanship*, pp. 19, 20.

43 Robert Dodgshon *Land and Society in Early Scotland* (Oxford, 1981), p. 277.

44 Ibid. pp. 289, 292.

45 Kula, *An Economic Theory of the Feudal System*, pp. 15, 17.

46 Ibid., pp. 17, 49, 62.

47 Macinnes, *Clanship*, pp. 210–34; Dodgshon, *From Chiefs to Landlords*, pp. 159–97; T. M. Devine, *Clanship to Crofters' War. The Social Transformation of the Scottish Highlands* (Manchester, 1994), pp. 32–53. For a brief introduction to the issue of the market in traditional peasant societies, see Tom Scott, 'Introduction' in Scott ed., *The Peasantries of Europe*, pp. 7–9.

48 Hagen, 'Village life', p. 170.

49 Rutkowski, 'Poddaństwo włościan', p. 85.

50 Dodgshon, *From Chiefs to Landlords*, p. 137.

51 Rutkowski, 'Poddaństwo włościan', p. 133.

52 Devine, 'The Highland Clearances', p. 137.

53 Dodgshon, *From Chiefs to Landlords*, p. 152.

54 Ian Whyte, *Scotland's Society and Economy in Transition c.1500–c.1760* (Basingstoke, 1997), p. 29.

55 T. C. Smout *A History of the Scottish People 1560–1830* (Edinburgh, 1969), p. 131; see also pp. 115–18.

56 Andrzej Wyczański, 'Czy chłopu było źle w Polsce XVI wieku?' *Kwartalnik Historyczny* 85 (1978), pp. 627–41.

57 J. Rafacz, *Sąd referendarski koronny. Z dziejów obrony prawnej chłopów w dawnej Polsce* (Poznań, 1948). See the many petitions in I. T. Baranowski, ed., *Księgi Referendarskie 1582–1602* (Warsaw, 1910).

58 For example, Aniela and Antoni Walawender, eds, *Księga Ławnicza wsi Kargowej w powiecie Kościańskim 1617–1837* Studia z Dziejów Gospodarstwa Wiejskiego III,2 (Warsaw, 1960); Adam Vetulani, ed., *Księgi wiejskie Klucza Łąckiego I 1526–1739* (Wrocław, 1962); S. Płaza, ed., *Księga sądowa wsi Iwkowej, 1581–1809* (Wrocław, 1969); L. Łysiak ed. *Księga sądowa wsi Wary, 1449–1623* (Wrocław, 1971).

59 Bernard Connor, *The History of Poland in Several Letters to Persons of Quality*, 2 vols (London, 1698), II, pp. 181–2.

60 Connor, *The History of Poland*, p. 183.

61 Ibid., p. 186.

62 Ulrich von Werdum, 'Reisen durch Ober- und Niederdeutschland, Preussen, Polen, Frankreich, England, Dänemark und Schweden, in den Jahren 1670–1677', in *Johan Bernoulli's Archiv zur neuern Geschichte, Geographie, Natur- und Menschenkenntniß* VI (Leipzig, 1787), p. 234; see also pp. 268–9, 277.

63 Rutkowski, 'Poddaństwo włościan', pp. 31–2.

64 Wyczański, 'Czy chłopu było źle', p. 628.

65 Connor, *History of Poland* II, p. 185; Stefan Inglot, 'Z życia codziennego chłopów polskich od XVI do XVIII wieku', in *Z dziejów wsi polskiej i rolnictwa*, Stefan Inglot (Warsaw, 1986), pp. 285–6.

66 Wyczański, 'Czy chłopu było źle', pp. 634–5.

67 Rutkowski, 'Poddaństwo włościan', p. 176.

68 A. Wawrzyńczyk, *Gospodarstwo chłopskie na Mazowszu w. XVI w XVI i początkach XVII wieku* (Warsaw, 1962), pp. 41–2, 84; Piotr Guzowski, 'Sytuacja ekonomiczna chłopów polskich w XV i XVI w. na tle europejskim', in *Między Zachodem a Wschodem. Tom IV, Życie gospodarcze Rzeczypospolitej w XVI–XVIII wieku*, ed. Jacek Wijaczka (Toruń, 2007), pp. 10–11.

69 Krzysztof Mikulski and Jan Wroniszewski, 'Folwark i zmiany koniunktury gospodarczej w Polsce XIV–XVII wieku', *Klio* 4 (2003), pp. 25–39.

70 Rutkowski, 'Poddaństwo włościan', p. 65.

71 Macinnes, 'Clanship', pp. 210–11.

72 Stanisław Śreniowski, *Zbiegostwo chłopów w dawnej Polsce jako zagadnienie ustroju społecznego* (second edition, Łódź, 1997), p. 26.

73 Guzowski, 'Sytuacja ekonomiczna', p. 34, table 1; p. 34, table 3.

74 Dodgshon, *From Chiefs to Landlords*, p. 63.

75 See Robert Frost, 'The nobility of Poland–Lithuania 1569–1795', in *The European Nobilities* vol II, *Northern, Central and Eastern Europe*, ed. H. M. Scott (Basingstoke, 2007), pp. 284–5.

76 Teresa Zielińska, 'Ordynacja w dawnej Polsce', *Przegląd Historyczny* LXVIII (1977), pp. 17–30.

PART TWO

POLES IN SCOTLAND, 1940–2010

9

'Bonnie Fechters'

The Polish Army and the Defence of Scotland, 1940–1942

Allan Carswell

On the evening of 31 October, Halloween, 1941, Colonel J.M.B. Scott opened the inaugural meeting of the Edinburgh branch of the Scottish–Polish Society. Being a time of year particularly associated with remembrance, especially for Poles – *zaduszki* or All Souls' Day was on 2 November – those present observed a minute's silence 'in homage to those who were in the maelstrom of the fight' against the occupation of their homeland. Colonel Scott, a former Scottish soldier and rugby internationalist, then began proceedings by observing that there were two things which he thought might bring the Scottish and Polish people closer together: both were 'bonnie fechters'[1] and both loved an argument.[2]

The latter is no doubt still true and was certainly a trait that would get an ample airing before World War II came to an end, even if, as we shall see, it achieved the opposite of bringing Scots and Poles together. The former, also undoubtedly true, recalls that both countries had a strong military tradition closely bound up with ideas of national identity. During the course of World War II, the military traditions of both nations would be both severely tested and enhanced. If the sense of mutual respect which emerged between these 'comrades-in-arms' withstood the storm of political argument which for a time soured relations between the two peoples, it was due in no small way to the impressions formed of the Poles during their first few months in Scotland.

The circumstances which led to the creation of a Scottish–Polish Society are among the most particular in Scotland's experience of World War II. They also form one of the most significant and intense episodes in the long history of engagement between the two countries. Rather than summarise all aspects of the Polish presence in wartime Scotland, this chapter will look mainly at the military aspects of the story, in particular the first phase between July 1940 and early 1942, when Polish troops played a vital role in defending Scotland from the threat of a German invasion.[3] In contrast to the later stages of the War, when Britain's reliance on the Soviet Union and the latter's attitude to Poland's future placed an unbearable strain on Britain's relations with the Polish government, this was a period of hope and cooperation in the face of shared adversity.

As will be clear, there were inevitable tensions between the two allies. Britain had gone to war in 1939 to preserve Polish independence, but neither at the time, and certainly not in retrospect, can many now claim that this goal was achieved in 1945. The sense of betrayal, bitterness and disappointment created amongst Poles who had fought alongside Britain would last a long time, even if it was overlaid in time with feelings of resignation and a need to move on with individual lives. It is therefore useful, and not simply nostalgic, to look back a little to the early period, before the Grand Strategy of the emerging super-powers dictated the future of Europe, to a time when Britain, and Scotland, faced a crisis for their very existence, when Polish soldiers were deeply appreciated as 'bonnie fechters' and made very welcome in what, for many, would become their adopted home.

An army in exile

The story begins with the fall of Poland in September 1939 after its joint invasion by the forces of Hitler's Germany and Stalin's Soviet Union. Unable to accept the obliteration of their country, elements of the Polish Government and Armed Forces escaped to the west, mainly to France, their long-time ally, or to French-held territory in the Middle East. By prior agreement, several warships of the Polish Navy also headed for British naval bases, including Rosyth in the Firth of Forth. The Poles then set about reconstituting their forces as an 'Army in exile', a familiar concept which had played a crucial part in defining ideas of modern Polish nationhood.

Ever since the 'partitions' of 1795, when the three empires of Austria, Prussia and Russia (in anticipation of Hitler and Stalin) had conspired to erase Poland from the map, Polish patriots had taken service with whichever foreign state seemed most likely to help them restore their independence. The service of these Polish Legions, particularly under French command – both revolutionary and Napoleonic, and again during World War I – inexorably linked the Polish Army with ideas of national salvation and imbued it, in the eyes of the Polish people, with an aura of extraordinary prestige.[4] The Army's role in the defence of a newly resurgent Poland during the Polish–Soviet War of 1919–21 bolstered this position further, ensuring that it emerged as a dominant institution of the Polish Republic. Even though the Army's defeat in 1939 was a national catastrophe, its resurrection was therefore far from unexpected.

What was unexpected, however, was that in the spring of 1940 France would fall victim to the German onslaught as quickly as Poland had the previous autumn. The Polish operational formations which had been organised under overall French command during the winter – two infantry divisions, an armoured brigade and a 'highland' brigade, which had only recently seen service in Anglo–French operations in Norway – were effectively destroyed in the brief campaign of 1940. This second catastrophe cost

Poland dear. Out of a total of 38,000 men, 32,000 (84.4 per cent) were either killed, wounded, taken prisoner, or interned.[5]

The defeat of France was a particularly stunning blow for the Forces' commander-in-chief and Poland's latest political leader, General Władysław Sikorski, a prominent soldier and politician, but one who had fallen foul of the pre-war Polish Government. Like many Poles, Sikorski was an ardent Francophile and had spent much of the previous fourteen years living in Paris. Again, like many Poles, he had an almost unlimited admiration for the prowess of the French Army and its leadership. In the aftermath of defeat, Sikorski's critics argued, many with the benefit of hindsight, that his misplaced and unquestioning confidence in the French Army had led him to squander Poland's precious military resources when it was clear the campaign was already lost. Similar accusations were soon levelled against another newly appointed war leader, Winston Churchill (who, like Sikorski, was a strong Francophile who had also recently been rehabilitated from the political wilderness). In particular, these concerned the loss of over 10,000 men of Scotland's 51st Highland Division, forced to surrender at St Valéry-en-Caux while still left fighting under French command several weeks after the main British Army had been evacuated at Dunkirk – a blow to Scotland's military prestige which was to have unforeseen consequences for both Scots and Poles.

Nevertheless, the Poles were determined to fight on. As French resistance collapsed, the Polish Government-in-Exile threw in its lot with Britain and arrangements were made to evacuate what was left of their forces to Britain. During late June/early July 1940, 19,451 Polish troops arrived at British ports (23.5 per cent of the Polish forces formed in France).[6] The War Office's immediate concern was to get the Poles as far away as possible from the congested south-east of England where Britain's own Army was still untangling itself after the confusion of Dunkirk. West-central Scotland offered the best solution. There was a main railhead at Glasgow, reasonably close to large areas of open country where the Poles could be sent to regroup and begin the next stage of their struggle.

In later life, many Poles recalled their first impressions of what, for many, was to become their adopted home. The first thing that struck them was the contrast between the chaos of their last weeks in France and the calm, orderly reception that awaited them on the quayside. The Women's Voluntary Service distributed tea and cigarettes while British officers directed them onto specially prepared troop trains. Perhaps, they thought, as the trains left the docks and headed north to Glasgow, here was a country that might yet stand a chance against Hitler's *Blitzkrieg*.

The war comes to Scotland

Regardless of the initial impressions of the Poles, coloured as they were by months of frustration, disappointment and uncertainty, life in Scotland in the summer of 1940 was a strange mix of the normal and the extraordinary. Although the War had been going since the previous September, its effects had been strangely muted in the North. Unlike in 1914, there had been no great release of patriotic fervour in September 1939; no rush of volunteers to the Army, nothing of the unreal 'holiday' atmosphere of the first months of the Great War. Neither had the skies filled with fleets of enemy bombers, despite the dire predictions of the pre-war strategists that mass bombing of civilian targets would be the overture to any 'modern' conflict. Instead, the War was something that was largely happening elsewhere – until the Fall of France, it was a foreign news story from far away places in Eastern Europe and Scandinavia.

This is not to say that things had remained unchanged at home. By the early summer of 1940, food and fuel rationing were starting to bite as more and more essentials were put 'on the ration'. The unfamiliar bureaucracy and seemingly petty intrusions of 'Air Raid Precautions' and the 'black-out' were a source of daily concern, and not a little irritation, especially in the absence of the much-heralded bombers. The planned mass evacuation of mothers and children from the cities to the countryside had been tried and then abandoned, with less than fifty per cent of those eligible presenting themselves in most Scottish cities, even though the evacuation of children overseas to Canada was still being actively considered. Italy's opportunist declaration of war on Britain and France on 10 June 1940 led to vicious attacks on Italian shops and businesses in Glasgow and Edinburgh. Such violence was further fuelled by a widespread and officially supported belief that Britain was harbouring a strong 'fifth column' of ruthless enemy agents, ready and able to subvert and attack the nation's defences. Draconian steps were taken to intern all enemy 'nationals' as a threat to security, regardless of any evidence to the contrary.

The War was also having other less direct consequences. Increased demands on industry had led to a sharp increase in output from Scotland's factories resulting in a flood of work. Suddenly young men had more money in their pockets and there was a marked rise in public disorder, with frequent incidents of drunkenness, brawling and general 'rowdiness' being reported in many Scottish towns. Other instances of violent crime also seemed to be on the rise. One night in late July 1940, an Assistant Chief Constable of the Edinburgh police was shot dead while riding in a police car through the 'black-out' in what appeared a random attack by a drunken soldier. As people awaited the next turn of events, a mood of nervous apprehension hung in the air.

General Sikorski's tourists

On their arrival in Glasgow, the bulk of the Polish troops evacuated from France – now scornfully dubbed as 'Sikorski's Tourists' by German propaganda – marched through the streets to the various locations where they were to be temporarily accommodated: halls, schools, parks and sports grounds. To raise their spirits in yet another foreign city, the men began to sing the old songs of Poland's long and bitter struggles for independence, just as earlier generations of Polish exiles had done. This demonstration of spirit seemed to strike a chord with the local people. After months of defeat, frustration, danger and uncertainty, the Poles found themselves being cheered by onlookers – another sign, perhaps, that this time they had fallen amongst a kindred people.

As for the Scots, the arrival of these foreign soldiers was a tangible sign that the War was finally reaching them. It was also an opportunity to show clearly whose side they were on.

On 24 June 1940, three days after his arrival in Britain, General Sikorski broadcast a radio message via the BBC to the people of Poland:

At a time when the great body of our armies safely back from France is landing on the shores of Great Britain I would like to declare solemnly in the name of the President of the Polish Republic and of the Polish government, that, animated by an indomitable will, we shall continue to fight shoulder to shoulder with the powerful British Empire for a free and independent Poland.

As Sikorski's words reached occupied Poland, most of the Polish troops had arrived in Scotland. The remaining personnel either went to London to man the main Polish HQ, or were transferred to units of the Polish Air Force being organised in England. Although the Poles in Scotland numbered around 17,500 men, few were organised into front-line units. Instead, it was mostly partly-formed units, training schools and headquarters personnel that had escaped, one consequence of which was a disproportionate number of officers. Sikorski's description of 'the great body of our armies' was therefore an exaggeration; in truth the 'great body', in terms of operational units, had either been lost in France or was now interned in Switzerland, even though many men from these formations were to make it to Britain over the coming months.

The Polish Air Force had fared better than the Army and had managed to get a large part of its trained front-line personnel out of France. They joined a significant contingent who had been serving with the RAF since the fall of Poland, and were soon either integrated into existing front-line squadrons or organised into new all-Polish units. According to some sources, by the end of the Battle of Britain in October 1940, Polish fighter pilots had accounted for up to twelve per cent of all German aircraft destroyed – a remarkable achievement which did much to promote the Poles' fighting reputation in British eyes.[7]

Meanwhile, in Glasgow, the initial spark of admiration grew into a genuine feeling of welcome. The City Corporation, under the leadership of the Lord Provost, Patrick Dollan, did all it could to provide hospitality for the Poles. Local people too were soon inviting them into their homes. One Polish soldier recalls venturing out with a couple of friends on their first Sunday morning in Glasgow and taking shelter from the rain in a local church:

> When we came out we were surrounded by people. Of course the problem was they couldn't understand us like we could understand them but there was one family with two young schoolgirls. One spoke German, one spoke French. We gathered enough words to more or less converse and they took us to their home, a beautiful home. Such a luxury we didn't see for months and months. The table was quite laden – the lunch ready with salad and salmon sandwiches and the glitter of the china and cutlery. It took us quite a while to remember the table etiquette after being in the wilds. The girls were such a good help to us. They were asking us questions about where we came from and who we were and where is Poland? We had to tell them the story how we came from Poland through Hungary and now we are in England and they said no, no, not England, this is Scotland.[8]

In as much as wartime censorship would permit, the local papers covered the story. On 25 June 1940 the text of Sikorski's radio message to Poland was printed in the *Glasgow Herald* under the headline 'Poles Remain Our Allies'. On the 27th the *Evening Times* printed a photograph of a group of cheerful-looking Polish soldiers above the caption: 'Polish troops who have been fighting in France have arrived in this country. Judging by the smiles they are not downhearted.' A few days later, another photograph of a Polish soldier in heroic pose was printed on the front page with the bold caption: 'The Spirit of Poland still lives'.

However, not everything was straightforward. The preponderance of unattached and seemingly surplus officers amongst the Poles was causing serious concern in British military and security circles, alert as they were to the threat of enemy infiltration. On 5 July 1940, the British Army's Area Commander for Glasgow, Brigadier F. H. Witts, contacted Scottish Command regarding a proposal to move some of the Polish troops back into Glasgow from outlying areas. He wrote:

While I have no direct evidence, I am not at all satisfied that these surplus officers – whatever their rank may be – are in reality officers at all. I know anyhow that they have no control over their men, who openly despise them. Until therefore our security officers are absolutely satisfied that they are not enemy agents or fifth columnists, I would protest most strongly against bringing them back into the Glasgow industrial area where there are so many opportunities for them to cause irreparable damage.[9]

Military retreats are rarely occasions when humanity shows its best and it is conceivable that amongst the Poles there were some who had taken advantage of circumstance to make a swift escape from France. It is also the case that the British authorities were particularly suspicious of any foreign presence which might constitute a threat to security, even if they had 'no direct evidence'. The surplus of officers was to dog the reputation of the Poles throughout their time in Scotland. To a large extent it can be explained by the presumption, begun in France, that the Polish Army in exile would be largely recruited from Polish emigrant communities, either in the host country or from other well-disposed nations. The key personnel evacuated from Poland were therefore, in theory, the trained professionals who would organise and lead these new forces. Nevertheless, in a few cases, British suspicions regarding impostors appear to have been well-grounded. Accounts of clandestine executions in secluded corners of the Scottish countryside over subsequent weeks have occasionally been recounted by Polish veterans. It was also the case that a significant minority of senior Polish officers now in Scotland believed their allegiance was due to the pre-war Government, not to the usurping General Sikorski. In due course, around 590 of these officers were sent to special camps at Rothesay and Tighnabruaich, well away from the rest of the Polish Forces.

Yet it was the Poles' own experience of the undertones of war which was to have a lasting effect on the people of Glasgow. On 2 July 1940, the *Glasgow Herald* published a long article by the city's socialist Lord Provost, Patrick Dollan, in which he calls for a wholesale change in attitude towards the War and an end to defeatism and the 'whisperers of dissension'. The influence of Dollan's contact with the Poles is clear:

The overseas soldiers who have been in our midst, including representatives of all ranks, have expressed their surprise to me that we have not been more vigilant in our ways of living. I am confident that this city, now that it is warned, will become fully conscious of all its responsibilities as the most important industrial centre in the Empire, and give of its whole strength in achieving the triumph that is essential to world peace.

Whatever effect this had on the people of Glasgow was overtaken on the night of 19 July by the appearance of the first German bombers over the city. Three people were killed and 31 injured – many more were to suffer in the following months.

Gallant Allies

The bulk of the Polish Army could not stay long in Glasgow and was soon moved out of the city to tented camps in rural Lanarkshire and Dumfriesshire. Yet not all went to plan. A combination of primitive conditions in the new camps at Crawford, Douglas and Biggar (including the supply of British Army rations) and the Scottish weather began to affect morale. Nevertheless, the Poles had begun to reorganise themselves and two infantry battalions were quickly formed. Although they were still armed with French rifles, enough suitable ammunition had been gathered for the British to regard these troops as fit for immediate operational duty. As for the rest, which included an overwhelming number of officers, the future was less clear. The British saw them as 'a valuable source of labour which can be most usefully employed in defence works and wood-cutting'.[10] Unsurprisingly, this was not what the Polish command had in mind.

Although Churchill and Sikorski had formed an almost instant rapport during the last turbulent days of the campaign in France, and the British premier was effusive in his public (and private) statements expressing support and respect for the Poles' fighting spirit, his senior military commanders were, on the whole, less sure. For one thing, the two armies were strangers to one another, Poland having seen France as its principal military ally, not Britain, who, traditionally, had taken little close interest in the affairs of Central and Eastern Europe. In a force now numbering 1.6 million men, the British Army had only three officers who were qualified as interpreters in Polish. Nevertheless, a joint military agreement had been signed on 5 August which placed the Polish Forces in Scotland under British command, in itself something of a diplomatic achievement. However, it also stated that in contrast to the Polish elements now serving with the Royal Navy and RAF, all Polish land forces, in any single theatre of operations, were to be kept together as a separate formation led by a Polish commander. For the Commander-in-Chief Scottish Command, Lieutenant General R. H. Carrington, this was not particularly welcome news as he prepared his forces for a possible German invasion, especially when it became clear that Sikorski himself planned to take command in Scotland should the Germans arrive. As early as 14 July, Carrington had reported that the Poles' insistence that they could not be deployed in any defensive role until they were re-equipped and reorganised as a single formation meant that 'it would be many months before these Polish troops can be anything but a drain on our resources'.[11]

To understand the British attitude, it is necessary to examine the overall military situation facing Britain in the late summer of 1940. Foremost was the fact that the Fall of France and the Low Countries had given the Germans access to vital ports and air bases from which to launch an invasion of southern Britain, just as the Fall of Norway, a few weeks earlier, enabled them to attack the north of the country. It was even conceivable that a separate invasion could be launched at the Scottish east coast.

Up until this point, neither eventuality had seemed anything other than a very remote possibility in the minds of the British Government, the military, or the general public. After its recent losses in the Norwegian campaign, the Royal Navy, which had previously been the guarantor of Britain's security, now realised that its warships were too vulnerable to air attack to provide unlimited control of the sea, while the resources of the RAF, on paper at least, failed to provide a wholly credible alternative. In light of the highly mobile, mechanised and airborne tactics used by the Germans in Poland, the Low Countries and France, it was also now apparent that the Army's existing (and in part, embryonic) defensive plans, based as they were around static defensive lines and fortifications, were seriously flawed. It was also clear that Britain simply did not have enough troops to even man such defences, given the many directions from which an invasion might come.

To make matters worse, although significant numbers of men had been evacuated from France, the British Expeditionary Force (BEF) had left colossal (and, at this point, irreplaceable) quantities of equipment behind – 88 per cent of its artillery and 93 per cent of its motor vehicles, as well as most of the Army's limited reserves of ammunition.[12] Given the perilously low level of preparedness to which the Army had dropped during the pre-war era of 'disarmament', and the stripping out of the rest of the Army which had been required to kit out the BEF, such losses had a disproportionate impact. The shortage of vehicles, for example, was particularly acute as it threatened to deprive most of the twenty-eight under-strength divisions which now made up Home Forces of any real degree of mobility. With nearly every available factory being turned over to aircraft production, it was also going to be some considerable time before the losses could be replenished. And it was not just military hardware that was in short supply; stocks of construction materials like cement, bricks and steel, required to reinforce existing defences (or build new ones), were also severely limited.

Other factors besides the loss of vital equipment were threatening the Army's future effectiveness. In the face of a fast-moving and aggressive enemy, the British, like their French allies, had been too slow to react and the campaign in France had shown up serious flaws in the way the Army was trained and organised, as well as in its tactics and systems of command. Perhaps more seriously still, it had suffered a massive blow to its self-confidence. A thorough shake-up was required and as a first stage new appointments were made at senior levels. One of the most crucial was a new Commander-in-Chief for Home Forces, General Sir Alan Brooke, whose first step was to abandon any idea of linear defence. Instead, he wanted to concentrate on identifying and defending key landing points, while building up strong mobile reserve forces to launch swift counter-attacks. Rather than let the enemy land and wait for them to attack the fortified 'stop' lines located several miles inland, Brooke reckoned that the only chance of success lay in defeating an invasion either on the beaches or on the landing grounds.

Defending Scotland

In Scotland, the main defence was the partially constructed 'GHQ Line', a supposed barrier which ran up the entire east of Britain about thirty miles inland from the coast. It consisted of a mix of concrete 'pill-box' positions and substantial anti-tank ditches, one of which followed a line right through the Howe of Fife from Kirkcaldy through Ladybank to Newburgh. Other defences had begun to be placed on certain beaches, but work over the previous months had been slow and haphazard. The main problem was a shortage of trained manpower. Although the loss of the famous 51st Division in France was soon made good, on paper at least, by taking the partly trained 9th (Scottish) Division and renaming it, it would be many months before it would match the standard of its predecessor. Of the two other infantry divisions in Scotland in the late summer of 1940, the 46th was described as being 'in a lamentably backward state of training', while the 5th, although in better shape, had just come back from Dunkirk.[13] There were no armoured units whatsoever. The arrival of the Poles, whose numbers were roughly equal to a British division, was therefore timely.

How real then was the threat to Scotland? Clearly, with the Germans only a few miles away across the English Channel, any invasion was most likely to fall on the south-east of England, with the capture of London as its principal objective. Certainly this was the conclusion of GHQ Home Forces, the only doubt being whether the projected main landings would occur on the south or the east coast. If a landing took place anywhere else, it would most likely be as a diversion. While it therefore appeared that Scotland was not in immediate danger of a primary assault, the risk of some kind of ancillary attack still remained. An appreciation prepared by Scottish Command over the coming winter presents a number of possible scenarios, all of which would have existed in the previous autumn.[14] The main object of a German attack would be two-fold; first, 'to contain the military forces on the mainland of Scotland', in other words, to prevent them from reinforcing other parts of the country; second, to threaten either of the Royal Navy's two significant Scottish naval bases – Scapa Flow in Orkney (the Home Fleet's main anchorage) and Rosyth in Fife.

In addition to threatening the naval bases, a landing in the Fife/Angus area could also endanger the main industrial areas of the central belt, therefore occupying all the field formations in Scotland as well as running the risk of necessitating reinforcement from England. The Fife/Angus coast also offered an invader a choice of excellent landing beaches – at St Andrews, Tentsmuir, Buddon Ness, Lunan Bay and Montrose, plus several airfields and a major port facility at Dundee. To compound the threat, the region's hinterland was seen as suitable for the deployment of tanks. In the view of the report, the Fife/Angus area should be the main defensive priority for the Army in Scotland.

As is now well known, the Germans did indeed prepare an invasion of Britain. Operation *Seelöwe* was aimed at the south coast and was due to have begun in mid-September 1940 after the *Luftwaffe* had eliminated Britain's air defences. Its failure to do so is accepted as the main reason for the operation's cancellation even though strong doubts have existed over its chances of success had it gone ahead. The shortage of naval resources, which was one of the main deficiencies in the German plan, would also almost certainly have precluded any major diversionary attacks on places like Scotland's east coast. However, at the time the British did not know this, and indeed had consistently overestimated Germany's naval strength.

It is also interesting to note that an attack on Scotland, either by parachutists, seaborne invasion, or by subversion, was a regular theme in German attempts at strategic deception, made through either propaganda broadcasts or 'special' operations (German intelligence mistakenly believed that extreme nationalist feeling in Scotland offered fertile ground for such efforts). For example, if *Seelöwe* had gone ahead, part of the plan was for a mixed fleet of warships and empty passenger liners to sail from ports in southern Norway two days before the actual invasion. They were to head towards the British coast between Aberdeen and Newcastle only to turn back under cover of darkness, the intention being to fool the British into thinking that an attack in Scotland was imminent.[15] Even if such attempts at deception were only partially successful, given the situation as it was understood at the time, British concerns over the east coast of Scotland would appear to have been justified.

Polish plans

It was essential therefore that the defence of this area be improved and the Poles appeared to offer a useful solution, if only they could be talked round. Yet static defence duties were not the Poles' main priority – what Sikorski wanted was tanks, or at least the promise of them, so that he could begin re-equipping and retraining his forces as offensive modern armoured formations. This conviction was not just the consequence of having been twice defeated by Germany's *panzer* divisions; Sikorski had himself written about the importance of armoured warfare during his exile in France. It was also clear that the liberation of Poland wasn't going to be achieved by an Army solely trained and equipped to defend Scotland.

However, tanks, like most other types of equipment, were in very short supply in 1940, so, after some three-way haggling between Sikorski, the British War Office and Winston Churchill, a compromise was hammered out. From 18 October 1940, the Poles, now reorganised into two brigades, would take over the defence of a stretch of the Scottish east coast from Rosyth on the Firth of Forth north to just beyond Montrose – the vital Fife/Angus area. In return, largely through Churchill's intervention, the Poles were promised a higher priority for new equipment than other British formations carrying out similar defence duties. Sikorski's objective, at least in the short term, was to get all or part of his forces moved away from this static defence role as soon as possible and into that of a mobile reserve in preparation for his long-term goal of the creation of at least one Polish armoured division.

Equipment was just one side of the equation; manpower was also needed. Sikorski's plan was once again to recruit from Polish emigrant communities, this time in Canada and the United States. While he and his government put out diplomatic feelers across the Atlantic, the forces in Scotland, now designated as the 1st Polish Corps, were reorganised in anticipation of a rapid expansion. In addition to the two full-strength brigades, each of around 4,000 men (the 1st Rifle Brigade now based at Cupar in Fife, and 2nd Rifle Brigade, soon to be renamed as the 10th Mechanised Cavalry Brigade, based at Forfar), four 'cadre brigades' were created. These were roughly of battalion strength (around 500 men), but were made up almost entirely of officers, the idea being that they would expand as recruits became available. Another 570 officers were temporarily used to man a group of armoured trains based throughout eastern Britain as part of the invasion defences, while 300 more were 'loaned' to British colonial forces in West Africa.

While the Polish troops moved into their new camps in and around the towns of Fife and Angus, Polish engineers, who had already been working under British command, quickly made an appreciation of the work required to improve the defences of their new area. Originally written in Polish, a rather patchy translation of this report was sent to Scottish Command in early December 1940.[16] Like many early communications between (or about) the two armies, and in contrast to the polished diplomatic language of their respective senior commanders, the report lacks a certain tact. Existing British-built defences are described as having been 'laid out and carried out in haste' and having 'neither a homogeneous nor an accomplished character' – all no doubt true, given the circumstances of May/June when a German assault anywhere in Britain would have been met with the most depleted resistance. The report then stresses various considerations for the defences of the area: the relative shortage of manpower and the need therefore to make the best use of strong defensive positions, the effect winter storms would have on defences placed too near the high tide mark, and the economic use of scarce material resources. It then itemises 57 new emplacements to be built, to Polish designs not British, followed by the moving of 700 anti-tank obstacles to better positions, the laying of 150,000 yards of new barbed wire, the laying of 18,600 mines and the erection of 4,750 anti-aircraft poles.

The British response, both to the criticism and the list of hardware, was mixed. While it was accepted that the defences had to be improved, such steps were 'necessarily limited by considerations of materials and finance'. British designs were also to be adhered to and a conference arranged to decide what work should be planned. The remains of the defences the Poles then went on to construct over the coming months can be seen to this day – for example, anti-tank obstacles along the beaches at St Andrews, the grid layout of anti-aircraft poles still discernible in the sands at low tide off Kinghorn and Burntisland, and concrete emplacements at Fifeness.

One of the most awkward tasks which faced the Polish engineers, but one which was to have beneficial consequences for the Allied war effort, was the need to locate and move hundreds of landmines which had been laid during the immediate invasion scare in May/June, but which had not been adequately mapped. The problem was not confined to the Fife/Angus area and the War Office in London had asked for designs for a new 'detector'. A Polish engineer officer now based in Scotland, Lieutenant J. S. Kozacki, came up with a new electronic design, based on designs begun in Poland. His prototype was immediately accepted, put into production and issued throughout the British Forces as the 'Mine Detector (Polish) Mk I'. Its first major success came in October 1942 when it was used to clear paths through German minefields in preparation for the massive British offensive at El Alamein. A refined version was still in use by the British Army until 1995.[17]

In addition to the engineering works, the Poles were busy drawing up overall defensive plans for their area. The threat was now defined as a likely attack from Norway of around four German divisions. This included an initial airborne assault – a threat which was significantly upgraded following the successful German invasion of Crete in May 1941. The Polish plans are remarkable documents, the meticulous level of detail of which far surpasses similar documents drawn up by adjacent British Forces. After the defence of vulnerable beaches and airfields, the strategic importance of the rivers Forth and Tay was paramount. Every road and rail bridge in the Fife/Angus area was carefully drawn and measured, plus the amount of time and explosive required to destroy it calculated and recorded. A survey was even carried out of all the available boats on the Firth of Tay which could be used to transport troops should the rail bridge be blown. Again, each vessel, right down to the lowliest rowing boats, was sketched, measured and its troop-carrying capacity noted. In the towns and villages, whose actual defence in the event of an invasion would be in the hands of the local Home Guard, all prominent or strategically important buildings were surveyed and sketched, showing the optimum defensive positions and arcs of fire. Such precision was partly a consequence of the Polish Army's cultural roots in the former professional armies of imperial Austria, Russia and Germany, in which many senior Polish officers had begun their careers, and where preparatory 'staff' work was placed among the highest of military virtues. It was also, no doubt, affected by the large numbers of officers now in Scotland with little to occupy them.[18]

Amongst the local population, such energetic preparations provoked occasional bemusement, and even annoyance, as favourite beaches and, more alarming still, golf links, were either dug up or placed 'out of bounds' by these strange foreign soldiers. It took the first attack by German aircraft on the Fife town of St Andrews to convince some local people that the Polish troops truly were helping to defend them from a very real enemy; as a result, relations with the Poles improved dramatically.

The road home

An army can only plan for so many eventualities, and there were other priorities to consider. When not providing manpower to watch the coast, the two full-strength brigades trained hard. Here the Poles were greatly assisted by having their own Polish 'Army cooperation' squadron of the RAF, No. 309, based in Fife. The 10th Brigade in Forfar, already seen by Sikorski as part of his first armoured division in embryo, was particularly active under the hand of its experienced commander, Major General Stanisław Maczek. All that was needed were actual tanks. But Sikorski's repeated attempts to both 'jump the queue' for equipment and to get his forces transferred to the mobile reserve were met with polite refusal by the British. General Alan Brooke, Commander-in-Chief Home Forces, records in his diary for 8 February 1941, the effect of Sikorski's 'charm offensive':

> The lunch had been settled as a bargaining meeting in which the Poles were to try and extract equipment, especially tanks! I was given excellent caviar to soften my heart, but went away with the caviar and my tanks! I did however part with a few light automatics, MGs (machine guns) and Tommy guns.[19]

The same month, the Commander-in-Chief Scottish Command was asked to make an assessment of the Poles' suitability for a new mobile role. His response was that he did not yet consider the Poles to be sufficiently organised, trained, or equipped for such a role. He also felt that they were now so well established in their vital defensive area that to move them would sacrifice all the knowledge and local contacts that they had built up since October. He did, however, concede that a blank refusal would be too discouraging so offered the compromise that 'whenever it is operationally possible, portions of the Polish forces will be withdrawn from their defences for short periods, and exercised in a mobile role in conjunction with British troops'.[20]

Meanwhile, the Polish recruiting campaign in North America was faltering. It became apparent that both the US and Canadian governments were now unwilling to risk depriving their own Armed Forces of any source of manpower. Although around 800 personnel came forward from Polish communities in South America, the overall number was nowhere near what had been hoped for. There was, however, another strand to Polish strategy that did not rely on an influx of new recruits and which required a different type of assistance from her allies – the organisation of a 'Home Army' in preparation for a future uprising against the occupying German and Soviet forces. Vital to this were efficient communications between the Government-in-exile in London and Poland, together with the supply of training and arms. If Britain would supply aircraft and training, partly through the newly formed Special Operations Executive (SOE), the Polish Forces had sufficient personnel in Scotland to carry out this dangerous work.

In early September 1940, a group of officers and NCOs from the 4th Cadre Brigade, then based at Eliock in Dumfriesshire, and waiting in vain for the arrival of Canadian recruits, were sent to Inverlochy Castle near Fort William in the West Highlands. Here they underwent a gruelling special training course in guerrilla warfare in preparation for their return to Poland. Over subsequent months, many more Poles would follow before going on to the RAF's parachute training centre at Ringway near Manchester. From there, these men would await orders to deploy to Poland as couriers, training officers, saboteurs, or local commanders to the *Armia Krajowa*.[21] This special role was also reflected in the transformation in September 1941 of the entire 4th Cadre Brigade (now based in Leven in Fife) into the 1st Independent Polish Parachute Brigade. Unlike the rest of the Polish Forces in Scotland, this brigade did not come under British command. Instead, it remained under the direct control of the Polish Government for possible use in support of an uprising in occupied Poland. Tragically, the Brigade was never deployed in this role and was eventually put under Allied Command for use in the ill-fated operation at Arnhem in 1944.

In June 1941, the issue of the Poles' role was revisited when the War Office's Inspector of Allied Contingents, Lieutenant General Sir George Cory, made a tour of inspection of various Polish units in Scotland. His report includes a strong recommendation that the Poles should now be withdrawn from the beaches and equipped and used as a mobile reserve. This view was based on having seen the two main brigades on exercise. Cory was so impressed by the skill shown by the senior officers and by the aggressive movements of the troops that he thought the Poles were very suitable for, as he put it, 'use as storm troops'.[22]

His recommendation was also influenced by a realisation that the threat of invasion had reduced, even if it had not disappeared completely. Opinions had also developed in Scotland and several Polish formations were now particularly highly regarded. For instance, the 10th Mechanised Cavalry Brigade had, in the opinion of a senior British liaison officer, 'considerably greater value as a mobile striking force than any other Polish unit or formation'.[23] Another War Office report of September 1941 into the practicality of moving the Polish Corps away from Scotland now openly recognised the potential of the Poles:

> They are capable of carrying out mobile offensive operations with considerable initiative, speed and exceptional resource. Morale is undoubtedly high although it is probable that the Poles would display this quality to a greater advantage in offensive roles than those implying a measure of static defence.[24]

Interestingly, amongst the administrative arguments for and against moving the Poles, the report dismisses the assertion that to take them away from an area 'where they are known individually to the local inhabitants and the Home Guard would render them indistinguishable during operations from the enemy'. In other words, if the Poles were not in Scotland, and the Germans landed, nobody (it was argued) would be able to tell friend from foe! Despite such misgivings, the path was at last clear for the Poles to be shifted away from the coastal defences and given the opportunity to start serious training for a new mobile role and the fulfilment of Sikorski's ambition for a Polish armoured division.

Meanwhile, events on the wider stage were about to change the course of the War, as well as Poland's place within it. Germany's invasion of the Soviet Union in June 1941 seemed, at first, to promise the realisation of Sikorski's plans for the forces in Scotland. Since the Soviet invasion of Poland in 1939, thousands of Polish prisoners of war and internees had remained in captivity. If they could now be released, a second Polish Army could be created in Russia. In addition, if sufficient numbers could be brought to the west, the

Polish Forces there could also be rapidly transformed. After protracted negotiations with the Soviet Government, agreement was reached in December 1941 to create a Polish Army of 96,000 men and evacuate a further 25,000 to Britain and the Middle East. Consequently, in February 1942, Sikorski ordered the formation of the 1st Polish Armoured Division in Scotland, to be based around the former 10th Brigade and the recently created 16th Tank Brigade (partly manned by the recruits from South America), with Major General Maczek in command. The new division soon left Angus and its coastal defences and moved to the area of East Lothian and the Scottish Borders to be closer to more suitable training areas. For the Poles it seemed a step nearer home.

Local relations

In October 1941, a year after the Poles had moved to the Fife and Angus area, the senior British liaison officer in Scotland, Colonel G. H. B. De Chair, a former Deputy Assistant Commissioner of the Metropolitan Police, submitted a special report to the War Office on relations between the Poles and the local population – both civil and military.[25] De Chair presents a remarkably candid picture of the situation, both the positive and the negative. According to the report, relations in the country districts and small towns remained very good, although 'the previous cordiality, which bordered on effusiveness, has generally worn off'. The billeting of troops greatly helped relationships, as did the assistance which the Poles had provided at harvest time, given the agricultural labour shortages caused by the War. The response of the local police was also favourable in that 'the general behaviour of the Poles is exceptionally good and that the incidence of misbehaviour, with the exception of traffic offences, is lower in their case than is the case with British troops'.

In the larger towns, like Dundee, and in the mining districts of Fife, things were not so good. In De Chair's view, relations were being undermined, in part, by the large number of officers in the 'cadre' brigades who appeared to have little role. A more serious factor was the entry of the Soviet Union into the War on the Allied side. This led to strong support for the Soviet war effort amongst the left of British politics which drew some of its staunchest support from the mining areas of Scotland. The Poles' general and long-standing anti-Soviet feeling was therefore at odds with much local opinion; it was also out of step with the tone of much official British propaganda, now striving to portray the Soviet Union in as positive a light as possible. De Chair quotes a remark overheard in a mining district: 'Why should we be working all out for Russia, while these bloody Poles walk about with nothing to do.'

Yet it is clear that some of the criticism levelled against the Poles was founded less upon ideological argument than on plain ignorance, prejudice and the continuing paranoia about subversion. By way of example, the report quotes extracts from various anonymous letters sent to the local police:

> Why don't they send them all out to Russia, where they should be, and give our boys a rest? They are going about here like gentlemen, with their kid gloves, brown shoes and cigarette holders. They are not soldiers, they are only fifth columnists or German spies.

The report does, however, criticise the Poles over the 'cadre' brigades and the way some of their officers occasionally conducted themselves:

> These 'officer' units are an embarrassment; they have admittedly been short of equipment, which has restricted their training, and the rather jealously guarded status of the Polish officer has prevented them undertaking certain work which would have kept them occupied as well as being generally helpful. It must be admitted that the personnel of these Brigades are not the best example of Polish officers, and in my opinion the Polish Higher Command has been insufficiently firm with them. Had they exacted a higher standard of efficiency and refused to listen to a series of somewhat puerile complaints about accommodation, which though not perfect has been the best possible, it would have been better for everyone, and I think we should have heard less outside criticism.

Relations between the Poles and British troops were seen, on the whole, as being good, especially where the two armies had worked closely together: 'In such cases British soldiers recognise the inherent value of the Poles as soldiers.' However, there were problems over the Poles' apparent success in attracting local women:

> There is no doubt that the Pole possesses a superior technique with the ladies, and consequently is getting the pick of the basket. This jealousy has, I think, been the origin of a certain number of complaints, many of them anonymous, about the morality of the Poles, but in my submission the standard of morality of the Polish soldier does not fall short of that of the British soldier and opportunities for criticism of the Poles are often looked for and made full use of, for motives not always ethical.

To staff at the War Office, the comparison between Polish morals and those of the ordinary British soldier might have been seen as rather faint praise. There were also problems with the attitudes of 'certain Scottish troops, who are habitually resident in this area'. In the opinion of De Chair, himself not a Scot: 'the Scotchmen regard the Poles as invaders of the stronghold, but I feel it is likely that any troops from elsewhere would be regarded in the same way, though in the case of the Poles this is a particularly unfortunate situation, since they are particularly sensitive and friendly'. The report concludes that the Poles were extremely anxious to behave themselves and be thought well of by their hosts.

Colonel De Chair's report reveals much about the Polish presence in Scotland. The 'effusiveness' of the early months, first seen in Glasgow, can, in part, be explained by a desire on the part of Scots to be seen to be playing their part in the War. Undoubtedly, these early relations were also helped by the sheer novelty of the Polish presence. To many Scots, particularly women, the Poles appeared extraordinarily exotic, especially so given the preponderance of educated young officers. Their generally impeccable manners and behaviour, matched by their elegant appearance, evoked the popular stereotypes of continental European sophistication encouraged by the cinema – a popular film showing in the summer of 1941 was *Dangerous Moonlight*, the unlikely story of a Polish concert pianist who joins the RAF. The film's ultra-romantic theme music entitled the 'Warsaw Concerto' became enormously popular throughout early wartime Britain.

The Poles, being far from home and often lonely as well as bored, were happy to make contact with local people, if only as a means of improving their English. They were also proud of their country and keen that their hosts formed a positive impression of its achievements as well as an understanding of its plight. The War also brought about shifts and relaxations in the rigid social conventions which dominated much of Scottish life, especially as they affected the lives of women. This was certainly a factor in the large number of liaisons and eventual marriages which occurred between Poles and Scots throughout the War. The absence of local men was obviously another factor, as it was in the attitude of some older Scottish women who had sons away at the War. The plight of so many young Poles, separated from their own families, led to a particular feeling of compassion and it was often older women who helped the Poles most, inviting them into their homes even when the political opinions of their husbands were often at odds with the experience of their guests.[26]

It was to build on these informal contacts, that the Scottish–Polish Society was created in 1941. A whole range of activities were initiated, organised by both communities, including lectures, exhibitions, concerts, language classes (particularly for those Scots who had recently married Poles), film shows and, especially around Christmas, events for local children.[27] The propaganda organisations of both governments also produced bilingual books, magazines and films which highlighted both the shared wartime goals of Scotland and Poland, as well as celebrating historical links between the two countries. The education of many of the Polish soldiers had also been interrupted by the

War, so special courses were set up in Scotland's universities so that these students could finish their degrees. The principal of these was the Polish Medical School set up at the University of Edinburgh in February 1941[28]. Other courses were organised in law, veterinary medicine and agriculture, all in preparation for the post-war reconstruction of Poland. Amongst the Polish Forces there were also numerous artists who were often commissioned to produce work which was then presented as tokens of gratitude to various Scottish communities, organisations and individuals. In return, Scottish towns would invest individual Polish units with the right to wear particular Scottish badges. Several Polish regiments were also presented with standards, or flags, by Scottish towns or communities with which they had become closely associated. One Polish battalion even went the length of creating its own pipe band.

Yet the cultural mix within the Polish Forces also affected their relations with local people. While the Poles' strong Roman Catholicism helped bring them closer to the Catholic community in Scotland, it occasionally distanced them from the more entrenched Protestants. The attitude of the Polish authorities towards the many Jews within the Polish Forces occasionally led to sharp criticism in both the British press and by some politicians, particularly later in the War when many Jews wished to transfer to units of the British Army such as the Jewish Brigade. The landed background (and equestrian interests) of some Polish officers also made them many friends amongst the local Scottish gentry. Similarly, while the Poles' strong antipathy towards the Soviet Union made them many enemies on the left, it generally endeared them to the right wing of British politics.

Overall, however, the Scottish response to the Poles in the early years of their presence was positive. Besides the complexities mentioned above, relations were strongly influenced by what many Scots, to this day, like to see as their innate sense of justice. This was matched by a widespread respect for resolute fighters and, perhaps, by a sense of fellow-feeling for a people as romantic as themselves. All of which led many Scots to feel a strong sympathy for the Poles, a people who were clearly the victims of unjust aggression, yet at the same time, just as clearly, were refusing to accept defeat. It was a fortitude that was to be tested even further before any sense of victory came to Poland and her soldiers.

Defeat in victory

It was Poland's tragedy that it was not the men of the Polish Army in exile who finally defeated the Germans in their country, but Stalin's Red Army – the same force which had invaded Poland in September 1939. Sikorski's dream of a Polish Army in Russia had ended when, in contradiction of previous agreements (and after suffering appalling privation), the survivors of the Soviet prison camps were evacuated to the Middle East in August 1942. Welcomed by the British as valuable reinforcements, these troops became part of the 2nd Polish Corps which fought with the Allies in the Italian campaign, most famously at Monte Cassino in May 1944. The Poles therefore knew there would be no free and independent Poland to return to as long as Stalin had power. For the Polish soldiers who had trained for so long in Scotland, and who fought through the Allied campaign in north-west Europe in 1944–5 with the 1st Armoured Division and the 1st Parachute Brigade, this outcome was a bitter blow. They believed they were allies of Britain, they believed their cause was Britain's cause, yet in the end, the Western Allies' reliance on the Soviet contribution to the War forced Poland's fate to the margin – an outcome foreshadowed by the untimely death of General Sikorski in July 1943.

For many in Britain in 1944–5, Poland's future was as yet unclear, and so the rising volume of Polish anguish fell largely on deaf ears. To a minority, who either saw the Soviet Union as a beacon of progress, or for whom the Poles appeared fractious, capricious, or hopelessly romantic, their protests could be dismissed with contempt. However, for some, including many in Scotland who had known the Poles the longest, the outcome was a tragedy, and Britain's acquiescence to it brought both a sense of shame and a realisation that their nation's status as a power in the world had fallen far. For many Scots, fidelity to the Poles was more than just a matter of treaty obligations and alliances; it was a debt of gratitude for a time when Polish soldiers had stood guard on Scotland's shore, ready to give their lives in its shared defence – 'Bonnie Fechters' indeed.

Notes

1 'A bonnie fechter is someone who puts up a determined struggle, often in the course of some kind of campaign [The phrase was popularised by Robert Louis Stevenson in his novel *Kidnapped* when he used it with reference to Alan Breck]', Betty Kirkpatrick, *Concise Dictionary of Scottish Words and Phrases* (Edinburgh, 2006).

2 National Library of Scotland, A8419(1), Minute Book of the Edinburgh Branch of the Scottish–Polish Society, 1941–1958.

3 For a general account of the Polish presence in wartime Scotland see A. Carswell, *For Your Freedom and Ours: Poland, Scotland and the Second World War* (Edinburgh, 1993) and 'Gallant Allies', in *Scots and Slavs: Cultures in Contact 1500–2000*, eds Mark Cornwall and Murray Frame (Newtonville, MA, 2001), pp. 241–67.

4 John Stanley, 'The Polish Military in the Napoleonic Era' in *Armies in Exile*, ed. David Stanfancic (Boulder, CO, 2005), pp. 3–51.

5 P. A. Szudek, 'Sikorski as Strategist and Military Thinker' in *Sikorski: Soldier and Statesman*, ed. Keith Sword (London, 1990), pp. 75–97.

6 T. Kernberg, 'The Polish Community in Scotland' (Unpublished PhD thesis, University of Glasgow, 1990), p. 57.

7 Adam Zamoyski *The Forgotten Few. The Polish Air Force in the Second World War*, (Barnsley, 2010), note on sources p. 221.

8 National Library of Scotland, A11307, transcript of interview with Mr Wladslaw Maronski for the television series *Scotland's War*, 1995. Extract published by permission of STV, Glasgow.

9 National Archives, Kew, WO 199/602, Area Commander Glasgow to HQ Scottish Command, 5 July 1940.

10 National Archives, Kew, WO 199/602, Commander-in-Chief Scottish Command to GHQ Home Forces, 14 July 1940.

11 Ibid.

12 David French, *Raising Churchill's Army: The British Army and the War Against Germany 1919–45* (Oxford, 2000), p. 156.

13 Alex Danchev and Daniel Todman, eds, *War Diaries, 1939–1945, Field Marshal Lord Alanbrooke* (London, 2001), p. 95.

14 Archives of the Polish Institute and Sikorski Museum, London, A.VI.1/15, 'Invasion of Scotland. Appreciation of the Situation of Army Commander, Scottish Command, 1st March 1941.'

15 Peter Fleming, *Invasion 1940* (London, 1958), pp. 111, 235, 241.

16 Archives of the Polish Institute and Sikorski Museum, London, 1/28.XI.Sap, 'Report from C-in-C Polish Engineers'.

17 Mike Croll *The History of Landmines* (London, 1998), p. 54.

18 Archives of Polish Institute and Sikorski Museum, London, A.VI.1/78.

19 Danchev and Todman, *War Diaries*, p. 139.

20 National Archives, Kew, WO 199/602, 10 March 1941: C in C Scottish Command to GHQ Home Forces.

21 Stuart Allan, *Commando Country* (Edinburgh, 2007), pp. 161–6.

22 National Archives, Kew, WO199/602, Inspector of Allied Contingents to Vice Chief of the Imperial General Staff, 25 June 1941.

23 National Archives, Kew, WO199/2675, OC No. 4 Liaison Headquarters to HQ Scottish Command, 21 June 1941.

24 National Archives, Kew, WO199/581, report on 'The effect of moving the Polish Corps from Scotland to Yorkshire', 18 September 1941.

25 National Archives, Kew, WO199/602, OC No. 4 Liaison Headquarters to Inspector of Allied Contingents, War Office, 16 October 1941.

26 Jozef Tarnowski, *Walking with Shadows* (Kirkudbright, 2009), p. 69.

27 See L. Koczy, *The Scottish Polish Society. Activities in the Second World War. An Historical Review* (Edinburgh, 1980).

28 W. Tomaszewski, ed., *The University of Edinburgh and Poland* (Edinburgh, 1968).

10

'God, Honour and Fatherland'

The Poles in Scotland, 1940–1950, and the
Legacy of the Second Republic

Peter D. Stachura

A substantial Polish military presence in Scotland originated with the arrival
in September 1939 in the Firth of Forth of sailors from three Polish destroyers
which had managed to evade the German Navy in the Baltic Sea. The number
of Poles soon increased as a consequence of Poland's defeat by Nazi Germany
and the Soviet Union, the Fall of France – Poland's ally since 1921 – in June
1940, and, to a much lesser extent, of the Polish–Soviet Pact of July 1941.
Through a variety of circuitous routes and circumstances, therefore, around
20,000 Polish soldiers, who were almost entirely male and Catholic, socially
diverse and largely under the age of forty, eventually reached Scotland. They
were then organised into military units under the overall command of their
British allies, except for the 1st Independent Polish Parachute Brigade, created
in September 1941 under Colonel Stanisław Sosabowski, and based in Leven,
Fife. The most important, and ultimately the most successful, unit was the
16,000-strong (by 1944) 1st Polish Armoured Division, set up in February
1942 under General Stanisław Maczek.[1]

The Poles were made to feel most welcome as 'gallant allies' against
Germany by many official bodies, prominent public figures, some aristocratic families of invariably Catholic background, and the general public in
Scotland. A typically warm expression of support was: 'The Poles are a
delightful, naturally charming people . . . Their intense love of music, their
keen sense of humour, and their unquenchable determination to fight on
until freedom is restored . . . these are among their chief qualities.'[2] The
Poles, well-disciplined, well-mannered and smartly turned out, fully recipro-
cated this friendliness, and cut something of a dash, especially with the
ladies. Marriages during and after the war were not uncommon.[3] One Pole
fondly recalled: 'We smiled at this serene country. From the first day, we felt
surrounded by a warm and exciting atmosphere of cordiality. We saw a
country more civilised than many of the continental states, bright, pictur-
esque and extremely attractive.'[4] Among the outstanding manifestations of
this genuine support was the establishment of the Scottish–Polish Society
(1941–8) under the energetic chairmanship of John J. Campbell, a Glasgow
solicitor,[5] and the Polish Medical School in the University of Edinburgh
(1941–9).[6]

The Polish contribution to final Allied victory in Europe was impressive. It had actually begun before the war, when mathematicians in the Polish Cypher Bureau broke the German Enigma Code, passing on the secrets to Britain[7] and France, which was then complemented by the outstanding role of Polish pilots in the Battle of Britain, and by the actions of the Polish Navy and Army in various theatres of conflict, particularly at Monte Cassino in May 1944 and the Falaise Gap in the Normandy Campaign.[8] Moreover, Poland boasted the largest and most effective underground resistance movement in occupied Europe, the *Armia Krajowa* (Home Army), ably supported by some other, smaller groups, like the National Armed Forces (NSZ), culminating in the ill-fated Warsaw Rising in 1944.[9]

None of this, however, counted for anything much with Poland's allies when the major political decisions were taken, especially at the conferences at Tehran in late 1943 and, above all, at Yalta in February 1945. The latter was *the* defining moment for Poland because it endorsed what President Franklin D. Roosevelt and Prime Minister Winston Churchill had conceded previously to Marshal Josef Stalin, that the Soviet Union would be free to dominate Eastern Europe unopposed, including Poland, after the war.[10] In practice, this resulted in the speedy imposition of a Communist regime in Warsaw that was subservient to the Kremlin, accompanied by a wholesale reign of Red Army and NKVD (Soviet Secret Police) terror, and the Soviet Union's annexation of Poland's pre-war Eastern Provinces (*Kresy*), including the historically and culturally Polish cities of Wilno and Lwów. Thus, while a minority of the 249,000 Poles in the UK by 1946 opted to return to this Soviet-controlled Poland – invariably for family rather than political or ideological reasons – and a smaller number emigrated in due course to the United States, Canada, Australia, New Zealand and South America, some 157,000 decided to remain in Britain, mainly in England. Of these, roughly 20 per cent were in Scotland.[11] However, according to the 1951 National Census, that number had declined to 10,603 Polish-born persons in Scotland, who were concentrated in the Central Belt and Fife, reflecting wartime ties and, more mundanely, job opportunities. There were 1,200 Poles in Edinburgh (of whom 895 were male), 1,164 in Glasgow (975 males), 660 in Stirlingshire (608 males), 332 in Kirkcaldy and 309 in Dundee.[12] Unfortunately, for several reasons, the wartime goodwill towards the Poles in Scotland had changed too frequently by then into outright antipathy.

Firstly, after Germany's attack on the Soviet Union, its erstwhile ally, in June 1941, Churchill had made strenuous efforts to bring Stalin into the anti-Nazi coalition, which emerged in 1942 as the 'Grand Alliance'. Thereafter, it became increasingly apparent that Britain and the United States, convinced that Germany could not be defeated without Soviet military assistance, were appeasing Stalin at just about every turn, especially where Poland and Eastern

Europe, in which they had no essential interest, were concerned. Abandoning moral principle and ignoring their own guarantees for a Free Europe after the war, as enunciated in the 1941 Atlantic Charter, they were guided instead by political expediency. The cause of a Free Poland, represented by the Polish Government in London since June 1940, became expendable within the exigencies of *Realpolitik*.

In any case, the Poles had been from the beginning mere junior partners in the Western Alliance, a point which was even more painfully obvious after the death in July 1943 of General Władysław Sikorski, their Prime Minister and Commander-in-Chief. After all, the exiled Polish Government was based in a foreign capital, had only restricted and irregular contact with the homeland, was often riven by acrimonious political factionalism and personality clashes, and could provide only comparatively small numbers of military personnel. Behind the numerous public and private pledges of support for the Poles from both Roosevelt and Churchill, the reality was that the Polish cause, like that of Czechoslovakia in the crisis over the Sudetenland in 1938, mattered little in the eyes of those dictating priorities in international diplomacy as the war wore on. The Polish Government was powerless to oppose successfully developments and decisions inimical to the national interest.[13]

Secondly, this diplomatic balance of power also found expression in the development of public opinion in the Britain. From 1942/3, the Soviet Union was depicted in important parts of the media and by government and political sources in the most favourable terms – hence the manufacture of the cosy image of 'Uncle Joe' Stalin – while the Poles were portrayed more and more as the antithesis: reactionary, troublesome, unrealistic, anti-Soviet and, for good measure, anti-Semitic. These attitudes were disseminated vigorously not only by sections of the British left, that is, by important trade unions, notably the National Union of Mineworkers (NUM) and the Amalgamated Union of Engineering Workers (AUEW),[14] sections of the Labour Party and pro-Soviet, Marxist intellectuals, but also by the Beaverbrook press (not least the *Daily Express*) and the normally stuffy, conservative BBC.[15] It is also relevant to note in this regard the alarmingly deep penetration of both the British and American administrations at the highest levels by Soviet intelligence agencies. The British Foreign Office, the US Department of State, the atomic facility at Los Alamos, the Office of Strategic Services (OSS: the US intelligence agency) and even the White House itself were specially targeted.[16] Despite the support of several right-wing Conservative MPs, the Poles lacked the substantive means, of course, to counter effectively this rising tide of vituperative propaganda.

In certain parts of Scotland, conspicuously in the Central Belt and Fife, was also added, inevitably perhaps, a certain sectarian dimension to this hostility. Although Protestant bigotry of the type crassly exhibited towards Irish Catholic immigrants in the interwar era by the General Assembly of the Church of Scotland (as in 1923 and 1935, for instance) and the powerful Orange Order appears not to have been extended to the overwhelmingly Catholic Poles in the early years of the war, the situation changed at its end,[17] not least in the capital, Edinburgh. Anti-Polish feeling was running so high that the *Scotsman* was moved to issue an appeal for calm, reminding its readers that most of the Poles chose to remain in the city because they 'distrust profoundly, not without reason, the present political dispensation in Poland . . .'[18]

The appeal was not universally heeded. In June 1946, Protestant Action, an extremist body with close links through its disreputable, rabble-rousing leader, John Cormack, to the Orange Order and the NUM, which had already displayed strong opposition to Poles being employed in the mines,[19] organised an anti-Polish rally in Edinburgh's Usher Hall. Its message to the 2,500 people present was that the Poles should return home without delay because they, as 'foreign papists', constituted 'a malign influence' on the 'Scottish way of life', and besides, provided competition for jobs and housing.[20] The Poles' dignified response was to assure their critics that they would 'not stay one day abroad after the real liberation of Poland'.[21]

Tensions were evident in various other parts of the country. In September 1945, in Peebles, a town where, as in the rest of the Borders, the Poles had enjoyed an especially warm welcome earlier in the war, the town council passed a resolution, in response to a petition signed by many of the locals, that the Poles had overstayed their welcome and should return home, especially as they had 'plenty of money to burn, unlike our own fellows'.[22] The following year, miners in Fife organised a 'Poles Go Home' campaign,[23] and the NUM Scottish Executive urged the Government to remove all Polish troops from Scotland. Scottish delegates at an AUEW conference in Blackpool on 26 June 1946 followed suit.[24] The same month, a Labour MP declared in the Commons that the Poles in Scotland were 'greatly resented' and 'unwelcome'.[25] One of the few sources of public support for the Poles came from the Catholic Church, which published a number of statements strongly condemning the attacks on them.[26]

Many Poles subsequently articulated their personal post-war experience of racist-sectarian hostile behaviour in the street from Scots, as well as gratuitous insult and outright discrimination in the workplace from colleagues and employers. One lamented:[27]

I refused to return to Poland after the war because it was under Soviet and Communist control, and I decided to find work in Glasgow. Most of the jobs involved heavy physical work, but I could cope because I was strong . . . Glasgow was a dreary place, and the people were generally distant and uncooperative. Many didn't like us at all. At work, in a machine-tool factory, some of the workers completely ignored me and the few other Poles employed there. We were obviously not wanted, also, apparently, because we were Catholics. At that time, I was renting a shabby, ill-furnished room, and there were neighbours who sometimes shouted at me, 'Go back to Poland!', or, 'When are you going back to your own country?' After a time, I was so pleased to leave 'Bonnie Scotland' behind for a better job in London.

Another told a similar story:[28]

After the war and Yalta, my home was in Russia, so I couldn't return. I found a job on a farm in Stirlingshire, then in a steelworks outside Glasgow . . . Some of the Scottish workers made it clear, usually in small ways, that they didn't like us, me and several other Poles there. I think they were Communists, for they sometimes whistled the *Internationale*, just to annoy us. There was also the religious thing: they said they were Protestants and that we were Catholic. One time, it ended in a fight, which was easy for us, battled-hardened veterans. After that, we were left in peace, though not in a friendly atmosphere.

Thirdly, the social tension generated unavoidably by Britain's painful transition from wartime to peacetime was a significant contributory factor. At a time of severe rationing, widespread poverty, acute housing shortage and uncertainty in the labour market, the country was worn-out, dull, fractious and scarred by xenophobic resentment towards 'bloody foreigners'.[29] The official atmosphere was hardly improved by Foreign Secretary Ernest Bevin's exhortations to the Poles to return home, as their 'patriotic duty', to help rebuild their war-ravaged country.[30]

Moreover, a Gallup Poll in June 1946 revealed that 56 per cent of British people opposed the Government's recent decision to allow Polish troops to remain in the UK,[31] and numerous articles highly critical of the Poles were published in the national and local press.

At various levels and from diverse sources, it is obvious that the Poles in certain parts of post-war Scotland were subjected to overt, populist antagonism, which was reinforced by official attitudes. These included the Government's issue of an Aliens' Registration Certificate, requiring Poles to report weekly to their local police station with details of their address and employment, a somewhat fraught situation that continued for many years thereafter. It also quickly became apparent that, with the exception of some doctors, dentists and architects, very few of them with pre-war Polish professional qualifications would be able, or even allowed by the British authorities, to pursue their career in this country. They, along with former high-ranking professional military personnel, who were usually older, had to endure downward social and professional displacement in poorly paid, low-status, unskilled manual work.[32]

The post-war challenge confronting the Poles, therefore, was how to find a place in a society blighted by austerity and other inauspicious historical baggage. It begs the leading question: what were the principal immediate and longer-term formative influences on these Poles, as distinct from organisational initiatives, such as the British Government's introduction of the Polish Resettlement Corps (PRC, 1946–9), designed to facilitate their demobilisation and integration into the workforce?

For a start, the Poles' legitimate pride in their military contribution to Allied victory in 1945 served as a positive platform. King George VI, who had visited Polish troops in Scotland in March 1941 with Queen Elizabeth, expressed his 'sincere admiration' for 'the courageous Polish soldiers, sailors and airmen' and 'their bravery and sacrifice'.[33] Indeed, they were encouraged to believe by senior Army figures, notably General Władysław Anders, that they would probably be recalled to the colours in the near future in a war against the Soviet Union as part of a new Western Alliance within the context of the intensifying Cold War. The tantalising prospect was extended to them that they would soon have the opportunity of liberating their beloved Poland from the nefarious Soviet Communist yoke.[34] Thus, their sojourn in Britain was to be viewed as merely temporary.

An equally significant influence was the Polish soldiers' profound sense of betrayal over Yalta: they had not fought for a Soviet-dominated, Communist Poland, or, of course, for the loss of the Eastern Provinces of the Second Republic. In fact, Poland, despite being on the 'winning' side of the war, had ended up a principal 'loser'. As one Pole recalled bitterly: 'Settlement in Britain was made all the more difficult by our feeling of betrayal . . . We felt extreme bitterness towards our allies, who recognised the puppet Polish government which was killing people who'd fought for the freedom of our country . . . We were completely lost and this didn't help us to settle.'[35]

The Polish Government-in-Exile immediately and vociferously denounced Yalta as an unacceptable sell-out,[36] a stance it resolutely adhered to right up to December 1990, when it handed over the Seals of Office of the Polish Republic to Lech Wałęsa, the first, freely elected President of post-Communist Poland. Apart from a handful of renegades and Communist sympathisers, all Poles in Scotland (and Britain) remained loyal to the exiled Government's outlook, which was reinforced by their anger at further post-war humiliations at the hands of their erstwhile allies: the withdrawal in July 1945 by the British and American Governments of their recognition of the exiled Government in favour of the new Warsaw regime, and Britain's accession to Stalin's demand that Polish troops be excluded from the Grand Victory Parade in London in June 1946. Also, the Polish Consulate in Glasgow from 1946 was staffed mainly by Communists, including Consul Emil Woynarowski and his successor, Józef Teliga, some of whom were not even Polish, but Soviet agents who engaged in intensive political propaganda among former Polish soldiers.[37]

From a more positive direction, the leadership and role provided by the most important voluntary lay Polish organisation, the Polish Ex-Combatants' Association (*Stowarzyszenie Polskich Kombatantów*: SPK), was crucial. It has to be borne in mind that the traditional ruling élites of pre-war Poland – the large landowners, industrialists, the armed forces, the Catholic clergy and the educated, professional middle classes – had been decimated by Nazi and Soviet mass murder, deportation, imprisonment, as well as racial and class discrimination, a tyranny that continued in Poland after the war under Soviet and Communist auspices. The Katyń massacre in 1940 of some 25,000 Polish officers and others of the pre-war élites, which was carried out on Stalin's orders by the NKVD, symbolised the enormity of the catastrophe that had befallen Poland.[38] Fortunately, a large number of survivors from the most able groups of the nation were now exiled in Britain and became involved in the SPK as a way of sustaining the traditional values and heritage of their country.

Formed in May 1946 in London from several existing Polish military self-help groups, the SPK had established within five years 202 thriving, well-organised branches across the UK with some 14,500 members, a fifth being women.[39] In Scotland, branches appeared, for example, in Edinburgh, Glasgow, Perth, Aberdeen, Dundee, Galashiels, Kirkcaldy, Falkirk and Alloa.[40] While the Edinburgh branch enjoyed the patronage from the outset of the legendary General Maczek, who had settled in the city with his family, the Glasgow branch, established on 2 November 1947 under chairman Zbigniew Rażniewski, had the largest membership in Scotland.[41] The SPK not only initiated a host of Polish social, economic, cultural, charitable, welfare, sports and educational activities (for example, the Polish Saturday Schools), but also provided a vital patriotic point of reference that was inextricably connected to both the Catholicism and anti-Communism/Sovietism of its members. And, although above émigré party politics, the SPK's political mission was clear and unambiguous: uncompromising repudiation of Yalta, and no recognition, therefore, of the illegitimate, Soviet-imposed Communist regime in Warsaw. Its unshakeable objective was to work towards the regaining of Poland's freedom, independence and sovereignty, and the recovery of the Eastern Provinces. This was not so much an outlook as a veritable article of faith.

Furthermore, the SPK embodied the intrinsic ethos of the Second Republic that had been embraced enthusiastically by the great majority of its ethnic Polish citizens before the war, regardless of their party political loyalties, and despite the bitter divisions between the two most prominent political camps, the nationalist *Endecja* and the followers of Marshal Józef Piłsudski. They could all now subscribe to a common cause. Accordingly, any understanding of the post-war development of the Polish community in Scotland, and indeed in the UK as a whole, must take due account of the indispensable longer-term role played by the legacy of the Second Republic, and the main-tenance and perpetuation of that legacy after 1945 by, above all, the SPK.

It has to be admitted, however, that the historiography of the Second Republic has been largely unfavourable, for a number of reasons, not least the Soviet/Polish Communist disparagement of so-called 'white, bourgeois Poland', whose genesis lay in the period following the end of World War I, with particular reference to the defeat of the Bolsheviks by the Polish Army in 1920.[42] Thwarted in their plans to destroy Poland's newly regained independ-ence and to extend their revolutionary ideology into the heart of Europe, the Bolsheviks never forgot or forgave this momentous setback. Stalin personified this pernicious attitude, which was simply incorporated later into Soviet interpretations of Poland and her history in the wake of their control of the country after 1944–5.[43]

Moreover, the puppet regime the Soviets installed in Warsaw, soon to be termed 'People's Poland', danced obediently to the Soviet historical tune and promoted an unremittingly negative view of the Second Republic. 'People's Poland' claimed to be a new and better Poland, even if, in stark reality, it was nothing of the sort. Much of historical importance in the twentieth century, such as the Polish–Bolshevik War of 1919–20, the 1921 Treaty of Riga that had demarcated Poland's eastern frontier, the Nazi–Soviet Pact of 1939, the mass deportations to the Gulag, and Katyń – what came to be termed the 'Blank Spots' – was either ignored, manipulated, or wantonly falsified in order to comprehensively blacken the Second Republic's reputation:[44] it was depicted as having been reactionary, quasi-Fascist, priest-ridden, backward and anti-Semitic. This erroneous view was, and continues to be, embraced by many Marxist and left-wing/liberal historians of Poland in the West, espe-cially in the United States.[45]

The historiography began to change noticeably only after the collapse of the Warsaw regime in 1989/90, though not as quickly or as extensively in Poland as might have been anticipated. After all, two post-war generations of Poles had been educated in a totalitarian system, while regime-change did not result, unfortunately, in a clear-out of Communists from the most influential institutions of the Polish state, including not only the universities and schools, but also central and local government, the media, foreign service, judiciary, the army, security services and some political parties.[46] Instead, the truth was pursued by a few courageous and talented Polish historians, such as Wojciech Roszkowski,[47] and, in due course, by the newly founded Institute of National

Remembrance (IPN), but mainly by a small group of determined historians, usually of Polish background, in the West, employing proper methods and criteria of historical enquiry, and untainted by political or ideological bias.

As a result, they have delved into archival records in Poland and abroad, unearthing new and significant material. For instance, it has now been revealed that British consular and later embassy officials in Warsaw frequently produced favourable reports on Poland for the Foreign Office. Thus, Mr Frank Savery commended the economic and social progress in Poland's provinces, notably since the Piłsudski coup of 1926.[48] Another official noted Poland's fair treatment of her ethnic minorities,[49] and, against a background of alleged anti-Semitism, the position of the Jews was specifically mentioned: 'The Jews are vastly better off than they were under the Russian empire, and they know it.'[50]

The same report highlights that Poland has 'a new spirit of order and efficiency' in 'an atmosphere of prosperity, contentment and confidence'. Also, Sir William Erskine, the British Ambassador in Warsaw, wrote of the Poles' response to the Great Depression: 'The Polish people generally have shown the same surprising fortitude in adversity . . . and merit one's admiration for the manner in which they have proved their determination to tighten their belts and withstand the crisis.'[51] Nor were the British alone in expressing positive views. The Italian Foreign Minister, Dino Grandi, formed 'distinctly favourable impressions of Poland' during an official visit, adding, tellingly, that 'he had found Poland a more sober, steady and stable country than he had been led to believe'.[52]

The overall outcome of this fresh approach has been to allow historians to produce an eminently more credible re-interpretation of the Second Republic which, while not overlooking its undeniable weaknesses and failures, such as the political and governmental instability that prevailed until the mid-1920s, has at last emphasised its many positive features.[53] There was a reasonable degree of economic growth, despite the disastrous legacy of the long partitionist period, the physical ravages of World War I, the retardative role of an overblown and outdated agricultural sector, hyperinflation in the early 1920s, a protracted tariff war with Germany (1925–34), and the Great Depression. By the late 1930s, partly as a result of state intervention, which included the creation of the new, bustling Baltic port of Gdynia and the Central Industrial Region, major spheres of the economy were showing renewed growth. Prices stabilised, some real wages rose, the budget was returned to surplus in 1938, transport and communications were improving and living standards were beginning to improve, particularly in western Poland. These advances were assisted by the creation of modern administrative, judicial and public welfare systems at national and local levels, and by the successful launch of a new currency (złoty).[54]

In addition, it was not surprising, in view of the Poles' long-standing regard for education and learning, and the patriotic desire to build up and strengthen the country, that the means were found to bring about an impressive expansion of the entire educational system. Thousands of new schools, teachers and university students, drawn from a widening social spectrum, appeared, prompting a dramatic fall in what had been in 1918 high illiteracy rates, especially in the former Russian partition. The universities in Warsaw, Cracow, Poznań, Lwów and Wilno, in particular, were rapidly earning an international reputation as centres of excellence, above all in mathematics, philosophy and literature. Allied to this was the development of a vibrant cultural scene, centred in the attractively revitalised capital, Warsaw, and incorporating both conservative and progressive movements, the latter influenced in part by corresponding trends in Weimar Germany. The Skamander group of poets and the challenging works of Stanisław Ignacy Witkiewicz ('Witkacy') are but a few prominent examples.[55]

It is also now more widely acknowledged that the Second Republic was characterised by a high standard of public and private morality. Although there were several notorious episodes of financial corruption, incompetence and nepotism involving governmental and political figures, as well as examples of blatant electoral vote-rigging, the overall picture of public life compared favourably with that in most other contemporary European countries. Criminal gangs existed in Warsaw and some other major cities, but the incidence of crime was, on the whole, low. The family unit, championed by the Catholic Church as the essential basis of society, was very much the norm and constituted in an otherwise often economically unstable period a solid point of moral and ethical reference in everyday life. As the 1928 programme of the nationalist movement (*Endecja*) enunciated:

> The National Democratic Party adopts the principle that Roman Catholicism should occupy the leading role in Poland . . . The laws and actions of the state, particularly regulations concerning the family and marriage, which are the foundation of society, must conform to the principles of Roman Catholicism, whose principles must also pervade public life in Poland.[56]

The elderly and authority were respected within a wider social environment of civility, good manners, and a gentry-derived (*Szlachta*) appreciation of quality and style. 'Progressive' ideas regarding divorce, abortion and sexual licence attracted minimal popular sympathy because these were perceived as pernicious and 'un-Polish'. In short, the Second Republic had a definite, admirable moral compass.

One of the most sensitive and contentious aspects of the Second Republic concerns its relationship with the approximately one-third of its population of 32 million, according to the National Census of 1931, which was not ethnically Polish, including the 3.5 million Jews (by 1939, when the total population had risen to 35 million).[57] The old historiographical consensus, that the German, Ukrainian, Byelorussian and Jewish minorities were discriminated against, even persecuted, by the Polish state, is no longer tenable.[58] More recently available empirical evidence has uncovered a quite different story. For instance, the large majority of Germans and the many Ukrainians who had made no secret of their resentment at being Polish citizens following the Treaty of Versailles in 1919, were allowed, nonetheless, wide-ranging constitutional and legal freedoms to pursue their own activities and interests, whether that entailed religious, economic, educational, press, sports, cultural, or even political matters.[59] Neither the German minority's staunch Protestantism nor its subsequent mass susceptibility to Nazism, or the involvement of some Ukrainians in underground anti-Polish terrorism, persuaded the Government of the Second Republic to alter that munificent prescription.

The same latitude, and much more, was accorded the Jews, with the result that they were able to develop as the largest and most innovatively creative Jewish community in Europe before the War.[60] This is not to deny the regrettable fact that in interwar Poland anti-Semitism existed, as it did in just about every other European country, including Britain, but its prevalence in Poland has undoubtedly been exaggerated. Many memoirs written by both Polish Catholics and Jews stress the peaceful, if separated, co-existence between them.[61] What is truly remarkable is the general tolerance, moderation and fairness displayed towards all these minorities by the Second Republic. It invariably chose to disregard the provocation of their all too frequent, ill-concealed animosity, propensity to confrontation and recalcitrance, even, indeed, their rejection of the very notion of Poland's right to independent nationhood. In fact, too many of them, it appears, were disloyal citizens of the Republic.

Perhaps the most salient and lasting achievement of the Second Republic was its nurturing among ethnic Poles of a profound, passionate but wholesome belief in and love of their country. Their patriotism during the nineteenth century, when there was no longer a Polish state, had been sustained through their language, culture and religion, and after independence had been recovered in 1918, it provided the most powerful ingredient of a maturing national consciousness. Institutionally, this patriotism was embodied above all by the Catholic Church and the revered Polish Army – the 'school of the nation' – particularly following its stunning victory over the Soviet Bolsheviks in 1920 and instrumental role in securing Poland's borders in a series of enforced wars in the early 1920s with her neighbours.[62] The Army's Commander-in-Chief, Marshal Piłsudski, was, and remains to this day, a national hero and father-figure for many Poles, personifying the national spirit of pride, vitality and creativity, and the accomplishment, against the odds, of establishing Poland's status as a viable and respected independent state in the comity of European nations.[63] It was this Catholic-inspired patriotism, which had been further intensified in response to the overt enmity of Germany and Soviet Russia in the interwar period, as well as by the unprecedented tribulations suffered by Poles and Poland during and after World War II, that informed the SPK's *raison d'être* in a foreign, somewhat unpropitious and generally unwelcoming environment in post-war Scotland.

In conclusion, the Second Republic can now be more accurately depicted as an era of relatively substantial achievement and fulfilment, which, in turn, explains why, after 1945 in Scotland, the SPK could invoke the best tradi-tions of the Republic. Its steadfast Catholicism,[64] legitimate pride and unquenchable patriotism – expressed in its inspirational motto, 'God, Honour and Fatherland' (*Bóg, Honor i Ojczyzna*) – formed the basis of its quest to help construct a settled and successful Polish community in Scotland. Integration into indigenous society, however, had to be complemented by the maintenance of the Poles' own cherished national identity. Over the longer term, the SPK, by remaining unswervingly loyal to its founding principles, was able to make a significant contribution to the eventual demise of the Communist regime in Warsaw and the re-establishment of a Poland once more free and independent, though not yet in repossession of the Eastern Provinces.

Notes

1 P. A. Szudek, 'The First Polish Armoured Division in the Second World War', in *Themes of Modern Polish History*, ed. P. D. Stachura (Glasgow,1992), pp. 33–64; Z. Mieczkowski, ed., *The Soldiers of General Maczek in World War II* (London and Warsaw, 2004); on Maczek, P. D. Stachura, *Poland in the Twentieth Century* (London, 1999), pp. 83–96.

2 *Scotsman*, 14 November 1940. Also see *Scotsman*, 17 April 1940; *Glasgow Herald*, 8 and 9 July 1940.

3 J. Gula, *The Roman Catholic Church in the History of the Polish Exiled Community in Britain (1939–1950)* (London, 1993), p. 161.

4 *Glasgow Herald*, 20 August 1940.

5 Archive of the Research Centre for Modern Polish History (ARCMPH), *The Thornton Private Papers*, Membership Registers of the Scottish–Polish Society, 1941–8. By 1945, the Society had nearly 50 branches with 9,800 members. For an outline history, L. Koczy, *Kartki z Dziejów Polsko-Szkockich: Nakładem Społeczności Polskiej w Szkocji* (London,1980).

6 W. Tomaszewski, *The University of Edinburgh and Poland* (Edinburgh 1968), and W. Tomaszewski, ed., *In The Dark Days of 1941: Fifty Years of the Polish School of Medicine, 1941–1991, The University of Edinburgh, Jubilee Publication* (Edinburgh, 1992).

7 See Peter Wescombe's interesting letter in *The Times*, 3 September 2009, p. 27.

8 A. Zamoyski, *The Forgotten Few: The Polish Air Force in World War II* (London, 1995); L. Olson, and S. Cloud, *For Your Freedom and Ours* (London, 2003); E. Maresch, ed., *Polish Forces in Defence of the British Isles, 1939–1945* (London, 2006), especially pp. 92–107; K. K. Koskodan, *No Greater Ally: The Untold Story of Poland's Forces in World War II* (Oxford, 2009); J. Garliński, *Poland in the Second World War* (London, 1986), pp. 139–48, 230–62, 300–20.

9 *Armia Krajowa w Dokumentach 1939–1945*, 6 vols (London,1970–1989); B. Chiari, ed., *Die Polnische Heimatarmee: Geschichte und Mythos der Armia Krajowa seit dem Zweiten Weltkrieg* (Munich, 2003), pp. 111–49, 169–86, 255–74; M. J. Chodakiewicz, *Narodowe Siły Zbrojne: 'ZĄB' Przeciw Dwu Wrogom* (Warsaw, 1999), pp. 183–230.

10 P. D. Stachura, 'Towards and Beyond Yalta', in *The Poles in Britain, 1940–2000: From Betrayal to Assimilation*, ed. P. D. Stachura (London, 2004), pp. 6–20; for Roosevelt's role *vis-à-vis* the Poles, P. D. Stachura, 'Rozczarowanie i Zdrada: Franklin Delano Roosevelt i Polacy (1941–1945)', *Glaukopis: Pismo Społeczno-historyczne*, numer 7–8 (2007), pp. 124–43.

11 *House of Commons Debates (HCD)*, fifth Series, vol. 427, column 790; J. Zubrzycki, *Polish Immigrants in Britain: A Study of Adjustment* (The Hague, 1956), p. 62.

12 National Archives of Scotland (NAS), GRO 006/00289, Census of Scotland 1951, vol. 3, General Volume (Edinburgh, HMSO, 1954), Table 36, pp. 55–6; vol. 1, Part 1, City of Edinburgh, Table 30, p. 30; Part 2, City of Glasgow, Table 16, p. 32; Part 4, City of Dundee, Table 16, p. 34; Part 17, County of Fife, Table 16, p. 36; Part 31, County of Stirling, Table 16, p. 31.

13 P. D. Stachura, *Poland, 1918–1945: An Interpretive and Documentary History of the Second Republic* (London, 2004), pp. 164–6, 167–71.

14 On anti-Polish sentiment in the trade unions, see National Archives, Kew (NA), A, FO371/56630, Joint Consultative Committee, 59th Meeting, 17 May 1946; and *Report of Proceedings at the 78th Annual Trades Union Congress* (London, 1946), pp. 357–64; *The Labour Party, Report of the 44th Annual Conference* (London, 1945), p. 108.

15 K. Sword, *The Formation of the Polish Community in Great Britain, 1939–50* (London, 1989), p. 261; *Glasgow Herald*, 8 January 1943 and 1 May 1944.

16 J. E. Haynes, H. Klehr, and A. Vassiliev, *Spies: The Rise and Fall of the KGB in America* (New Haven, 2009), pp. 195–291; C. Andrew and V. Mitrokhin, *The Mitrokhin Archive: The KGB in Europe and the West* (London, 2000), pp. 55–179.

17 ARCMPH, *Thornton Private Papers*, correspondence file, letter of 19 March 1947 to John J. Campbell; T. Kernberg, 'The Polish Community in Scotland' (PhD thesis, University of Glasgow, 1990), pp. 231ff; Stachura, *Poland in the Twentieth Century*, pp. 117–18.

18 *Scotsman*, 22 August 1945.

19 R. Page Arnot, *A History of the Scottish Miners* (London, 1955), p. 271; T. Gallacher, *Edinburgh Divided: John Cormack and No Popery in the 1930s* (Edinburgh,1987); *Glasgow Herald*, 14 June 1946, report on anti-Polish speeches at the Scottish NUM annual conference in Rothesay on 13 June 1946.

20 ARCMPH, A.4: corroborated eye-witness statement to author, 14 June 2003.

21 Ibid., *Thornton Private Papers*, statement by the Polish Press Agency, 'To Our Scottish Hosts', 8 August 1946.

22 *The Voice of Poland*, 18, 9 September 1945, p. 14.

23 D. M. Henderson, ed., *The Lion and the Eagle: Reminiscences of Polish Second World War Veterans in Scotland* (Dunfermline, 2001), p. 25; note the proliferation of Orange and Masonic lodges in coalmining areas, where membership of the lodge and the NUM often went hand in hand – an incongruous *mélange* of the Red and Orange: see G. S. Walker, 'The Orange Order in Scotland between the Wars', *International Review of Social History*, 28, no. 2 (1992), pp. 193, 196.

24 *Scotsman*, 6 August 1946; *Glasgow Herald*, 27 June 1946.

25 *HCD*, fifth series, vol. 423, column 2233, 6 June 1946.

26 ARCMPH, *Thornton Private Papers*, correspondence file, memorandum of 14 February 1949 from the Catholic Council for Polish Welfare, London; the *Tablet*, 7 May 1949.

27 ARCMPH, A.1., author's interview with Zbigniew Bienek (pseudonym), 24 April 2003. For more examples of anti-Polish sentiment in Scotland and the UK, see B. J. Wojciechowska, ed., *Waiting To Be Heard: The Polish Christian Experience Under Nazi and Stalinist Oppression, 1939–1955* (Bloomington, Indiana, 2008), pp. 275–83, 285–318, 362.

28 ARCMPH, A.2., author's interview with Stanisław Grabowski (pseudonym), 10 September 2005.

29 D. Kynaston, *Austerity Britain, 1945–51* (London, 2008), pp. 93–128, 270–77; C. A. Holmes, *A Tolerant Country? Immigrants, Refugees and Minorities in Britain* (London, 1991), p. 104.

30 An example in *HCD*, vol. 420, column 1877, speech, 20 March 1946.

31 Sword, *Formation*, pp. 472–7.

32 S. Patterson, 'The Polish Exile Community in Britain', *The Polish Review*, 6, no. 3 (1961), p. 221; T. Smith, and M. Winslow, *Keeping the Faith: The Polish Community in Britain* (Bradford Heritage Recording Unit, Bradford, 2000), p.100; T. Ziarski-Kernberg, *The Polish Community in Scotland* (Sussex, 2000), p. 123.

33 Archive of The Polish Institute and Sikorski Musuem (PISMA), A.48. Z.II, King George to Polish President Władysław Raczkiewicz, 8 May 1945.

34 W. Anders, *An Army in Exile: the Story of the Second Corps* (London, 1949), pp. 349–50; J. Pyłat, J. Ciechanowski, and A. Suchcitz, eds, *General Władysław Anders: Soldier and Leader of the Free Poles in Exile* (London, 2008), pp. 183–90; S. Patterson, 'The Poles: an Exile Community in Britain', in *Between Two Cultures: Migrants and Minorities in Britain*, ed. J. L. Watson (Oxford, 1977), p. 216.

35 Smith and Winslow, *Keeping the Faith*, p.76.

36 Z. C. Szkopiak, ed., *The Yalta Agreements. Documents prior to, during and after the Crimea Conference 1945* (London, 1986), pp. 30–1, declaration of 18 February 1945.

37 ARCMPH, *Thornton Private Papers*, correspondence file, letters between John J. Campbell, H. Przyborowski and Frank Harrod, July 1949; *Glasgow Herald*, 22 June 1946; T. Kondracki, *Historia Stowarzyszenia Polskich Kombatantów w Wielkiej Brytanii* (Warsaw, 1996), p. 381.

38 A. M. Cienciala, N. S. Lebedeva and W. Materski, eds, *Katyn: A Crime Without Punishment* (New Haven and London, 2007), pp. 121–205, 229–64; G. Sanford, *Katyn and the Soviet Massacre of 1940: Truth, Justice and Memory* (London, 2005), pp. 124–233; K. Kersten, 'The Terror, 1949–1954', in *Stalinism in Poland, 1944– 1956*, ed. A. Kemp-Welch (London, 1999), pp. 78–93.

39 A. Suchcitz, *The Polish Ex-Combatants' Association in Great Britain 1946–2003* (London, 2003), pp. 10–11.

40 PISMA, A.XX. 1/1: SPK, Komitet Wykonawczy, London, 5 March 1947, Provisional Regulations for SPK branches in Scotland, and list of SPK branches, 9 May 1947; and list of branches in Scotland, 21 July 1947. My thanks to Dr Andrzej Suchcitz and Mr J. M. Bernasiński for providing documents and other information concerning the SPK.

41 ARCMPH, A.3: The Poles in Glasgow, 1945–90: Miscellaneous data; Kondracki, *Historia*, pp. 381–2.

42 P. D. Stachura, 'The Second Republic in Historiographical Outline', in *Poland Between The Wars*, ed. P. D. Stachura (London, 1998), pp. 1–12.

43 E. K. Valkenier, 'Stalinizing Polish Historiography: What Soviet Archives Disclose', *East European Politics and Societies*, 7, no. 1 (winter 1993), pp. 109–34.

44 G. C. Malcher, *Blank Pages: Soviet Genocide against the Polish People* (Woking: Pyrford Press, 1993); A. Ajnenkiel, 'Blank Pages in Polish History', *The Polish Review*, 33, no. 3 (1988), pp. 333–41.

45 The most notorious recent example is J. T. Gross, *Neighbors: The Destruction of the Jewish Community in Jedwabne, Poland* (Princeton, 2001), which has been comprehensively discredited by M. J. Chodakiewicz, *The Massacre in Jedwabne, July 10, 1941: Before, During, and After* (New York, 2005).

46 M. J. Chodakiewicz, 'Transformation', unpublished paper, 11 November 2009, kindly provided by the author; Polish version, 'Transformacja: Przekształcenie ku ocaleniu', in *Dwie koncepcje państwa* (forthcoming, Warsaw, 2010). See also A. Dudek, *Reglamentowana rewolucja: Rozkład dyktatury komunistycznej w Polsce, 1988–1990* (Cracow, 2004). Despite regime-change, every Polish Consul General in Scotland from 1990 until the present was a member of, or at least very closely associated with, the former Polish Communist Party (PZPR).

47 For example, his *Historia Polski, 1914–2000* (Warsaw, PWN, 2001), and *Landowners in Poland, 1918–1939* (Cambridge, 1991).

48 NA, FO 417/24, Document no. 24, report of 14 June 1929.

49 Ibid., FO 417/27, Document no. 44, Sir William Erskine to Arthur Henderson, British Foreign Secretary, Warsaw, 2 July 1930.

50 Ibid., FO 417/22, Document no. 38, report by R. C.Thomson, 23 November 1927.

51 Ibid., FO 417/33, Document no. 32, report to Foreign Secretary Sir John Simon, 24 October 1933.

52 Ibid., FO 417/27, Document no. 42, report of 20 June 1930.

53 English-language examples include P. Latawski, ed., *The Reconstruction of Poland, 1914–23* (London, 1992), and Stachura, *Poland, 1918–1945*.

54 Stachura, *Poland*, pp. 45–52.

55 C. Miłosz, *A History of Polish Literature* (London, 1969); B. Carpenter, *The Poetic Avant-Garde in Poland, 1918–1939* (Seattle, 1983); Stachura, ibid., pp. 101–6.

56 *Gazeta Warszawska*, 16 October 1928. Similar viewpoint in R. Dmowski, *Kościół, Naród, Państwo* (Warsaw, 1927), p. 25; see also K. Krasowski, *Episkopat katolocki w II Rzeczpospolitej* (Poznań, 1992), pp. 176ff.

57 E. Szturm de Sztrem, ed., *Statistical Atlas of Poland* (London, 1942), pp. 19–31.

58 See S. Horak, *Poland and Her National Minorities, 1919–1939* (New York, 1961); A. Micewski, *Z geografii politycznej II Rzeczpospolitej* (Warsaw, 1964); J. Tomaszewski, *Ojczyzna nie tyłko Polaków: Mniejszości narodowe w Polsce w latach 1918–1939* (Warsaw, 1985).

59 Stachura, *Poland Between the Wars*, pp. 67–73, and pp. 79–86 for full bibliographical references.

60 N. Davies, *God's Playground: a History of Poland*, vol. 2, *1795 to the Present* (Oxford, revised edition 2005), pp.190–93, 302; M. J. Chodakiewicz, *Żydzi i Polacy 1918–1955* (Warsaw, 2000), pp. 38–77, 82–91, 98–105.

61 For example: T. S. Hamerow, *Remembering a Vanished World: A Jewish Childhood in Interwar Poland* (Oxford, 2001); E. Hoffman, *Shtetl: The History of a Small Town and an Extinguished World* (London, 1998); A. Tarnowski, *The Last Mazurka: A Tale of War, Passion and Loss* (London, 2006).

62 See A. Zamoyski, *Warsaw 1920: Lenin's Failed Conquest of Europe* (London, 2008); N. Davies, *White Eagle, Red Star: The Polish–Soviet War, 1919–20* (London, 1983).

63 NA, FO 417/23, Document 1, report of 26 December 1927 from R. A. Leeper to Austen Chamberlain, British Foreign Secretary, on Piłsudski's stature among Poles. See also W. Jędrzejewicz, *Piłsudski: A Life for Poland* (New York, 1982), pp. 370–4, and H. L. Englert, *Józef Piłsudski: Komendant – Naczelnik Państwa Pierwszy Marszalek Polski* (London, 1991).

64 The Polish Catholic Mission in Scotland was set up in 1948 with several Polish priests, including Father Ludwik Bombas in Edinburgh and Father Jan Gruszka in Glasgow (ARCMPH, *Thornton Private Papers*, correspondence file, 1948–9).

11   Press Reception of Polish Migrants in Scotland, 1940–2010

Rachel Clements

This chapter considers the reception of Polish migrants in Scotland by the Scottish press during and around the end of World War II. An analysis of the reception of the British press, following the more recent wave of Polish migration subsequent to the enlargement of the European Union in 2004, ensues. Particular reference is made to representations in the Scottish press which make significant departures from those typical in the British press. Such commonalities and differences in the representation of Polish migrants are subsequently discussed, as are possible reasons for these similarities and variations. The chapter examines the type of reception Poles received, and the significant moments when reception changed in relation to political and economic influences.

While it is recognised that press reception is not an accurate reflection of public attitude, as is discussed shortly, analysis of the press still offers considerable value to migration and historical studies. Press analysis in migration studies aims to retrieve and evaluate the historically documented context from which migrants are hosted. By focusing on the Scottish specific account of this context we are able to identify hegemonic ruptures from the British frame, reflecting on Scotland's relatively recent devolution. Themes emerging include Scottish multiculturalism and citizenship. Initially, this analysis began as a contextual precursor to my doctoral research on Polish migration to Glasgow, Scotland. While my interests and research have consequently evolved into a study of Polish families in Newcastle Upon Tyne, England, representations of Polish migrants in the press continue to inform my understanding of Polish reception at large.

Research methodology

As Stevenson and Cole note, content analysis is a pragmatic methodology which benefits the researcher by being both simple to use and making concepts easily comparable.[1] By quantifying content into predetermined categories, the technique proves fairly systematic and replicable, offering a high level of reliability. It is exhaustive, consistent and repetitious, taking frequency as an indication of significance and attitude. Bryman feels that one of the main advantages to this approach is that the physical gathering of evidence is unobtrusive and non-reactive, so research can be conducted without disruption to the research setting in any way.[2] It might be argued, however, that objectivity is compromised due to reliance on the interpretation of the data, and it is important to keep any conjectures, linkages and conclusions within the historical and cultural context of the original material. It might be suggested therefore that the material gathered for this study would benefit from analysis by historians, and hence there is scope for further research in this field.

Ninety-eight newspaper articles concerning Polish migration to Scotland between 1940 and 1946 were sourced for analysis. The material was retrieved using archives stored on microfiche in the University of Glasgow Library and the Mitchell Library, Glasgow (this material has subsequently been digitised and is available at the British Library in London). My sample concentrated on the *Glasgow Herald* (based in Glasgow and now known as the *Herald*) and the *Scotsman* (based in Edinburgh) as archives for these newspapers were full and complete. The main complication in viewing the data was the quality of the print; wartime paper rationing meant the newspapers researched were only five to seven pages in length and used a tiny font, the layout and spread of pages were crammed and, despite enlarging the material, occasionally photographs remained unclear. The second part of the research was sourced predominantly, but not exclusively, using online press articles, retrieved via search engines, alert services and online archives.

When analysing material in the British press, 160 articles were found to concern Polish migration to Britain in the period 2006–9, with a further 64 articles concentrating on Polish migration to Scotland in the period 2006–9 sourced from the Scottish press. My analysis begins in 2006, a reflection of when I began collecting data at the beginning of my project award, but plans are afoot to source material from 2004 and 2005 to reflect press reception immediately after Poland's accession to the European Union in May 2004. Both stages of data collection may have been subject to human and mechanical error, sources may have been missed, overlooked, or remained unfound for instance, though I made every attempt to avoid this. A disclaimer should also be made about overall usefulness of press analysis; readers are inevitably responsible for the selection and consumption of articles and readership can be assumed but is not known to any accuracy. Press attitude therefore, is not a true reflection of public reception and should not be interpreted as a synonym for such. Press analysis does, however, serve the purpose of beginning to unpick the historical documentation of a specific period of time.

The reception of Poles in the Scottish press 1940–1946

Stachura estimates that, in June 1940, 20,000 Polish troops together with 3,000 civilian refugees were sent to camps in Scotland.[3] They arrived in Liverpool and were directed on to trains bound for Glasgow. When they eventually arrived on 18 July 1940, the sight of Polish troops marching through Glaswegian streets was said to be met with enthusiastic applause from bystanders, according to Stachura. The Scottish press, however, remained fairly mute on this event and it was not widely covered; this might be explained by reports of a flurry of war developments engaging reporters at the time of the Polish arrival, so, for example, the evacuation of Dunkirk, the evacuation of Scottish children, Italy joining the war and the arrival of Norwegian refugees in Scotland consumed the *Glasgow Herald*'s column inches at that time. Soon after their initial arrival in Scotland the portrayal of Poles in the Scottish press was on the whole very sympathetic; Poles were described as living in 'proud grief', being 'musically minded', 'impressive', 'delightful' and 'charming'. Poles were most commonly ascribed the attribute of 'determination', an important and prestigious wartime media characterisation. Later in the decade Poles were described rather uniformly as 'loyal' and 'gallant', and the press actively refuted claims that Poles were 'anti-Semitic'. Cynically, however, it might also be argued that by reporting these allegations the press merely helped to re-associate the accusation.

Stachura cites the so-called 'turning point' of the reception of Poles to Scotland as late 1941, when the Soviet Union became part of the Allied Grand Alliance.[4] This left Poles, many of whom held anti-Soviet feelings, 'liable to get insulted in the street and be subject to petty discrimination'.[5] Although the British government led a pro-Soviet propaganda campaign to sway support for the new Allies from 1941 onwards, pro-Soviet reports did not appear in the Scottish press until the summer of 1942. From here on, pro-Soviet sentiments were evident, especially in Glasgow. Glasgow University Students' Union, for example, reported having entertained a well-known Soviet sniper ('Russian Heroes Feted by Glasgow Students', the *Glasgow Herald*, 24 November 1942), a Russian exhibition was reported as having been hosted in the city (12 June 1943), and Glasgow City Council was said to have considered adopting the 'Russian Example' for post-war planning, including the laying down of a maximum city population (23 February 1943). In January 1943, Red Cross appeals for Russia were published across the Scottish press. It was not until 1946, however, that negative Scottish press coverage about Polish exiles began to outweigh the positive. It should be noted too, that while there was significant increase in negative reception toward Poles, not all press articles held one-sided portrayals. The *Glasgow Herald* for example, described Poles as 'inconvenient foreigners', but in the same article recalled how they 'fought splendidly' ('Poles in Scotland', the *Glasgow Herald*, 30 May 1946).

Other subtle indications that Polish exiles began to lose favour in the press include an increasing use of statistical information regarding their presence in Scotland. In 1940, just over 20 per cent of articles about Poles in Scotland included estimates of how many Poles were stationed in Scotland. Between June 1942 and June 1943, this rose to over a third of all articles, and in 1946 almost 50 per cent of all articles on Poles in Scotland featured statistics. Increased use of statistics suggests that Polish exiles were considered ever more in terms of their economic value. In 1940, this value was measured by the Polish contribution to the war effort; 'Heroic Polish Generals' touts the *Glasgow Herald* (2 November 1940), '6,000 Polish soldiers killed and wounded in operations'. By 1946, however, the article 'Scots Criticise Poles' in the *Glasgow Herald* (27 June 1946) compared '75,000 unemployed Scots' with '28,517 Poles in Scotland'. The reception of Poles in relation to economic worth is a phenomenon revisited by the press in the 21st century also, as is discussed later.

The format in which articles on Poles appeared also changed, so, for example, in 1940, Polish exiles featured in appeals, news items, memoirs, reviews and summaries. In the latter stages of the decade, however, coverage of Poles in Scotland featured only in news columns. The use of photographs to illustrate articles diminished too, meaning Polish exiles were increasingly represented non-visually. The length of column inches devoted to Poles in Scotland remained roughly the same throughout the period; an average of 3.5 paragraphs per article in 1940 compared to 3.8 paragraphs per article in 1946. In the early stages of the War, articles about Poles featured in the 'West Scotland' community pages, mid-war coverage commonly links their portrayal to foreign policy articles, and the post-war press located Poles in the national news, almost exclusively relating to their repatriation or in relation to housing and employment, 'Poles to Vacate Houses' (*Glasgow Herald*, 8 January 1946) and 'Poles Working in Pits' (*Glasgow Herald*, 16 February 1946), for example. In 1946, therefore, Polish exiles were presented as an alleged threat to the interests of a majority group, putting pressure on post-war resources, in this case jobs and housing. This technique is commonly used in the press to discredit minority groups, creating an implicit connotation that 'we' (the majority group) will get less (or worse) because of 'them' (the minority group) as is discussed by van Dijk.[6]

In 1940, Poles frequently featured in stories about recreation and social interaction: they were shown to be involved in Scottish exhibitions, concerts, parties and celebrations. The Polish role in the defence of Scotland was also recognised and welcomed. These home front stories link to the founding of the Scottish–Polish Society in 1941 and its prolific early heyday when language classes, concerts, dances and conferences were organised. Sir Patrick Dollan, or 'Dollanski' as he became known, was Lord Provost of Glasgow from 1938 to 1941, and a prominent community leader throughout the 1940s. He had a keen association with the Scottish–Polish Society, and as such, the press made him a spokesperson for the Polish community based in Scotland. Dollan is referenced in almost 20 per cent of all press concerning Poles in Scotland from 1940–6, hence he provides a good barometer against which to measure attitude toward Polish exiles. In the early 1940s, for example, Dollan was featured attending social events and presented as a benevolent and welcoming champion of Poles. An article in February 1941, for example, saw Dollan donating his car to the war fund following his appreciation of a Polish operatic concert. By 1946, however, Patrick Dollan's presentation becomes politicised and serious, as does press attitude toward Poles. In October 1946, for example, Dollan is described as refereeing a dispute between this Polish community in Scotland and the Trade Union Congress.

In 1940, other notable Polish community spokespeople in the Scottish press, if not the British press at large, included the Polish Government-in-Exile leaders Władysław Sikorski and Władysław Raczkiewicz. This technique by news agencies to call on 'accessed voices' is used to legitimate stories and reinforce a dominant idea.[7] Hegemonic ideas can therefore be seen to shift in 1946 when the press began to favour Polish military leader General Władysław Anders as an 'accessed voice'. While Sikórski and Raczkiewicz were portrayed as cooperative, Anders was portrayed as demanding and uncompromising. Stanisław Kot, the Polish Ambassador in Italy, for example, was quoted saying: 'I am convinced that behind all these misunderstandings is General Anders.' (*Glasgow Herald*, 19 February 1946). The portrayed incompetence of Anders was paralleled against the diplomatic, reserved and calm depiction of British Foreign Secretary Ernest Bevin, shown to be offering controlled 'assurances' regarding the repatriation of Poles (*Glasgow Herald*, 16 February 1946). Newsworthiness is reliant on stories of conflict, threat and deviancy.[8] So by placing Anders and Bevin in binary opposition, Polish repatriation became ever more newsworthy, eventually making the front page of the *Glasgow Herald* (23 May 1946). An increase in letters published in the newspapers about Polish resettlement is further indication that Polish migration gained prominence on the news agenda at this time.

In 1943, the Scottish press took a particular interest in the rising number of marriages between Scots and Poles. These were viewed optimistically but with the noted clause that the couples' residence would be temporary; 'until victory comes and their husbands are able to make homes for them in their own country' (*Scotsman*, 26 July 1943). Scottish women meanwhile were depicted as stoic wives ready to help 'in the reconstruction of Poland' (*Glasgow*

Herald, 10 January 1943). By 1946 it was clear that some of these couples would probably stay in Scotland rather than take up residence in Poland as was supposed earlier. While the Scottish press showed some concern for the safety of Scottish wives in Poland, reiterating the Earl of Craven's fears that life would be very hard, possibly dangerous for them (*Glasgow Herald*, 12 April 1946) and quoting the Vice Premier of Poland saying, 'a tolerant outlook and an open mind were the two qualities which Scottish wives of Poles should posses if they intended to settle with their husbands in Poland' (22 April 1946), there was no regard for the safety of Polish husbands. Moreover, a growing interest by the press in whether to absorb Scottish–Polish marriages in Scotland was symptomatic of wider calls for a 'Scottish quota of Poles' (*Glasgow Herald*, 23 May 1946). Even though a quota was subsequently set, the Scottish press by 1947 felt that this figure was too high. An article in the *Scotsman* (21 April 1947), for example, insisted that 'it will not be possible to place in Scotland more than a small proportion of the Poles at present here . . . The bulk will have to be absorbed in England, or possibly overseas.' Demands for 'quotas' and insistence that England should take a fairer proportion of newcomers is a discourse which reappears in post-2004 Polish migration press coverage.

Growing angst in the Scottish press over the numbers of Poles ascribed to settle in Scotland coincided with the description that Poles were 'intensely nervous about their reception in Britain' (*Glasgow Herald*, 19 June 1946). Moreover, a steady rise in the number of articles which related Polish exiles to crime then proceeded: 'Pole Denies Murder Charge' (*Glasgow Herald*, 20 February 1946), for example. A series of reports about a missing Polish paratrooper meanwhile characterised the Polish exile as dangerous: 'he called at Firkin farmhouse, Luss, and asked the farmer's wife, Mrs McDonald, for a razor blade' (*Glasgow Herald*, 30 May 1946). Likewise, Poles began to be described as 'politically minded' and 'dabbling in local politics' which was said to cause 'unrest and minor incidents' (*Glasgow Herald*, 24 May 1946). Including Poles in stories on crime and politics presented them as deviant and a threat to the *status quo*. Poles went from being portrayed as 'gallant heroes' (*Scotsman*, 13 July 1942) to increasingly dysfunctional. The *Glasgow Herald*, for example, covered a story about a Polish man convicted of murdering his wife and being an 'emotionally unstable type' (21 February 1946). In 1940, articles involving Poles frequently referred to Polish children denoting a sense of victimhood and innocence, whereas in 1946 the youthfulness of resident Poles was received negatively, aligning youth to a lack of training and skill. In post-war Scotland, with growing unemployment, industrial and economic decline and growing social unrest, concern that new arrivals had appropriate job skills is yet another discourse shared with the representation of Polish migrants today.

The reception of Poles in the British press 2006–2009

In 2006, the British press was in agreement that Eastern European migrants, who had arrived in Britain following the expansion of the European Union in May 2004, were taking the 'right' jobs (low-paid or skilled work), were the 'right' ages (young and financially independent adults) and were going to the 'right' places (London, East Anglia, the Midlands, the North East and Scotland) (*Independent*, 22 November 2006, for example). Amidst this applause there also lay concern that the 'guest workforce' would not 'stay long' (*Guardian*, 23 August 2006) and that despite the 'great Polish influx' (*Independent*, 30 December 2007), the Polish presence was still not great enough to meet 'London's needs' with regard to completing the 2012 Olympic stadium (ibid.). The overworked use of the puns 'Poles of growth' and 'Pole position' demonstrated how the tabloids primarily deemed Polish migration as economically beneficial, generally praising first the incoming cheap migrant workforce, latterly celebrating the so-called 'Polish pound'. Even *The Times*, which had been the least welcoming of all the broadsheets toward the Poles, referred to Polish migration as part of a 'worker-consumer' cycle in the early days of post-2004 Polish migration. The newspaper featured articles about banks promoting mortgages to Poles (18 June 2006) and the introduction of Polish food in leading British supermarkets (28 August 2006), for example. Once again we see how the press greeted Polish migrants by holding a debate about their economic worth.

In August 2006, the representation of Poles in the British press was at its most prevalent, due to a series of special supplements the broadsheets ran regarding migration in general. *The Times*, for example, produced a special focus on population statistics bearing an image of a sardine can shaped like Britain with the heading 'Can we squeeze in?' (as a reference to incoming migrant groups). Likewise, the *Independent* (23 August 2006) dedicated itself to a demographic analysis of the 'immigrant nation'. Within these supplements and across the press *en masse*, Polish migrants were commonly described as 'young', 'fit', 'educated', 'skilled', 'keen' and 'eager to work'. The *Mirror* often ran with more aged stereotypes of Poles being a 'tough and proud people' (*Mirror*, 1 August 2008), while the *Guardian* led the way in reproducing the idea that Poles had a cultural predisposition to working long hours and being especially efficient and fast workers with a 'superior work ethic' and 'more skills than their UK counterparts' (*Guardian*, 24 August 2008). *The Times* was the only broadsheet to present a particularly derogatory portrayal of Polish migrants as early as 2006, running an article which offered readers 'essential phrases' when employing Polish builders, including 'Are you sure you want all that money in cash?' and 'Do you take vodka in your tea?' (*The Times*, 10 September 2006). By 2007, however, all the British broadsheets had negated their former position on Polish migration to some extent. While it may set itself up to be the more leftist broadsheet of choice, even the *Guardian* was culpable of running a series of articles (24 January 2007–31 January 2007) which outlined the pressures Eastern European migrants put on local councils in rural counties. Though the series was clearly not intended to emit a negative portrayal of Polish migration, it did linger on the sadder, darker, and more desperate circumstances of migration.

In 2007 (just as Romania and Bulgaria joined the EU), amidst fear of further new member state immigration, the phrase 'Poles apart' became popular press coinage, accentuating the 'difference' between 'Poles' and 'Brits'. There was also a marked increase in the use of the terms 'foreign invasion', 'sheer/unprecedented scale', 'soaring population' and 'influx', and an almost hysterical fear or 'moral panic'[9] that demographic statistics were inadequate and immigration figures unreliable. With regard to these statistics, criticism was levelled at the Government from all sides of the British press, and once again, even the more left-wing newspapers presented Polish migration as spontaneous and ill-thought-through. The *Guardian*, for example, says 'Poles 'swanned off to the UK and Ireland' and went 'AWOL' (29 September 2007). Between 2007 and 2008, every article on Polish migration analysed mentioned to some degree, the 'pressure' Polish migrants put on British housing, policing, education and health services. The *Guardian* was particularly interested in the rise in homelessness among Eastern Europeans in Britain (21 February 2008, for example). The *Telegraph* took a stand on the breakdown of marriage in Poland and the increasing pressure put on education in Britain (13 February 2009, for example). The tabloids concerned themselves with 'soft-touch Britain' (*Daily Mail*, 14 April 2009) in relation to a reported 'surge in euro migrants on UK benefits' (*Daily Express*, 14 April 2009). The *Sun's* right-wing mantra was probably the most overt, having produced a so-called 'sponger's guide for UK Poles: a dossier on how to avoid paying bills' (22 August 2008), whereas it was the *Daily Mail* which was publicly accused of racism by the Federation of Poles in Britain. In turn, the *Daily Mail* (4 June 2008) was busy covering the story of Conservative MP Daniel Kawczynski's criticism that the BBC was responsible for racism against Poles. Incidentally, the *Daily Mail* (22 October 2008) described 'the Poles, Czechs, Latvians and Lithuanians' as 'probably the best group of immigrants any country could wish for', presumably because they feared how 'the immigration debate' would 'likely shift once again'.

As the economic downturn intensified in 2008 and 2009, articles on Polish migration generally approved of the departure of Poles from the UK, but then fretted about a possible ensuing skills shortfall. Concern about the 'influx' of migrants veered toward speculation about their 'exodus' and the idea that the 'tide' would 'turn' (*The Times*, 16 February 2008, for example). Polish migrants were hereby presented as deserters ('Poles catch the first coach out of a Britain mired in slump', *Independent*, 21 May 2009). Moreover, the 'Polish plumber' stereotype was resurrected ('Polish plumbers pack their bags as pickings get richer back east', *The Times*, 16 February 2008) as a means of construing how Britain was supposed to feel about the reported return of migrants ('finding a cheap, honest, eager-to-work builder in 2008 is going to be considerably harder', ibid.). In the wake of the recession, the British press re-equated 'migrant' with 'migrant worker', navigating representation away from that of the 'consumer'. Migrant experiences were downplayed as simply amounting to economic circumstance. *The Times* (ibid.), for example, quoted a number of Poles talking about their decision to return to Poland attributing their move to poor exchange rates ('Each pound I sent home could buy three or four loaves of bread . . . now it can buy only one . . . the exchange rate means it's not worth staying.'). Prior to 2007, moreover, press articles often mentioned how an aspect of Polish culture was practised in Britain (Christmas or Easter, for example), the successes of Polish entrepreneurialism and the service and debt Britain owed to Polish ex-servicemen following World War II. From 2007 onwards, these more embracing factual asides about Polish presence in Britain were too often replaced by a quote from right-wing campaign group Migrationwatch UK.

The reception of Poles in the Scottish press 2006–2009

The British press held very satirical views about the contribution Poles made to Scotland. The *Daily Mail* (21 June 2007), for example, noted that 'Eastern European immigrants have triggered a baby boom north of the border', 'with randy Poles leading the surge'. Sports columnist Stuart Cosgrove made a pretend 'campaign' for Scottish men to take Polish partners, saying it was likely to have a positive effect on Scottish football and so 'Scotland will have a superb team in time for the 2022 World Cup finals.' *The Times* meanwhile (31 December 2006) covered the story that VisitScotland used a Polish model as the face of their campaign. The journalist also seemed to revel in reiterating the more naïve comments made by Polish migrants about Scotland: 'The Scottish people are from mountains just as our people are from the mountains' (*The Times*, 16 April 2006), for example. The Scottish press were much less satirical, and received post-2004 Polish migration with great enthusiasm. At times, so ardent was the feeling toward Polish migrants in the Scottish press that it seems contrived, and a wider nationalist Scottish agenda can therefore be exposed. An article in the *Scotsman* (14 January 2008), for example, entitled 'New Scots from Poland doing us proud' accorded Poles with having 'helped to fill thousands of job vacancies', 'improving transport links', introducing 'a blossoming cultural scene', 'helping to save the Catholic Church' and changing 'Scotland's place in Europe.'

A quote from the *Herald* (18 October 2007) neatly demonstrates the most common adjectives associated with Poles by the Scottish press: 'single, young, healthy, well-educated, economically active and relying relatively less on public services than indigenous communities'. Although the Scottish press echoed the same fear in the wider British press that Poles would put pressure on public resources, the Scottish press framed Poles in a 'worker and consumer' dichotomy for longer; there was even praise for their 'positive contribution to the public purse' (*Herald*, 24 July 2009). As with the wider British press, Government oversight in terms of the numbers of migrants that arrived was a complaint shared in the Scottish press, and was commonly used by the Scottish press as a backdoor to comment on devolution and the need for greater devolved powers. In the *Herald* (7 June 2008), for instance, the 'planning difficulties' associated with the sheer volume of Poles resident in parts of Scotland was blamed on 'central government'. Although the Scottish press shared the same propensity as the wider British press to view the migrant as 'a migrant worker', journalists were generally more complementary: Poles are 'excellent uncomplaining workers' (*Highland News*, 22 June 2006), 'hardworking' and 'plugging vital gaps' [in the economy] (*Daily Record*, 2 June 2006), and are viewed as an 'essential part of the workforce' (*Herald*, 7 June 2008).

Polish presence in Scotland was resoundingly celebrated for addressing two Scottish specific issues, population decline and skills shortage. Poles were presented as the then First Minister, Jack McConnell's, ideal migrants; they were said to be 'helping Jack McConnell meet his target' and being 'just the kind of migrants Jack McConnell' wanted (*Herald*, 23 August 2006). This political seal of approval was also seen with regard to overcoming Scotland's dwindling and ageing population, for which 'the young Poles have come to the rescue' (*Herald*, 3 November 2007). Poles were credited with reversing a 'demographic time-bomb' (*Herald*, 15 May 2006) and 'doomsday scenario' (*Herald*, 27 April 2007), an analogy which ran short of presenting Poles as Scotland's modern saviours. The *Evening News* (7 September 2007), for example, depicted Polish migrants helping Edinburgh finally overcome its construction shortfall, and the *Herald* (18 October 2007) believed 'vital areas of life would experience difficulties without them [Poles]'. Predictably, therefore, the *Herald* acted with anger when it realised that this new migrant life-blood might return to Eastern Europe 'leaving employers in the lurch' (*Herald*, 7 June 2008). The 'Polish exodus', as it was also commonly described in the Scottish press, was met with fear rather than approval, with emphasis placed on resulting workforce shortages. The *Evening Times*, meanwhile, seemed to excel in uncovering 'hidden Polish talent', being a strong advocate of Polish Celtic footballer Artur Boruc, promoting the plight of a Polish canoeist wishing to compete for Scotland, and championing the discovery of a Polish concert pianist working as a cleaner.

The Scottish press described the 'problems' as well as 'benefits' that Polish migration brought, but rather than seeing these problems as being insurmountable, as they are often presented in the British press, the Scottish press reported problems generally involving Poles being preyed upon, rather than doing the preying. 'Criminal gangs are duping Poles into paying hundreds of pounds in fees to come to Scotland for nonexistent jobs', said the *Scotsman* (21 September 2007); Poles experienced 'exploitation at the hands of Scottish landlords and bosses', recalled the *Herald* (17 October 2006); and 'Polish brides in Glasgow marriage scam', recounted the *Evening Times* (22 October 2009), reporting that Polish women were being approached to marry asylum seekers and were being 'taken advantage of [because of] their desperation and need for money'. While some very serious social issues relating to the Polish community were reported in the Scottish press between 2006 and 2009, so for instance a 'rise in crime linked to attacks on Poles' (*Scotsman*, 28 June 2007), Poles were rarely portrayed as the instigators of crime (not so the case in the 1940s). Even when Poles were presented undertaking crime, 'Poles are warned on flouting drink-drive laws' (*Scotsman*, 23 December 2008), for example, the manner in which the article was presented was fairly jovial and forgiving; '*Kto ky jestes?* Stirling Moss!', for example, even if the journalist's attempt at Polish was not always that accurate. Moreover, when situations likely to cause tension between resident Scottish and Polish communities arose, the Scottish media helped to deflect negativism toward Poles by pre-empting response. In an article about a social housing project, 'Polish migrants given block of flats to call their own' (*Scotsman*, 28 April 2008), for example, Poles were presented as a deserving case.

The Scottish press presented Poles as being incredibly complimentary of Scotland: 'I really like the country, it's small but with many cultures' (*Scotsman*, 29 November 2008), and as having a desire to integrate into Scottish society, 'I'm in Scotland, I want to integrate' (*Scotsman*, 9 November 2005). Poles were commonly depicted as wanting to build 'a new life in Scotland' (*Scotsman*, 9 November 2005) and this was often portrayed as 'a better life' (*Herald*, 18 October 2007). While Poland was characterised as down-at-heel and a place from which Poles had escaped, Polish culture was still keenly promoted. Much, for example, was made of the Polish 'entrepreneurial spirit' which it was hoped would 'make Scotland a better, more cosmopolitan place' (*Herald*, 7 June 2008). The historical link between Scotland and Poland was also reported, with many references made to Bonnie Prince Charlie, Scottish traders in Poland and the resettlement of Polish troops in Scotland following World War II. Personal similarities between Scots and Poles were also drawn. The *Herald* (17 October 2006), for example, quoted the Consul General for Poland saying: 'both peoples understand each other very well as they are similar'. In fact, an opportunity was rarely overlooked to present the relationship with 'Scotland and Poland' or 'Scotland and Polish migrants' as somewhat different to that of England and the Poles. Polish migrants were frequently quoted demonstrating their allegiance to Scotland, 'We also thought Scotland was a cleaner country than England' (*Herald*, 18 October 2007), for example, echoing a nationalist fervent in the Scottish press at large. In return, Poles were branded the 'New Scots', a term manifest of the desire to maintain Scottish demographics without compromising 'Scottish' identity. While the Scottish press urged England to take a greater share of Poles in the 1940s, during the more recent wave of Polish migration it urged Poles to choose Scotland over England.

Conclusion

In 1940, the reception of Poles in the Scottish press was very positive and welcoming, reflective of political allegiances at the time. In the summer of 1943, pro-Soviet sentiment began to mount in the press, coinciding with a gradual demise in the portrayal of the Polish exile. By 1946, press articles highlighted pressures Poles placed on housing and the workforce, and this culminated in considerable debate and speculation as to the numbers of Polish exiles Scotland might have been expected to host. Following the accession of Poland to the European Union in 2004, a further wave of Polish migration was initially well received in the British press. While the British economy was buoyant, the press depicted the migrants as both workers and consumers, but, as the downturn proceeded, the reception of Polish migrants became more adverse. The Scottish press, however, consistently embraced Polish migration, promoting these 'new Scots' as a way of bolstering population growth and providing specific skills to a now devolved Scotland. The attempts of the Scottish press 2006–9 to deflect negative representation of Polish migrants is a marked change from the portrayal of Polish exiles as a threat to the *status quo* initiated by the post-war Scottish press. This discussion therefore asks wider questions about the nature of press representation, and as such, urges any further analysis of the relationship between Poland and Scotland in the press to be observed through a wary lens.

Notes

1   R. Stevenson and R. Cole, 'Some Thoughts on the Future of Content Analysis', *International Communication Gazette* 30 (1982), pp. 167–76.
2   A. Bryman, *Social Research Methods* (Oxford, 2004).
3   P. Stachura, ed., *Perspectives on Polish History* (Stirling, 2001).
4   Ibid.

5 P. Stachura, ed., *The Poles in Britain 1940–2000: From Betrayal to Assimilation* (London, 2004), 54.

6 T. van Dijk, 'Principles of Critical Discourse Analysis', *Discourse and Society* 4 (1993), pp. 249–83.

7 R. Fowler, *Language in the News, Discourse and Ideology in the Press* (London, 1991).

8 S. Cohen and J. Young, eds, *The Manufacture of News, Social Problems, Deviance and The Mass Media* (London, 1973).

9 S. Cohen, *Folk Devils and Moral Panics* (London, 2002).

Aleksander Dietkow

A Polish Consulate was established in Scotland in 1939 to deal with the thousands of Polish soldiers who came to the country during World War II. At that time there were more than 20,000 Poles in Scotland, mostly soldiers. Some of those soldiers were joined by their families in the 1960s. In 1985, the office of the Polish Consulate was transferred from Glasgow to Edinburgh and at one point, in the 1990s, the Polish Government even considered closing down the office. This, of course, never happened and with the current number of Poles in Scotland is unlikely to happen in the foreseeable future.

I was first appointed as the Consul General of the Republic of Poland in Edinburgh in the year 2000/2001. Back then there were around 8,000 Polish nationals living in Scotland, mostly families of veterans of the Polish Armed Forces in the West.

The office of the Polish Consulate employed four members of staff back then. This was more than enough to deal with the needs of the Polish nationals in Scotland. The Consulate concentrated on maintaining good relations with the Polish diaspora and the promotion of Polish culture and Polish history among the locals. The Poles were already well integrated into Scottish society and expected support in promoting national culture and traditions from the consular office. The work of the Consul General concentrated mostly on visiting the different Polish Ex-Combatants Associations spread throughout the country and attending the national celebrations organised by the Polish associations. The typical office work accounted for only a small part of the overall consular activities performed by our consuls. The number of registered cases did not exceed 500, of which 150 were passports issued for Polish nationals, another 150 were visas issued for people who wanted to travel to Poland. The rest were translations and legalisations of documents, confirmations of signatures, etc. Very rarely, Polish nationals asked our office for consular and legal help.

The lack of direct flights between Poland and Scotland meant relatively few Poles came to Scotland in the years 2000 and 2001, not even as tourists. Consequently, the consuls had plenty of time to attend cultural events, meet with the Polish and Scottish societies, and to get to know Scotland, its people, culture, and history.

The new millennium brought the signing of the Nice Treaty, the declaration to extend the European Union that brought hopes and lots of questions to Polish nationals. 1998 marked the beginning of preparations for negotiating the provisions of the Polish accession to the EU. When the final negotiations took place, on 13 December 2002, I was already back in Poland, involved in the accession work at the Ministry of Foreign Affairs in Warsaw. In 2002, our Government, many think tanks, research institutes, and other institutions did not have any idea what 1 May 2004 and the accession of Poland to the EU would bring in regard to the new freedom to travel beyond the previous limits. No one was able to predict the numbers of Poles who would want to look for better employment and study opportunities abroad. Of course, the numbers of people who decided to move to Britain to try a new life were determined by the fact that only three countries opened their borders for the new accession countries from the beginning: the UK, the Republic of Ireland, and Sweden.

When I arrived in Scotland in August 2005 to again take up the position of Consul General of the Republic of Poland in Edinburgh, I found a totally new situation from the one I remembered from 2001.

After the UK opened its borders to the A8 countries, hundreds of thousands of people from the new accession countries came to the UK to look for a better life, a huge percentage of whom were Polish nationals. In the beginning, Scotland did not seem to be so popular. There were no cheap direct flights to Scotland and a trip by bus from Poland was more than thirty hours long. Despite this, according to our statistics, around 10,000 migrants from the A8 countries came to Scotland in the year 2004.

The situation changed in autumn 2005, when new cheap air routes from the main Polish cities to Scottish airports were established. There were around thirty direct flights from Warsaw, Cracow, Katowice, Wrocław, and Gdańsk available by spring 2006. This was when the number of Polish people in Scotland increased significantly. The new air routes and the policy of the Scottish Government were the two significant factors that caused such a huge increase in numbers of migrants in Scotland.

The Scottish Government supports a policy of encouraging migration to Scotland. In 2004, the First Minister of Scotland, Jack McConnell, initiated the Fresh Talent for Scotland scheme that was aimed at Polish nationals as well. The current Government with the First Minister of Scotland, Alex Salmond, continues the policy set in 2004. As part of the programme a 'Welcome to Scotland' guide in the Polish language was prepared by the Scottish Government that included all the important information about life and work in Scotland for potential migrants. To prepare the guide, a special advice committee was created, which included representatives of the so-called 'old Polish emigrants' who came to Scotland during World War II and in the 1960s, the Rector of the Polish Catholic Mission in Scotland, and a representative from the Consulate General of the Republic of Poland in Edinburgh.

Also, most of the local authorities in Scotland prepared more detailed versions of welcome packs for new migrants in different languages, including Polish. Quite often the Polish Consulate in Edinburgh was consulted during the preparation process for these and other information packs prepared by different institutions, including the police, National Health Service, trade unions and other services. This allowed us to suggest the most sensitive issues to be included in the guides. Links to these guides were put on our consular website and on other popular Polish websites to allow Polish nationals to learn more about the life and work in Scotland before deciding to come here. To encourage migrants to come to Scotland the Scottish Government also ran an information campaign in Poland.

Subsequently, the number of Polish migrants in Scotland rose to around 50,000 by the end of 2006. Such a sudden wave of migration brought media attention and a general increase of interest in Poland, its politics, policies, people, culture, and traditions. Our office noticed increased demand for educational and promotional materials about Poland, especially among local schools that had some Polish pupils, local authorities, and Scottish people interested to learn more about Poland and potentially interested in visiting Poland as tourists.

The expanding numbers brought, of course, not only more interest in Poland, but also increased the demand and pressure on services as well. Many of our nationals were not fully prepared for emigration and the consequences of it. Quite a few of them had no knowledge of the English language, which put pressure on the services offered by our office and by the Scottish local authorities that were forced to set up provisions for translation services for new migrants. New translation and interpretation 24-hour help lines were set up to deal with the increased demand in this field.

There were some individual cases of Poles who came to Scotland without any knowledge of the country, with no money for the initial period of looking for a job, with no English, and no contacts. Some of these were quite often being brought by dishonest employment agencies or forged offers from non-existent employers in Scotland. The consular office needed then to deal with the consequences of these dishonest agencies' and employers' practices. However, over the last four years, the number of such cases has been fortunately low.

In 2006, our office still employed only four people as the number of Poles in Scotland grew. Without the help and support of many local organisations and institutions we would not have been able to deal with even the most critical issues, like exploitation of workforce, a small number of cases of discrimination at work, and the consequences of dealing with Poles brought here by illegal employment agencies. Regardless of not always having enough resources, the Polish Consulate and the local authorities and other bodies were always willing to help.

As the number of Polish migrants continued to increase, our office was forced to extend our services and increase the number of employees. By the end of 2008 we had thirteen employees at the Consulate to support 80,000 Poles in Scotland. The Polish Consulate in Edinburgh also took over the responsibility for looking after the 30,000 Polish nationals in Northern Ireland.

At this point it is not really possible to provide exact information on numbers with regard to the migrants in Scotland, as there is no separate data kept for Scotland. Our estimates come from information gathered from different sources: the local police, the NHS, the Border Agency, and the Home Office registration of workers under the Worker Registration Scheme that applies to all nationals of A8 countries. However, this registration does not apply to self-employed, spouses, children, or students and, of course, not everyone is aware that they should register with the Home Office.

Our office noticed systematic growth in the number of Polish migrants in Scotland until the second half of 2008, after which point the numbers stabilised. It is estimated that there are currently more than 70,000 Poles living in Scotland (some sources suggest that there are even as many as 85,000). The highest numbers of Polish people live in Midlothian, in Edinburgh, and the surrounding area (probably around 30,000). The second highest conglomeration of Poles is in Strathclyde, most of them living in Glasgow and the surrounding area (around 20,000), then around 10,000 live in the Grampian region, many of them in Aberdeen, around 8,000 live in the Highlands, with most of them in Inverness, and finally in Tayside (probably 5,000), with most of them living in Dundee.

The majority of so-called new migrant workers who arrived in Scotland after 2004 came from the new EU member states, with the majority of them (probably even as high as 80 per cent) from Poland. Currently, Polish nationals living in Scotland constitute the biggest ethnic minority in Scotland. According to research undertaken in Scotland by various local authorities, around 40 per cent of Polish economic migrants are less than 24 years old, another 40 per cent are aged 24 to 32. Eighty per cent of them have no family of their own. They are well educated: 15 per cent have a Bachelor degree and 20 per cent have a Masters degree from Polish universities. There is no data available at this point with regard to current occupation, but it is obvious that these young, well-educated people who came here would very much like to make use of their skills and use the qualifications they possess in a more appropriate and useful way. This is one aspect that should be further discussed and seriously considered by the Scottish Qualifications Authority and the Scottish Government.

Up until 2004 there had been only a few hundred Polish nationals living in Northern Ireland. Now there are 30,000. The largest concentration of Poles live in Belfast and its surroundings, their numbers approaching 8,000. There are around 5,000 Poles living in Newry, another 2,500 in Londonderry, around 2,500 in Dungannon, and 1,500 in Enniskillen. Poles are considered the biggest ethnic minority group in Northern Ireland. Unlike in Scotland, the majority of Poles who settled in Northern Ireland have minimum qualifications, and they are mostly unaware of the political and religious tensions in the region. The predominantly Catholic Poles generally use cheaper accommodation which is frequently offered in Protestant areas, which in turn can lead to experiences of religious bigotry. There have always been more racial attacks on Poles in Northern Ireland than in any other part of the UK, but then the Northern Irish authorities are better prepared to deal with such situations.

The increase in numbers of Poles living in Scotland and settling here – potentially for a slightly longer period – has been apparent in the consular workload. While before 2004 there were almost no passport applications for new-born children, we have noticed the gradual increase in the demand for passports and especially for passports for new-born babies; civil marriages at the Consulate and in the local registry offices, which meant that we needed to deal with higher number of requests for translation and legalisation of documents, obtaining documents like birth certificates and no-impediment certificates from Poland; legal help provided on request from Polish courts; transportations of ashes and bodies of Polish nationals to Poland; and also a slight increase in interest in obtaining or regaining Polish nationality among the second- and third-generation Poles.

In 2008, our office issued 4,000 passports for Polish children born in Scotland and a similar number for 2009. The number of marriages increased from around three in 2004 to twenty-eight in 2007 and fifty-three in 2008 and stayed at the same level in 2009. The same tendency was noticed by the General Registry Office of Scotland: the number of marriages where at least one party was Polish and in some cases both were Polish increased from forty-two in 2004 to one hundred and forty-five in 2007. According to General Registry Office statistics, the number of registered births of Polish origin was 37 in 2004 and grew to 976 in 2007.

The role of the Polish Consulate has evolved constantly, adapting the consular tasks according to the changing demand from Polish nationals. We started by offering basic advice and information for the newcomers, as this was the most important necessity in 2004 and 2005. We provided the support, especially for those who found themselves in trouble or difficulties. We then were forced to adapt to the needs through increasing the passport services, translation services and performing civil marriage ceremonies for Polish nationals.

Over the last four years, the demand for Polish schools, Polish classes and various cultural activities has been gradually increasing. This, of course, suggests that Polish nationals are slowly settling in Scotland, bringing their families, but still missing their native culture and wanting to maintain links with their home country and its culture, but also wanting to present their Polish culture to the locals.

The number of Polish supplementary, mainly Saturday, schools run by professionally qualified Polish teachers grew from three in 2006 to twenty-two in 2008, with 1,306 Polish pupils attending Polish classes. All of the schools are voluntarily run places that are not only dedicated to teaching Polish to children of migrants from Poland, but also to cultivating the Polish traditions and teaching the geography and history of Poland. Originally we noted the tendency for schools to be opened mostly in bigger Scottish cities, for example Glasgow, Edinburgh, Inverness and Aberdeen, but then the idea grew and new schools have been opened in Motherwell, Banff, Ayr, and Elgin.

At the moment there are around 1,400 Polish pupils attending the Polish Saturday Schools. According to the research undertaken in 2007 in Scottish schools and published on 26 February 2008 in the *Scottish Government Statistical Bulletin on Pupils in Scotland*, there were at least 3,347 Polish children attending publicly funded Scottish schools in 2007.[1] According to the same report, the Polish language is, after English, Punjabi, and Urdu, the fourth most popular language used in homes in Scotland. This number will, of course, grow once all the new-born Polish children reach school age.

For the last four years our office provided both practical and financial help and support for the Polish schools. We also tried to liaise with the Scottish Government, the Convention of Scottish Local Authorities and various school directors in order to highlight the cultural needs of migrants and the potential value of providing them with a certain level of support. According to the Council Directive of 25 July 1977 on the education of the children of migrant workers, the local authorities should provide the services to allow the children of migrant workers to gain access to learning their home language and culture.[2] This is a very important directive in the age of free movement and in the context of the number of migrants from different countries changing their place of stay on a more or less regular basis. Our office still has not managed to achieve the perfect solution in this field in Scotland.

We are glad though that knowledge about Poland and the other A8 countries has been increasing thanks to many programmes and activities and events organised by local institutions and organisations and also to the diplomatic representatives based in Scotland. The number of requests for educational and promotional material about Poland received by our office from different primary and secondary schools increased by 100 per cent in 2006 over the previous years. Different Unity and Diversity Weeks and International Days are still being held at schools and cultural centres.

However, the need for more action is still apparent as this is the only way to promote further understanding and smoother integration of Poles and other migrants with the locals.

In general the suggestions from different sources are that the Poles are integrating well. The Scottish employers consider the Polish migrant workers to have very high work ethics and welcome their services; they also proved to be extremely productive. According to research conducted in March 2006 in the Tayside area by the Dundee Business School at the University of Abertay, around two-thirds of migrant workers stated that relationships with their local co-workers are either good or very good. According to the same report, the Scottish employers stated that the main reason for employing migrant workers was a lack of supply in the local labour market, which, of course, contradicts all the press reports that the Polish people are taking away jobs from locals. The report also suggests that in the Tayside area, 19 per cent of businesses have improved their performance significantly after employing migrant workers, and in a further 47 per cent of businesses, there was visible improvement noticed.

Poles are mostly employed in the construction, hospitality and tourism sectors, in food-processing factories, and in seasonal work. In some cases, especially in bigger companies, migrants are given the chance to develop their skills and build a career.

The majority of Polish migrants who have come to Scotland are young and enthusiastic and open-minded, they are willing to learn new things and willing to teach new things to others, to teach about their country of origin and its culture.

In 2006, there were only a few Polish organisations in Scotland, most of them Ex-Combatants Associations and one cultural organisation. In 2008, the number of Polish organisations had tripled when compared to 2004, and the number continues to grow as many of the new emigrant Poles who have settled here are eager to introduce their culture and history to the Scottish society that became their host a few years ago. The number of Poles interested in joining existing societies or establishing their own societies, organisations, or other non-profit bodies dedicated to the promotion of different aspects of Polish culture and heritage to locals is still growing. There are currently more than thirty organisations and Polish media that we are aware of, among them cultural associations, Polish magazines, radios and web portals.

These organisations are quite often established by Poles who are university graduates, and are currently in jobs that are not commensurate to the qualifications they gained in Poland, although they still are considered to be reasonably good as they give them financial stability. Among the most active Polish cultural organisations are the Scottish–Polish Cultural Association and the Polish Cultural Festival Association in Edinburgh, the Social and

Educational Society in Glasgow, the Polish Association in Inverness, the Polish Association in Aberdeen, Polish Art Scotland, United Polish Falkirk, and the Polish Association in Fife 'MOST'. Among the Polish media and web portals created by the young Polish migrants are emito.net, Glasgow24, Scotland.pl, Edinburgh.com.pl, and Emigrant. There are also still three Polish Ex-Combatants Associations, in Edinburgh, Glasgow, and Kirkcaldy. In 2009, the Polish Naval Association, with only a few aged members left, decided to dissolve the organisation.

With the growing number of Polish students at various Scottish universities, the number of Polish student organisations is growing too. There are at least five Polish Students' Societies, at the University of Edinburgh, the University of St Andrews, the University of Aberdeen, the Robert Gordon University in Aberdeen and the University of Glasgow. The Congress of Polish Students' Organisations has become an annual event; it has taken place twice at Oxford University and once at the University of Glasgow.

With the number of Polish schools, there are naturally many organisations created to help to run the schools and to organise other types of activities for the pupils, two of the most active among them being the Polish Volunteers 'Świetlica' in Edinburgh and the Association of Teachers, Parents and Sympathisers of Polish Culture 'Children for Future' in Glasgow. These young Polish organisations have already managed to organise events that have brought Polish culture into Scotland and have helped with the integration process. The Polish Cultural Festival Association, which consists of members of so-called 'New Scots' – young Poles well-integrated into the Scottish society – organised the first Polish Cultural Festival in Edinburgh, which was very well received and attended by both Poles and locals. The Festival was part of a bigger event organised by the Adam Mickiewicz Institute in Warsaw in collaboration with the Polish Cultural Institute in London, the Polish Embassy in London, and the Consulate General of the Republic of Poland in Edinburgh – the POLSKA!Year – that aimed to present different aspects of Polish culture in British society, to highlight the fact that Poland can supply not only a reliable workforce but also an interesting culture.

The Polish Cultural Festival Association, established by Lidia Krzynowek and Joanna Zawadzka together with a group of more than forty volunteers, organised around twenty different events across the city, including concerts, lectures, film screenings and exhibitions. The events attracted almost 7,000 visitors of which 60 per cent were locals. The Festival received support from many Polish and Scottish institutions and proved to be an interesting area for cooperation between different Polish organisations.

This and many other events received positive media reviews, which balance out some specific examples highlighted by the media of negative behaviour of Polish nationals in Scotland.

More and more Polish businesses are being set up in Scotland. Of these, shops were probably first to appear. Before 2004 there were hardly any Polish shops and restaurants in Britain, but then Polish Deli, Deli Polonia, and Polish Delicatessen, to name but a few, were followed by the biggest supermarkets in offering Polish produce, allowing Scots to experience Polish culinary delights. *Barszcz, żurek, bigos, pierogi* and other delicacies which you can find in Polish delis and restaurants are no longer attractive only to Polish nationals, but are becoming more and more popular with the locals, happy to learn more about Polish cuisine.

The Polish shops were then followed by Polish painting and decorating companies, Polish plumbing services, and other small businesses established by new Polish migrants. This not only suggests that Poles are settling well, but that they are expanding their knowledge and achieving their goals.

Poland and Poles are now well established within Scottish society, and even the current financial crisis has not convinced them to go back to Poland. The local authorities and some of the Polish organisations noticed an increase in numbers of Polish families requesting social help due to financial issues as a result of a job loss. True, the number of homeless migrants and those threatened by homelessness has increased over the recession period, with many of them suffering from health and mental problems. Also, in some cases, Polish nationals have been victims of racial abuse as a result of the current crisis and worsening of community relations. The tensions are exaggerated, especially in situations when Scots, not Poles, are the first ones to lose their jobs through compulsory redundancies.

In general, the overall impact of Polish migrant workers in Scotland has been positive. The information received by our office from different sources suggests that the population growth that was so needed in Scotland was mostly achieved, the impact on communities, except for some initial racial issues in some areas, is positive and the overall economic benefit is significant. However, there has been an impact on services, including translation services.

Of course, the migration is also positive from a different perspective, as it broadens the views and cultural experiences of young Poles who came to Scotland, and brings positive changes to their local communities in Poland when they return to their home country, even if the return is not a permanent one.

This migration is being considered as a purely economic migration, but we have to remember that the reasons for coming to Scotland varied from necessity and purely economic reasons to a need for new experiences and more freedom.

The group of Poles who came here after World War II are still remembered in a very positive light because of their role in the defence of Scotland. The newcomers are mostly seen as hardworking individuals with high work ethics. In general, the image of a Polish person among the Scots is highly regarded. Even though the circumstances of the arrivals of these two groups are totally different, the Scottish people treat them with respect and understanding.

There are, however, certain reservations between the Poles who are well settled here and the newcomers. The role of our office is to help them to over-come the differences and encourage cross-generational dialogue. One of the ways to promote this is to enable the various organisations to gather together at events and celebrations. The extended knowledge about the history of migrations of different nations can help to achieve those goals.

The four years I spent in Scotland as Consul General of the Republic of Poland were interesting and challenging times for me, the consular staff and I am sure many Polish people who came here after 2004. In this period the number of consular tasks increased to up to twenty times in comparison with 2004. Poland and the Polish people have become vital parts of the Scottish landscape. For me, as the departing Consul General, it is important that these so-called 'New Scots' will cultivate their emotional and cultural ties with their native country and those who decide to go back to Poland will give testimony of the friendly country of Walter Scott.

Notes

1 Scottish Government Statistical Bulletin, Education Series Edn/B1/2008/1.
2 Council Directive (77/486/EEC), 25 July 1977.

Grazyna Fremi

Arriving in Edinburgh from Poland, via the USA, Germany and France, in the summer of 1991 with my Scottish husband and our one-year-old daughter, I had just one personal contact in Scotland. A Polish friend from Princeton had given me the telephone number of his aunt Krystyna, who ran a Polish delicatessen in Barony Street. Visiting her shop shortly after my arrival was like stepping back in time, into an old Poland which felt very familiar. She was wearing white overalls, had blonde curly hair and an open, good-natured face, and was surrounded by Polish produce, whilst British adverts from the 1950s decorated the shop's higher shelves. In the back room I was offered tea and sandwiches made with fresh Polish rolls (*kaizerki*) and Polish sausage. Familiar scents of old wood, Polish food and other indescribable aromas transported me back to my grandmother's old-fashioned kitchen in Poznań. Here was my Polish safe haven, no matter what the future in Scotland would bring.

Krystyna arrived in Paisley in 1948, liberated from a forced labour camp in Germany. She met her first husband, Stefan Olejnik, during a concert in the Polish Combatants Association in Glasgow. Stefan had arrived in Scotland in 1947, with the 2nd Polish Corps under the command of General Anders, along with thousands of Polish soldiers at the end of World War II. Like many others, they decided not to return to Soviet-controlled Poland at the end of the War and, relying on their skills, resourcefulness, and hard work, they opened a shop and a restaurant. In the basement of their second shop in Barony Street in Edinburgh, Stefan made sausages according to the Polish recipes. Demand for Polish produce and services amongst the exiled community were great enough to make a good living.

Krystyna told me about two Polish clubs in Edinburgh, one in Drummond Place and one in Great King Street, and she told me about the popular dances and dinners held there for many years after the War. In time, I met Krystyna's second husband, Władek, who was Ukrainian and who had a small shop repairing leather goods (a Polish widow marrying a Ukrainian was a courageous thing to do within the Polish community, even though Władek was part of the 1st Polish Armoured Division under the command of General Maczek). Although the Ukrainian Club, rather than the Polish clubs, became their social circle, Krystyna still went to the Polish chapel in Randolph Place.

I would meet her there on my occasional visits to the Polish Sunday mass, where a small group of around thirty to forty people gathered in the chapel to listen to the familiar chants of Father Puton who is still looking after the spiritual needs of what is now a much larger Polish community. The chapel, recently sold by the Catholic Church to the restaurant next door, functions as a smart wine bar today. It still bears witness to the days gone by, with the stained glass windows which remain, because they were too expensive to remove, and an inscription, *Kaplica*, at the entrance. I hear that the Polish mass in the St Mary's Cathedral takes place twice on Sunday, and there are at least three more Polish Catholic masses in Edinburgh. Father Puton's mass alone brings together approximately 250 Poles.

When my mother came to visit us in Edinburgh in the 1990s, with her suitcases full of fresh Polish cheese, meat, sausages, dried mushrooms, vodka and chocolates, I introduced her to Krystyna and her Ukrainian husband. My mother was from a Polish–Russian family from Zytomierz, a city in what is now Western Ukraine, and like Krystyna and Władek, she spoke fluent Russian and Ukrainian. In their discussion they switched easily from one language to the other, depending on how it suited the tone and the subject of the conversation. I was surprised and delighted to meet in Edinburgh people who were from the same area and shared similar heritage with my mother. I was beginning to learn the side of World War II history first-hand which was not taught at schools in post-War Poland.

In the 1990s, veterans' clubs were still important meeting points for the Polish community in Edinburgh. My memory of visiting the Polish Invalids' Club in 53 Great King Street is vague, but I remember friendly Polish guys standing at the bar and making gentle jokes in Polish. Some years later I heard that it was sold as it was no longer economically viable. My involvement with the Polish Ex-Servicemen's Club (SPK) in 11 Drummond Place was and, to some extent still is, much stronger. I remember my first visit well: one Sunday afternoon, I walked in to the club with my-one-year-old daughter in the pushchair, and to my delight I was offered a typical Polish lunch of home-made soup, pork chop cutlet, beetroot and mashed potatoes, with fruit compote for desert. Henry Biger, who volunteered as barman and waiter, announced that my lunch would be the last lunch ever to be served in the club. He explained that the kitchen was very old and in need of renovation, operated only on a part-time basis, without permanent staff, relying on a Polish lady visiting her family in Edinburgh, and she was going back to Poland. The meal was delicious and very affordable, with the added bonus of interesting Polish conversation. I was sad that it was the last lunch, as I would have been happy to come back for more! Later, I learned that Henry was a retired accountant who had worked for one of the most respected Edinburgh financial firms. I am still in touch with him, and he is a great source of knowledge about the post-war Polish community in Edinburgh. Eventually I was accepted as a Supporting Member of the Polish Ex-Servicemen's Club, on the basis that my father was a soldier during the War in the Polish People's Army which participated in the Prague operation.

At that time there was a well-organised library in the basement of the club, run by Irena Hurna. Sadly, it is no longer functioning, and many books were lost over the years. In 2004, when Poles were arriving in large numbers and desperate for accommodation, most rooms in the club, including the library, were rented out to the newcomers. When the last occupants had moved on to more permanent accommodation, the library, once neat and orderly, with beautiful, glass-fronted Georgian bookcases, looked like a location from *Trainspotting*. Later on it was used as a temporary wood workshop, covering what remained of the library in thick layers of sawdust.

I was a newcomer with a one-year-old toddler in Edinburgh, and my husband's social circle consisted mainly of his colleagues from work with whom I did not have very much in common. Conversation was often difficult as I was still getting used to the Scottish accent. I had no female friends with children who, like me, tried to combine studies with bringing up their children. Looking for Polish contacts seemed to be a natural thing to do. As I searched for Polish contacts, I attended one or two meetings of the Polish Women's Association held in the kawiarnia (coffee shop) of the Ex-Servicemen's Club. I was made very welcome, but the members were mainly retired Polish ladies who focused on charitable causes, which they supported by their home-baking and cooking. I was in the middle of my doctorate in art history at Princeton University and preparing for a one-year research scholarship in Paris.

Among my early impressions of the Polish community in Edinburgh are splendid carol-singing events led by Polish men with operatic voices, as well as comedy evenings staring Stefania Wawro, who, with the formidable talent and stamina of a professional stand-up comedian, kept her audience roaring with laughter for hours. There were, and still are in the Polish Ex-Combatants Association in 11 Drummond Place, indoor Christmas markets with home baking, including indispensable poppy seed and cheesecakes, along with a mixture of Polish and Scottish bric-a-brac.

At the end of 1992, we moved to the Scottish Borders and my participation in the Polish community in Edinburgh became much less frequent. I attended only occasional, very special events. One of those was the splendid funerary mass for General Maczek, held in St Mary's Cathedral in December 1994. It was a marvellous occasion, with Polish songs, patriotic speeches, flags, and Polish war veterans wearing military uniforms, commemorating a much beloved General and a wonderful man, shamefully neglected after the War by both the Polish and British Governments.

A true centre for Polish cultural and intellectual life was Crocket's Land in Victoria Terrace, the home of Krystyna and Jim Johnstone. Both architects with a passion for conservation and contemporary architecture, they often held receptions when Polish architects, artists, and intellectuals came to Edinburgh. I can still picture Krystyna dressed in fashionable black, with her hair cut short, and silver designer jewellery, in her stylish home, being a perfect host to the select members of the, at that time, very small Polish–Scottish community.

The Scottish Polish Cultural Association (SPCA) was founded in 1970 by the Scottish wife of a Polish man, in response to the fact that at Polish-speaking events the English-speaking spouses were totally ignored. The Association still meets in the Polish Ex-Combatants Association in 11 Drummond Place and holds most of its events there. Both groups are very close-knit, with a succession of very long-held chairmanships; they tend to be run almost as private organisations, and demonstrate nearly suspicious attitudes towards newcomers. A lack of effective publicity means that they are not visible enough to attract young Poles or Scots who may have a growing interest in Polish culture. Both organisations have small memberships with very low membership fees, and are unable and even reluctant to make a profit from their events; instead they rely on donations from the Polish Consulate and from SPK plc headquarters in London. SPK's splendid townhouse at 11 Drummond Place is in a sad state of neglect, and may be sold sooner rather than later, which would be an irrecoverable loss for the Polish community in Edinburgh and in Scotland. The townhouse was bought with the hard-earned savings of Polish soldiers and officers and is part of the Polish heritage in Scotland. Now, more than ever, such a base in Edinburgh is needed, but the vision and leadership to encourage collaboration between different Polish organisations has not yet emerged.

Our family's move back to Edinburgh from the Borders in 2004 coincided with Poland's accession to the European Community and the subsequent influx of 'New Poles' to Scotland. As a consequence, we easily found affordable Polish help for the renovation of our flat and in time we were able to access other services offered by Poles, for example a Polish joiner with a degree in divinity built our bookcase and the storage for my collection of paintings. We found that our Polish stair-cleaner is trained in drilling for oil, and he is just one of many keen and reliable (and often over-qualified) cleaning helps to be found. Not only private but also public institutions have benefited from Polish people with a good work ethic offering their service in a range of skills. The Polish language, as well as Polish swearing, is now heard on the street and buses of Edinburgh. My older daughter, whom I have managed to teach Polish through a string of Polish au pairs and by speaking to her in Polish, suddenly came home with a variety of Polish words picked up around town.

Her school had a young Polish teacher on the Erasmus student exchange programme who ran a Polish after-school club which attracted considerable attention.

Surprisingly, it was much more difficult to teach Polish to my second daughter who has been brought up mainly in Edinburgh. Polish language classes, made available by the City of Edinburgh Council, were suitable only for the Polish-speaking children who arrived here with their families and were already speaking Polish. My letters to the Council about the need for additional provision for Polish children who do not speak the language but who need to be encouraged to speak Polish, an important part of their heritage, remained unanswered. Now at the age of ten, my daughter is having private lessons, because there is no acceptable alternative in Edinburgh.

Young Poles who arrived in Edinburgh after 2004 are organising themselves in various creative groups sharing similar interests. Perhaps one of the most successful ones so far has been the Polish Cultural Festival, which culminated in a week of Polish cultural events in April 2009. It was a rich and colourful programme of events, organised to a professional standard and staffed by an outstanding team of volunteers. Depending on funding, the organisation may put on more events in the future.

For the past few years there have been two internet portals responding to the needs of the Polish community. Edinburgh.com.pl in Polish concentrates on cultural and social events, whilst emito.net in English is more commercial, but with good listings of associations, events, jobs and advertisements.

After 2004, Polish shops, delis, butchers, bakers, bars, pubs, restaurants, hairdressers and even a pet shop were gradually opening up in Edinburgh, Glasgow and in other Scottish towns. Much sought-after Polish gardeners, cleaners, plumbers, tilers and painters became so busy that it was hard to obtain their services. Our grand piano was moved by a professional piano-moving firm, where to get a job one had to have Polish because all the movers were Polish and communication in Polish was paramount in their business. Italian and French restaurants acquired Polish chefs, and ordering in Polish has become as common as ordering in English. Building firms and clothing alteration companies seem to be staffed mainly with Poles. Gradually, Poles began to be employed in high street shops, pharmacies, banks, hospitals, and even Edinburgh's sheriff court. Some Poles did not speak English or good enough English, so translation services became very much in demand, especially for medical appointments, at schools, and in courts of justice. Polish magazines emerged and disappeared, to be replaced by new titles. Polish students filled colleges and universities. Polish diaspora art begun to appear and young British curators interested in Polish art put on shows. In response to the overwhelming presence of Poles in Edinburgh and in Scotland, my daughter reassured me one day: 'Mummy, don't worry, you were here first!'

I thought that I was observing all this from the side-lines without getting directly involved. However, one day my daughter announced that she was going to write an article for her school magazine entitled 'My Mother's Polish Army'. It was going to be about all the Poles that I am in touch with in Edinburgh, which includes friends, people whom I am helping and people who work for us from time to time. It made me think that perhaps I was involved more than I thought I was. Eventually she decided that it was going to be too personal and instead she wrote about Polish Easter, where being soaked with water and drinking vodka are a crucial part of celebrations.

However, when I think about the Polish services we are using in Edinburgh, it comes to a small battalion: a Polish garage looks after our car, a Polish man looks after our staircase and our garden, a Polish computer shop fixes our computers and mobile phones, a Polish seamstress alters our clothes, a young Polish lady looks after our well-being at the gym. In addition, there seem to be numerous bonuses for being Polish: I was unexpectedly offered a 10 per cent discount at Harvey Nichols from a Polish sales assistant, and we got preferential treatment from another Polish assistant in the same store when buying accessories for my daughter. We also got a wonderful service in Zara from a Polish man, who, within minutes, undressed a window model to get us the right size. This is just some examples of the Polish clan at work in the Scottish capital.

The Polish community tries to open up and bring Poland to the Scottish people. In 2007, we set up *Zielony Balonik* with a friend, a Scottish–Polish Book Club, whose members read newly published Polish literature available in English translation; we aim to promote Polish culture through our formal and informal networks. We have about ten members, both Polish and British, meeting alternately in Edinburgh and Glasgow approximately once every two months. Recently we branched out into poetry with the help of Robyn Marsack from the Scottish Poetry Library.

As the British economy struggles and the Polish economy thrives, the number of Poles in Scotland would seem to be in decline. Friends living in small towns in Scotland tell me that young Poles have disappeared from their local shops and restaurants. I also hear less Polish on the streets of Edinburgh. Either they have learned English and are less visible or perhaps some have left Scotland and gone home. Those who stay are often the ones with children who, once at school, become part of the educational system and English is often their first language, even if Polish is spoken at home. Polish Saturday schools, supplementing Scottish education to keep the door open for families who may want to return, are a great idea and very much needed, but their implementation is slow, probably due to the considerable cost of setting up and running the programme.

When I think about my own family, I would like my two daughters to be able to function with ease and pleasure in both countries, to understand both cultures and to be able to take advantage of the best that both countries have to offer and at the same time to contribute to either or to both. After all, Poland and Scotland are both part of the European Union, and it is up to us what we make out of it.

Index